BUYING A HOME IN FRANCE

by

David Hampshire

SURVIVAL BOOKS • LONDON • ENGLAND

First Published 1996
Reprinted 1998
Second Edition 1999
Reprinted 2000 (twice)

Survival Books Limited, Suite C, Third Floor
Standbrook House, 2-5 Old Bond Street
London W1X 3TB, United Kingdom
☎ (+44) 020-7493 4244, Fax (+44) 020-7491 0605
E-mail: info@survivalbooks.net
Internet: www.survivalbooks.net

British Library Cataloguing in Publication Data
A CIP record for this book is available from the British Library
ISBN 1 901130 90 8

Printed and bound in Italy by LEGPRINT SpA

ACKNOWLEDGEMENTS

My sincere thanks to all those who contributed to the successful publication of this book, in particular the many people who provided information and took the time and trouble to read and comment on the many draft versions. I would especially like to thank Joanna Styles, Karen Verheul (proof-reading), John Beaumont (research), John Adams, Debbie Bartlett, Veronica Orchard, Julia & Michael Thorpe, Philip & Jane Read and Ron & Pat Scarborough for their help, and everyone else who contributed in any way whom I have omitted to mention. Also a special thank you to Jim Watson (☎ UK 01788-813609) for the superb illustrations, cartoons and cover.

By the same publisher:

The Alien's Guide to Britain
The Alien's Guide to France
Buying a Home Abroad
Buying a Home in Britain
Buying a Home in Florida
Buying a Home in Greece & Cyprus
Buying a Home in Ireland
Buying a Home in Italy
Buying a Home in Portugal
Buying a Home in Spain
Living and Working in America
Living and Working in Australia
Living and Working in Britain
Living and Working in Canada
Living and Working in France
Living and Working in Germany
Living and Working in Italy
Living and Working in London
Living and Working in New Zealand
Living and Working in Spain
Living and Working in Switzerland
Rioja and its Wines

What Readers and Reviewers Have Said About Survival Books

When you buy a model plane for your child, a video recorder, or some new computer gizmo, you get with it a leaflet or booklet pleading 'Read Me First', or bearing large friendly letters or bold type saying '**IMPORTANT** - follow the instructions carefully'. This book should be similarly supplied to all those entering France with anything more durable than a 5-day return ticket. – It is worth reading even if you are just visiting briefly, or if you have lived here for years and feel totally knowledgeable and secure. But if you need to find out how France works then it is indispensable. Native French people probably have a less thorough understanding of how their country functions. – Where it is most essential, the book is most up to the minute.

Living France

We would like to congratulate you on this work: it is really super! We hand it out to our expatriates and they read it with great interest and pleasure.

ICI (Switzerland) AG

Rarely has a 'survival guide' contained such useful advice – This book dispels doubts for first-time travellers, yet is also useful for seasoned globetrotters – In a word, if you're planning to move to the US or go there for a long-term stay, then buy this book both for general reading and as a ready-reference.

American Citizens Abroad

It's everything you always wanted to ask but didn't for fear of the contemptuous put down – The best English-language guide – Its pages are stuffed with practical information on everyday subjects and are designed to complement the traditional guidebook.

Swiss News

A complete revelation to me – I found it both enlightening and interesting, not to mention amusing.

Carole Clark

Let's say it at once. David Hampshire's Living and Working in France is the best handbook ever produced for visitors and foreign residents in this country; indeed, my discussion with locals showed that it has much to teach even those born and bred in l'Hexagone – It is Hampshire's meticulous detail which lifts his work way beyond the range of other books with similar titles. Often you think of a supplementary question and search for the answer in vain. With Hampshire this is rarely the case. – He writes with great clarity (and gives French equivalents of all key terms), a touch of humor and a ready eye for the odd (and often illuminating) fact. – This book is absolutely indispensable.

The Riviera Reporter

The ultimate reference book – Every conceivable subject imaginable is exhaustively explained in simple terms – An excellent introduction to fully enjoy all that this fine country has to offer and save time and money in the process.

American Club of Zurich

What Readers and Reviewers Have Said About Survival Books

What a great work, wealth of useful information, well-balanced wording and accuracy in details. My compliments!

Thomas Müller

This handbook has all the practical information one needs to set up home in the UK – The sheer volume of information is almost daunting – Highly recommended for anyone moving to the UK.

American Citizens Abroad

A very good book which has answered so many questions and even some I hadn't thought of – I would certainly recommend it.

Brian Fairman

A mine of information – I might have avoided some embarrassments and frights if I had read it prior to my first Swiss encounters – Deserves an honoured place on any newcomer's bookshelf.

English Teachers Association, Switzerland

Covers just about all the things you want to know on the subject – In answer to the desert island question about the one how-to book on France, this book would be it – Almost 500 pages of solid accurate reading – This book is about enjoyment as much as survival.

The Recorder

It's so funny – I love it and definitely need a copy of my own – Thanks very much for having written such a humorous and helpful book.

Heidi Guiliani

A must for all foreigners coming to Switzerland.

Antoinette O' Donoghue

A comprehensive guide to all things French, written in a highly readable and amusing style, for anyone planning to live, work or retire in France.

The Times

A concise, thorough account of the Do's and DONT's for a foreigner in Switzerland –Crammed with useful information and lightened with humorous quips which make the facts more readable.

American Citizens Abroad

Covers every conceivable question that might be asked concerning everyday life – I know of no other book that could take the place of this one.

France in Print

Hats off to Living and Working in Switzerland!

Ronnie Almeida

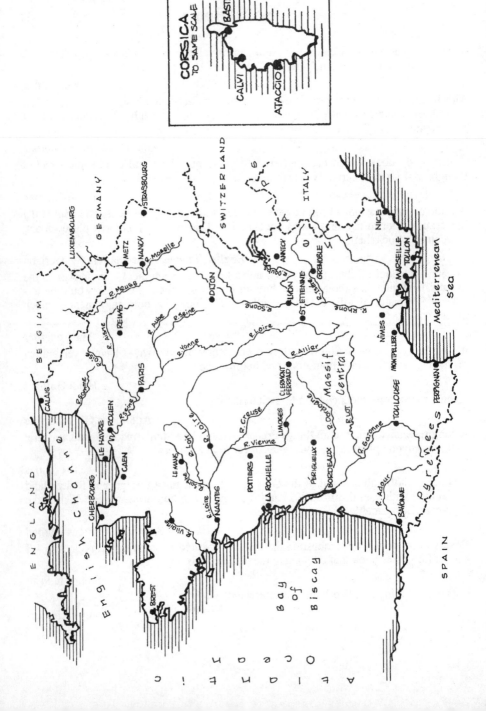

CONTENTS

4. FINDING YOUR DREAM HOME 111

5. ARRIVAL & SETTLING IN 201

APPENDICES 211

INDEX 233

ORDER FORMS 238

IMPORTANT NOTE

Readers should note that the laws and regulations for buying property in France aren't the same as in other countries and are also liable to change periodically. I cannot recommend too strongly that you check with an official and reliable source (not always the same) and take expert legal advice before paying any money or signing any legal documents. Don't, however, believe everything you're told or read, even, dare I say it, herein!

To help you obtain further information and verify data with official sources, useful addresses and references to other sources of information have been included in most chapters and in appendices A and B. Important points have been emphasised throughout the book **in bold print**, some of which it would be expensive or foolish to disregard. **Ignore them at your peril or cost.** Unless specifically stated, the reference to any company, organisation, product or publication in this book *doesn't* constitute an endorsement or recommendation. Any reference to any place or person (living or dead) is purely coincidental.

AUTHOR'S NOTES

- Times are shown using the 24-hour clock, e.g. 10am is shown as 1000 and 10pm as 2200, which is the usual way of expressing the time in France.

- Prices quoted should be taken as estimates only, although they were mostly correct when going to print and fortunately don't usually change overnight. Although prices are sometimes quoted exclusive of value added tax (*hors taxes/HT*) in France, most prices are quoted inclusive of tax (*toutes taxes comprises/TTC*), which is the method used when quoting prices in this book.

- His/he/him/man/men (etc.) also mean her/she/her/woman/women (no offence ladies!). This is done simply to make life easier for both the reader and, in particular, the author, and isn't intended to be sexist.

- The French translation of many key words and phrases is shown in brackets in *italics*.

- Warnings and important points are shown in **bold** type.

- Frequent references are made in this book to the European Union (EU), which comprises Austria, Belgium, Denmark, Finland, France, Germany, Greece, Ireland, Italy, Luxembourg, the Netherlands, Portugal, Spain, Sweden and the United Kingdom, and the European Economic Area (EEA), which includes the EU countries plus Iceland, Liechtenstein and Norway.

- Lists of **Useful Addresses** and **Further Reading** are contained in **Appendices A** and **B** respectively.

- A map of France showing the regions and departments is included in **Appendix C** and a showing the major cities and geographical features is shown on page 6.

- A list of property, mortgage and other terms used in this book is included in a **Glossary** in **Appendix D**.

- A **Service Directory** containing the names, addresses, telephone and fax numbers of companies and organisations doing business in France is contained in **Appendix E**.

INTRODUCTION

If you're planning to buy a home in France or even just thinking about it – this is THE BOOK for you! Whether you want a *château*, farmhouse, cottage or apartment, a holiday or a permanent home, this book will help make your dreams come true. The aim of *Buying a Home in France* is to provide you with the information necessary to help you choose the most favourable location and the most appropriate home **to satisfy your individual requirements.** Most important of all it will help you avoid the pitfalls and risks associated with buying a home in France, which for most people is one of the largest financial transactions they will undertake during their lifetimes.

You may already own a home in your home country; however, buying a home in France (or in any foreign country) is a different matter altogether. One of the most common mistakes many people make when buying a home in France is to assume that the laws and purchase procedures are the same as in their home country. **This is almost certainly not true!** Buying property in France is generally safe, particularly when compared with certain other European countries. However, if you don't follow the rules provided for your protection a purchase can result in serious financial losses as many people have discovered to their cost.

Before buying a home in France you need to ask yourself *exactly* why you want to buy a home there? Is your primary concern a good long-term investment or do you wish to work or retire there? Where and what can you afford to buy? Do you plan to let your home to offset the running costs? What about property, capital gains and inheritance taxes? *Buying a Home in France* will help you answer these and many other questions. It won't, however, tell you where to live and what to buy – or whether, having made your decision, you will be happy – that part is up to you!

For many people, buying a home in France has previously been a case of pot luck. However, with a copy of *Buying a Home in France* to hand you'll have a wealth of priceless information at your fingertips. Information derived from a variety of sources, both official and unofficial, not least the hard won personal experiences of the author, his friends, colleagues and acquaintances. This book doesn't, however, contain all the answers (most of us don't even know the right questions to ask). What it *will* do is reduce the risk of making an expensive mistake that you may bitterly regret later and help you make informed decisions and calculated judgements, instead of costly mistakes and uneducated guesses (forewarned is forearmed!). **Most importantly of all, it will help you save money and will repay your investment many times over.**

The recession in the early '90s caused an upheaval in world property markets, during which many so-called 'gilt-edged' property investments went to the wall. However, property remains one of the best long-term investments and it's certainly one of the most pleasurable. Buying a home in France is a wonderful way to make new friends, broaden your horizons and revitalise your life – and it provides a welcome bolthole to recuperate from the stresses and strains of modern life. I trust this book will help you avoid the pitfalls and smooth your way to many happy years in your new home in France, secure in the knowledge that you have made the right decision.

Bonne Chance!

David Hampshire
June 1999

1.

WHY FRANCE

France is one of the most beautiful countries in Europe, if not *the* most beautiful, and has the most varied landscape. It's a country of infinite variety, offering something for everyone: magnificent beaches for sun-worshippers; beautiful unspoilt countryside for nature lovers; magnificent historic towns and *châteaux* for history enthusiasts; an abundance of mountains and seas for sports lovers; vibrant Parisian night-life for the jet set; vintage wines and *haute cuisine* for gourmets; a wealth of culture, art and serious music for art lovers; and tranquillity for the stressed. Nowhere else in the world is there such an exhilarating mixture of culture and climate, history and tradition, sophistication and style. It's often said that when buying property in France you aren't buying a home but a lifestyle! As a location for a holiday, retirement or permanent home, France has few rivals and in addition to the incomparable choice of properties and excellent value for money, it offers a generally fine climate for most of the year, particularly in the south.

There are many excellent reasons for buying a home in France, although it's important not to be under any illusions regarding what you can expect from a home there. The first and most important question you need to ask yourself is *exactly* why do you want to buy a home in France? For example are you seeking a holiday or a retirement home? If you're seeking a second home, will it be mainly used for weekends or longer stays? Do you plan to let it to offset the mortgage and running costs? How important is the property income? Are you primarily looking for a sound investment or do you plan to work or start a business in France? Often buyers have a variety of reasons for buying a home in France, for example many people buy a holiday home with a view to living there permanently or semi-permanently when they retire. If this is the case, there are more factors to take into account than if you're 'simply' buying a holiday home which you will occupy for just a few weeks a year (when it may be wiser not to buy at all!). If, on the other hand, you plan to work or start a business in France, you will be faced with a whole different set of criteria.

Can you really afford to buy a home in France? What about the future? Is your income secure and protected against inflation and currency fluctuations? In the '80s, many foreigners purchased holiday homes in France by taking out second mortgages on their family homes and stretching their financial resources to the limits. Not surprisingly, when the recession struck in the early '90s many people had their homes repossessed or were forced to sell at a huge loss when they were no longer able to meet the mortgage payments. Buying a home abroad can be a good long-term investment, although in the last decade many people have had their fingers burnt in the volatile property market in many countries, including France.

Property values in France generally increase at an average of less than 5 per cent a year or in line with inflation, although in some fashionable resorts and communities prices rise faster than average, which is usually reflected in higher purchase prices. There's generally a stable property market in most of France (barring recessions), which acts as a discouragement to speculators wishing to make a quick profit, particularly when you consider that capital gains tax can wipe out much of the profit made on the sale of a home (especially a second home). You also need to recover the high costs associated with buying a home in France when you sell. **You shouldn't expect to make a quick profit when buying property in France, but should look upon it as an investment in your family's future happiness, rather than merely in financial terms.**

There are both advantages and disadvantages to buying a home in France, although for most people the benefits far outweigh any drawbacks. Among the many advantages are guaranteed summer sunshine (in most areas); excellent value for money, particularly if you want a house with a large plot of land; the solidity and spaciousness of rural homes; a huge variety of house styles; a stable property market; safe purchase procedure (providing you aren't reckless); the integrity of (most) licensed real estate agents and notaries; the availability of fresh food and excellent wines at reasonable prices; easy and inexpensive to get to (at least for most western Europeans); good rental possibilities (in many areas); excellent local tradesmen and services; the gentler, slower pace of life in rural areas; the friendliness of (most) French people; the timeless splendour of France on your doorstep; and, last but not least, a quality of life unmatched in virtually any other country.

There are of course a few drawbacks, not least the high purchase costs associated with buying; unexpected renovation and restoration costs (if you don't do your homework); the risk of overpaying for a home and being unable to sell it and recoup your investment; the risk of over-stretching your finances (e.g. by taking on too large a mortgage) and being unable to maintain the payments; the relatively high crime rate in some areas; the threat of storms and inclement weather in some areas which can severely damage your home; overcrowding in popular tourist areas; high traffic congestion and pollution in many towns and cities; relatively high running costs compared with some other countries and the heavy workload associated with running a large home and garden; high taxes for residents and an increasing cost of living; cool or unfriendly neighbours in some villages and areas; and the expense of getting to and from France if you own a holiday home there and don't live in a nearby country.

Unless you know exactly what you're looking for and where, it's advisable to rent a property for a period until you're familiar with an area. As when making all major financial decisions, it's never advisable to be in too much of a hurry. Many people make expensive (even catastrophic) errors when buying homes in France, usually because they do insufficient research and are in too much of a hurry, often setting themselves ridiculous deadlines (such as buying a home during a long weekend or a week's holiday). Not surprisingly, most people wouldn't dream of acting so rashly when buying a property in their home country! It isn't uncommon for buyers to regret their decision after some time and wish they had purchased a different kind of property in a different region (or even in a different country!).

Before deciding to buy a home in France it's advisable to do extensive research and read a number of books especially written for those planning to live or work there (like this one and *Living and Working in France*, also written by your author). It also helps to study specialist property magazines and newspapers such as *French Property News*, *Living France* and *Focus on France* (see **Appendix A** for a list), and to visit property exhibitions such as those organised by Outbound Publishing and French Property News in Britain. **Bear in mind that the cost of investing in a few books or magazines (and other research) is tiny compared with the expense of making a big mistake.** Finally, don't believe everything you read (even herein)!

This chapter provides information about permits and visas, retirement, working, buying a business, communications (e.g. telephones), getting to France and getting around, particularly regarding driving in France.

DO YOU NEED A PERMIT OR VISA?

Before making any plans to buy a home in France, you must ensure that you will be permitted to use the property when you wish and for whatever purpose you have in mind, and check whether you will need a visa or residence permit. While foreigners are freely permitted to buy property in France, most aren't permitted to remain longer than three months a year without an appropriate residence permit or visa. If there's a possibility that you or a family member may wish to work or live permanently in France, you should ensure that it will be possible before making any plans to buy a home there.

Citizens of European Union countries can visit France with a national identity card, while others require a full passport. A non-EU national usually requires a long-stay visa (*visa de long séjour*) to work, study or live in France. Note that there's no such thing as a work permit in France, where foreigners receive a residence permit (*carte de séjour*) permitting them to work, if applicable. All foreigners need a residence permit to live permanently in France and non-EU nationals may need a visa to enter France, either as a visitor or for any other purpose.

Visas may be valid for a single entry only or for multiple entries within a limited period. A visa is stamped in your passport, which must be valid for at least 60 days *after* the date you intend to leave France. EU nationals and visitors from a number of other countries don't require visas (see below). All non-EU nationals wishing to remain in France for longer than three months must obtain a long-stay visa (*visa de long séjour/longue durée*) and apply for a residence permit (*carte de séjour*) within one week of their arrival in France.

While in France you should carry your passport or residence permit (if you have one), which serve as an identity card, at all times. You can be asked to produce your identification papers at any time by the French police or other officials and if you don't have them you can be taken to a police station and interrogated. Immigration is an inflammatory issue in France and the government has introduced new laws to curb non-EU immigration in recent years, which were coupled with a crackdown on illegal immigrants, including forcible repatriation. **Permit infringements are taken very seriously by the French authorities and there are penalties for breaches of regulations, including fines and even deportation for flagrant abuses.**

Visitors

Visitors can remain in France for a maximum of 90 days at a time. Those from EU countries plus Andorra, Canada, Cyprus, the Czech Republic, Hungary, Iceland, Japan, Malta, Monaco, New Zealand, Norway, Singapore, Slovakia, South Korea, Switzerland and the USA *don't* require a visa for stays of up to 90 days. All other nationalities need a visa to visit France. French immigration authorities may require non-EU visitors to produce a return ticket and proof of accommodation, health insurance and financial resources.

EU nationals who visit France to seek employment or start a business have three months to find a job or apply for a residence permit, after which they must apply for a residence permit to remain (see below). If you haven't found employment or have insufficient funds, your application will be refused. If you're a non-EU national, it isn't possible to enter France as a tourist and change your status to that of an employee, student or resident. You must return to your country of residence and apply for a long-stay visa. It's possible to leave France, e.g. by crossing the border to a neighbouring country, before the 90-day periöd has expired and return again for another 90-days. However, if you wish to prove you have left, you must have your passport stamped. This is legal, although your total stay mustn't exceed six months (180 days) residence in a calendar year.

RETIREMENT

Retired and non-active EU nationals don't require a long-stay visa before moving to France, but a residence permit is necessary and an application should be made within one week of your arrival in France. Non-EU nationals require a long-stay visa (*visa de long séjour*) if they are planning to live in France for longer than three months and should make a visa application to their local French Consulate at least three months before their planned arrival date. All non-employed residents must provide proof that they have an adequate income or financial resources to live in France without working. The minimum amount necessary is roughly equivalent to the French minimum wage of 6,797F a month (around 82,000F a year), although it should be less if you aren't paying a mortgage or rent.

WORKING

If there's a possibility that you or any family members may wish to work in France, you must ensure that it will be possible before buying a home. If you don't qualify to live and work in France by birthright, family relationship or as a national of a European Union (EU) or European Economic Area (EEA) country, obtaining a work permit may be difficult or impossible. If you're a national of an EU country you don't require official approval to live or work in France, although you still require a residence permit. If you visit France to look for a job you have three months to find employment or set up in business. Once employment has been found you must apply for a residence permit within one week.

France has had a virtual freeze on the employment of non-EU nationals for many years, which has been strengthened in recent years due to the high unemployment rate. The employment of non-EU nationals must be approved by the French labour authorities (*Agence Nationale Pour l'Emploi/ANPE*), who can propose the employment of an EU national in place of a foreigner (although this is rare). Non-EU nationals are subject to restrictions on the type of work they can do and the department(s) where they can work. Exceptions are foreigners with a permanent residence permit (issued after three years residence), spouses of French citizens, and students who have studied in France for the preceding two years and have a parent who has lived in France for at least four years.

Before moving to France to work, you should dispassionately examine your motives and credentials. What kind of work can you realistically expect to do in France? What are your qualifications and experience? Are they recognised in France? How good is your French? Unless your French is fluent, you won't be competing on equal terms with the French (you won't anyway, but that's a different matter!). Most French employers aren't interested in employing anyone without, at the very least, an adequate working knowledge of French. Are there any jobs in your profession or trade in the area where you wish to live? The answers to these and many other questions can be quite disheartening, but it's better to ask them *before* moving to France than afterwards.

Many people turn to self-employment (see below) or start a business to make a living, although this path is strewn with pitfalls for the newcomer. **Most foreigners don't do sufficient homework before moving to France.** While hoping for the best, you should plan for the worst case scenario and have a contingency plan and sufficient funds to last until you're established (this also applies to employees). If you're planning to start a business in France you must also do battle with the notoriously obstructive French bureaucracy (*bonne chance!*). **Note that it's difficult for non-EU nationals to obtain a residence permit to work as self-employed in France.**

SELF-EMPLOYMENT

If you're an EU-national or a permanent resident with a *carte de séjour/résident* (see page 18), you can work as self-employed (*travailleur indépendant*) or as a sole trader (*entreprise individuelle*) in France. If you want to work as self-employed in a profession or start a freelance business in France, you must meet certain legal requirements and register with the appropriate organisations, e.g. the *Chambre des Métiers*, the *Registre de Commerce* and social security (*URSSAF*) within 15 days of starting a business.

Under French law a self-employed person must have an official status and it's illegal simply to hang up a sign and start business. Members of some professions and trades must have certain qualifications and certificates recognised in France, and all are required to attend a business administration course. Don't be in too much of a hurry to register as from the date of registration (when you receive your SIRET number) you must pay hefty social security, pension and health insurance payments, and are also liable for income tax and VAT. **However, you should never be tempted to start work before you're registered as there are harsh penalties that may include a large fine (e.g. 100,000F), confiscation of machinery or tools, and even deportation and a three-year ban from entering France.**

As a self-employed person you don't have the protection of a limited company should your business fail and there are few tax advantages (except for a business classified as a *petit commerçant* with a limited turnover). It may be advantageous to operate as a limited company, for example an *Entreprise Unipersonnelle à Responsabilitée Limitée (EURL)*. An EURL is a one-person limited company that allows a self-employed person to be taxed at a more favourable rate. Note that while an EURL protects your personal assets from your creditors, they may ask for a personal guarantee, thus negating this advantage. Obtain professional advice before deciding whether to operate as a sole trader or form a company, as it has far-reaching social security, tax and other consequences. Most new businesses enjoy a tax exemption for the first two years of trading, including sole traders, whose business and personal income are combined by the tax authorities. This means that as a sole trader you're unlikely to pay any income tax during your first two years in business. After the first two years, businesses are granted a tax exemption (*exonération*) of a percentage of their turnover.

There are, however, many drawbacks to being self-employed in France, which may outweigh any advantages. Social security contributions for the self-employed are much higher than for salaried employees and they receive fewer benefits, e.g. doctors' bills are reimbursed at 50 per cent only and not the 75 per cent paid to salaried employees. As a self-employed person in France you aren't entitled to unemployment benefits should your business fail and there are no benefits for accidents at work (except for artisans), although you're insured against invalidity. It's advisable to join a professional association as they provide valuable information and assistance and may also offer insurance discounts. One such organisation is the *Confédération pour la Défense des Commerçants et Artisans/CDCA* (Le Capoulie, 6, rue Maguelone, 34000 Montpellier, ☎ 04.67.58.24.90), which was formed to fight for better rights for the self-employed and small businessmen. (In recent years CDCA has encouraged small businesses to register abroad, e.g. in Britain, in order to save taxes.)

STARTING A BUSINESS

The bureaucracy associated with starting a business (*fonds de commerce*) in France is shocking and rates among the most pernicious in the world. France is a red tape jungle and French civil servants (*fonctionnaires*) can be inordinately obstructive, endlessly recycling bits of paper to create 'employment' for themselves. For foreigners the red tape is almost impenetrable, especially if you don't speak French, and you will be inundated with official documents and must be able to understand them. It's only when you come up against the full force of French bureaucracy that you understand what it *really* means to be a foreigner in France! However, despite the red tape, France is traditionally a country of small businesses and individual traders, where the economic philosophy actually encourages and even nurtures their creation.

Before undertaking any business transactions in France, it's important to obtain legal advice to ensure that you're operating within the law. There are severe penalties for anyone who ignores the regulations and legal requirements. It's also important to obtain legal advice before establishing a limited company there. All businesses must register for value added tax and there's no threshold below which you aren't required to register. Non-EU nationals require a special licence (*carte commerçante étranger*) to start a business in France and no commitments should be made until permission has been granted. Among the best sources of help and information are local chambers of commerce and town halls (*mairies*).

Generally speaking you shouldn't consider running a business in France in a field in which you don't have previous experience (excluding 'businesses' such as bed and breakfast or *gîtes*, where experience isn't necessary). It's often advisable to work for someone else in the same line of business in order to gain experience, rather than jump in at the deep end. Always thoroughly investigate an existing or proposed business before investing any money. **As any expert can tell you, France isn't a** country for amateur entrepreneurs, particularly amateurs who don't speak fluent French! Many small businesses in France exist on a shoe string and certainly aren't what would be considered thriving enterprises. As in many countries, most people are self-employed for the lifestyle and freedom it affords (no clocks or bosses!), rather than the financial rewards. It's important to keep your plans small and manageable and work well within your budget, rather than undertaking a grandiose scheme.

A useful guide for anyone starting a business in France is *Setting up a Small Business in France* published by the French Chamber of Commerce, 197 Knightsbridge, London SW7 1RB, UK (☎ 0171-225-5250). International accountants such as Price Waterhouse have offices throughout France and are an invaluable source of information (in English) on subjects such as forming a company, company law, taxation and social security. Many countries maintain chambers of commerce in France that are an invaluable source of information and assistance. The British Business Centre (BP 21, 14700 Falaise, ☎ 03.31.40.05.77) can also help you buy or establish a business in France. You can also enlist the services of a *Centre de Gestion*, which is a group of accountants, bookkeepers and administrative staff who specialise in assisting and establishing small businesses and providing financial services. See also **Self-Employment** on page 20.

Buying an Existing Business: It's much easier to buy an existing business in France than start a new one and it's also less of a risk. The paperwork for taking over an existing business is also simpler, although still complex. Note, however, that buying a business that's a going concern is difficult as the French aren't in a habit of buying and selling businesses, which are usually passed down from generation to generation. If you plan to buy a business, obtain an independent valuation (or two) and employ an accountant (*expert comptable*) to audit the books. **Never sign anything you don't understand 110 per cent and even if you think you understand it, you should still obtain unbiased professional advice, e.g. from local experts such as banks and accountants, before buying a business.**

Starting a New Business: Most people are far too optimistic about the prospects of a new business in France and over-estimate income levels (it often takes years to make a profit). Be realistic or even pessimistic when estimating your income and overestimate the costs and underestimate the revenue (then reduce it by 50 per cent!). While hoping for the best, you should plan for the worst and have sufficient funds to last until you're established (under-funding is the major cause of business failures). New projects are rarely if ever completed within budget and you need to ensure that you have sufficient working capital and can survive until a business takes off. French banks are extremely wary of lending to new businesses, especially businesses run by foreigners (would you trust a foreigner?). If you wish to borrow money to buy property or for a business venture in France, you should carefully consider where and in what currency to raise the necessary finance.

In best not to start a business until you have the infrastructure established including an accountant, lawyer and banking facilities. There are various ways to set up a small business and it's essential to obtain professional advice regarding the best method of establishing and registering a business in France, which can dramatically affect your tax position. It's important to employ an accountant to do your books, although you shouldn't expect him to be interested in reducing your social security charges and should question any costs that appear to be too high.

Location: Choosing the location for a business is even more important than the location for a home. Depending on the type of business, you may need access to *autoroutes* and rail links, or be located in a popular tourist area or near local attractions. Local plans regarding communications, industry and major building developments, e.g. housing complexes and new shopping centres, may also be important. Plans concerning new *autoroutes* and rail links are normally available from local town halls.

Employees: Hiring employees shouldn't be taken lightly in France and must be taken into account *before* starting a business. You must enter into an employment contract under French labour law and employees enjoy extensive rights. It's also *very* expensive to hire employees, as in addition to salaries you must pay an additional 50 per cent in social security contributions, a 13th month's salary and five weeks paid annual holiday. However, there are tax holidays for limited periods for newly formed companies, particularly regarding the first employee. During their first two years trading most new businesses enjoy a tax exemption and are required to pay only around 10 per cent of their first employee's wages in social security contributions.

Type of Business: The most common businesses operated by foreigners in France include holiday accommodation (e.g. bed & breakfast, *gîtes, chambres d'hôte,* chalets, apartments and cottages); caravan and camping sites; building and allied trades; farming (e.g. dairy, vineyards, fruit, fish, poultry, sheep, flowers, vegetables); catering (e.g. bars, cafés and restaurants); hotels; shops; franchises; estate agencies; translation bureaux; language schools; landscape gardening; and holiday and sports centres (e.g. tennis, golf, squash, shooting and horse-riding). The majority of businesses established by foreigners are linked to the leisure and catering industries, followed by property investment and development.

Companies: Companies cannot be purchased 'off the shelf' in France and it usually takes a number of months to establish a company. Incorporating a company in France takes longer and is more expensive and more complicated than in most other European countries (those bureaucrats again!). There are around 15 different types of 'limited companies' or business entities in France and choosing the right one can be difficult. Companies in France are either trading (*Société Commerciale*) or non-trading (*Société Civile*) companies. **You must never use a non-trading company to trade.**

The most common form of company created by foreigners in France is a SARL (*Société à Responsabilité Limitée*), a private limited company with a minimum share capital of 50,000F (part of which can be fixed assets) and at least two shareholders and a maximum of 50. Another common type of company is an SCI (*Société Civile Immobilière*), which is a property holding company. Note, however, that if you form a French company (e.g. a SARL) and pay yourself as an employee, you must pay an additional around 50 per cent in social security contributions. **Obtain professional legal advice regarding the advantages and disadvantages of different limited companies.**

Information: The interdepartmental economic agency (*Délégation à l'Aménagement du Territoire et à l'Action Régionale/DATAR*) is the major French government organisation concerned with attracting overseas investment and business ventures. DATAR provides comprehensive information regarding all aspects of doing business in France. It also implements the French government's policy of providing grants and investment incentives for certain businesses, particularly those located in depressed and under-developed areas. DATAR operates abroad as Invest in France (IFA) and has offices in Belgium, Germany, Italy, the Netherlands, Spain, Switzerland, the UK, the USA and in various Asian countries. Their head office is IFA, c/o DATAR, 1, avenue Charles Floquet, 75007 Paris (☎ 01.47.83.61.20 or 40.65.12.34).

Grants: There are over 250 different grants and incentives available for new businesses in France, particularly in rural areas. These include EU subsidies, central government grants, regional development grants, redeployment grants, and grants from departments and local communities. Grants include assistance to buy buildings and equipment (or the provision of low-cost business premises), subsidies for job creation and tax incentives. In areas designated as 'enterprise zones', new businesses may be exempt from corporation tax for up to ten years. Contact IFA (see above) and departmental and communal authorities for information.

Wealth Warning: Whatever people may tell you, working for yourself isn't easy and it requires a lot of hard work (self-employed people generally work much longer hours than employees); a sizeable investment and sufficient operating funds (most new businesses fail due to a lack of capital); good organisation (e.g. bookkeeping and planning); excellent customer relations; and a measure of luck (although generally the harder you work, the more 'luck' you will have). Don't be seduced by the apparent laid-back way of life in France; if you want to be a success in business you cannot play at it. Bear in mind that some two-thirds of new businesses fail within three to five years and that the self-employed enjoy far fewer social security benefits than employees.

KEEPING IN TOUCH

France enjoys a high standard of communications services such as telephone (including mobile phones), fax, mail and courier services.

Telephone: The French telephone service is run by France Télécom, partially privatised in 1998 in France's biggest ever sell-off, when two private companies (Cegetel and Omnicom) were created. France Télécom still maintains a monopoly on 'local' calls up to 52km (32mi) but all three companies offer services for inter-department and overseas calls. France has one of the most modern and efficient telephone services in the world and is fully automated. France Télécom is in the forefront of telephone technology and provides a wide range of services including the Internet. France also has an efficient car telephone service, encompassing the most populous areas of the country. **Emergency telephone numbers are listed at the front of telephone directories.**

Installation: When moving into a new home in France with a telephone line, you must have the account transferred to your name. If you're planning to move into a property without an existing telephone line, you will need to have one installed. To have a telephone installed or reconnected, contact your local France Télécom agent (*Agence Commerciale*), a list of whom is contained in telephone directories. If you're taking over a property from the previous occupants, you should arrange for the account to be transferred to your name from the day you take possession. **However, before you can do this the previous occupant must have already closed his account, therefore check in advance that this has been done.** If you move into a property where the telephone hasn't been disconnected or transferred to your name, you should ask France Télécom for a special reading (*relevé spécial*).

To contact your local Télécom agent dial 1014 and you will be connected. If you're applying to have a line connected or installed for the first time in France, i.e. you don't have an existing account with France Télécom, you must visit your local agent. To have a telephone connected or installed, you must prove that you're the owner or tenant of the property in question, e.g. with an electricity bill, confirmation of purchase (*attestation d'acquisition*) or a lease. You also require your passport or residence permit (*carte de séjour*). France Télécom publish a 'Set Up Guide' in English. If you wish to use Cegetel (☎ 08.00.77.77.77) or Omnicom (☎ 08.01.55.00.55) for long-distance and international calls you will need to subscribe to open a separate account with them (note, however, that you must still have an account with France Télécom for line rental and local calls).

Using the Telephone: Using the telephone in France is simplicity itself. All French telephone numbers have ten figures. Since 1996 numbers have incorporated the regional code (the first two digits, see below). Numbers beginning with 0800 are free (called a *Numéro Vert*), those beginning with 0801 (*Numéro Azur*) are charged at local rates and 0802/3 (*Numéro Indigo*) announce the rate at the start of the call.

If you're a Cegetel client you must replace the first zero of the area code with a 7 e.g. 01.40.20.70.00 becomes 71.40.20.70.00 and dial 70 instead of 00 for international calls. If you subscribe to Omnicom you replace the first zero of the area code with a 5 and for international calls you dial 05 instead of 00.

Code	Region	Departments
01	Paris	Essonne, Hauts-de-Seine, Paris, Seine-et-Marne, Seine-Saint-Denis, Val-de-Marne, Val-d'Oise, Yvelines
02	Northwest	Calvados, Cher, Côtes-d'Armor, Eure, Eure-et-Loir, Finistère, Ille-et-Vilaine, Indre, Indre-et-Loire, Loir-et-Cher, Loire-Atlantique, Loiret, Maine-et-Loire, Manche, Mayenne, Morbihan, Orne, Sarthe, Seine-Maritime, Vendée
03	Northeast	Aisne, Ardennes, Aube, Bas-Rhin, Côte-d'Or, Doubs, Haute-Marne, Haute-Saône, Haut-Rhin, Jura, Marne, Meurthe-et-Moselle, Meuse, Moselle, Nièvre, Nord, Oise, Pas-de-Calais, Saône-et-Loire, Somme, Territoire-de-Belfort, Vosges, Yonne
04*	Southeast	Ain, Allier, Alpes de Hte-Provence, Alpes-Maritimes, Ardèche, Aude, Bouches-du-Rhône, Cantal, Corse, Drôme, Gard, Hautes-Alpes, Haute-Loire, Haute-Savoie, Hérault, Isère, Loire, Lozère, Puy-de-Dôme, Pyrénées-Orientales, Rhône, Savoie, Var, Vaucluse
05	Southwest	Ariège, Aveyron, Charente, Charente-Maritime, Corrèze, Creuse, Deux-Sèvres, Dordogne, Gers, Gironde, Haute-Garonne, Hautes-Pyrénées, Haute-Vienne, Landes, Lot, Lot-et-Garonne, Pyrénées-Atlantiques, Tarn, Tarn-et-Garonne, Vienne
06	Mobile Phones	

* Note that Monaco now has its own country code of 377 instead of the regional code 04.

Extra Services: France Télécom provides a range of custom and optional telephone services (*services confort*). To take advantage of them your telephone must be connected to a digital exchange and you must have a touch-tone telephone. Custom calling or optional services can be ordered individually or as part of a package deal and include call transfer, third party call signal, three-way conversation and call memo.

Costs: Telephone charges in France include line charges; telephone, Minitel and other equipment rentals; credit card calls; Internet charges; and general call charges. The monthly line rental or service charge (*abonnement*) is 49.08F per month. If you use Cegetel or Omnicom, you must pay an additional 10F or 8F per month respectively. Tariffs depend on the time of calls (and the destination) as follows:

Tariff (*tarif*)	Period
Peak (*heures pleines/ tarif normal*)	Mondays to Fridays from 0800 to 1900 and Saturdays from 0800 to noon;
Reduced (*heures creuses/ tarif réduit*)	Mondays to Fridays from 1900 to 0800, weekends from noon on Saturdays and public holidays.

France Télécom's charge for local calls is based on a unit cost of 0.74F, which for a local call is equal to three minutes at full tariff (*normal*). Competition in the telephone market has brought much needed competition to 'long-distance' (inter-department) and international calls. For example, for long-distance calls France Télécom charges 1.14F per minute, Cegetel 1.02F and Omnicom 0.97F. Each company provides a range of packages and incentives and you should shop around for the best deal. For example, France Télécom offers a 'light user scheme' (*abonnement modéré*) with a lower service charge but higher call rates.

International Calls: It's possible to make direct IDD (International Direct Dialling) calls to most countries from both private and public telephones. A full list of country codes is shown in the information pages (*pages info*) of your local white and Yellow Pages, plus area codes for main cities and tariffs. To make an international call you must first dial 00 to obtain an international line. Then dial the country code, the area code (*without* the first zero) and the subscriber's number. For international dialling information and directory enquiries ☎ 00.33.12.

Deregulation of the telecoms market has resulted in an intense price war and considerable savings can be made on international calls by shopping around for the lowest rates. France Télécom has 16 tariff levels for international calls, listed in telephone directories, and are usually the most expensive. Calls to EU countries, Liechtenstein and Switzerland come under tariff one (the cheapest) and cost 2.10F per minute during normal tariff and 1.65F per minute during reduced tariff (*réduit*). Cegetel and Omnicom both charge the same rates of 1.59F normal (from 0800 to 2100 Mondays to Fridays and 0800 to noon on Saturdays) and 1.27F reduced (all other times). Calls to North America via France Télécom come under tariff six and cost 2.25F per minute during normal tariff, 1.80F per minute during reduced tariff. Cegetel and Omnicom charge

1.80F to North America during normal tariff (from 1300 to 1900 Mondays to Fridays) and 1.44F during reduced tariff (all other times).

Indirect Access or Callback Companies: The cheapest companies for international calls are usually indirect access companies (also called 'callback' companies when you need to ring a number and receive a call back to obtain a line), where you dial a freephone number to connect to the company's leased lines or dial a code before dialling a number. They may offer low rates for all calls or just national and international calls. Some charge a subscription fee. Calls are charged at a flat rate 24 hours a day, seven days a week. Calls may be paid for with a credit (charge or debit) card, either in advance when you must buy a number of units, or by direct debit each month. Alternatively you may be billed monthly in arrears. There are a number of indirect access companies in France including Riviera Communications SARL, BP 227, 92205 Nueilly-sur-Seine Cedex (☎ 04. 93.67.39.31).

Bills: France Télécom bills its customers every two months and allows you two weeks to pay your bill (*facture*). Bills include value added tax (TVA) at 20.6 per cent. If you're connected to a digital exchange you can request an itemised invoice (*facturation détaillée/annexe à la facture*). An itemised bill lists calls with the date and time, the number called, the duration and the charge, and is particularly useful if you let a second home in France or lend it to your friends (it isn't worth losing friends over a telephone bill). If you wish to find out how much you have spent on calls between bills, Âllofact (☎ 3653) will tell you for 0.74F.

Bills can be paid by post by sending a cheque to France Télécom, at a post office or at your local France Télécom office. Simply detach the bottom (pink) part of your bill and send or present it with payment. You can pay your telephone bill by direct debit (*prélèvement automatique*) from a bank or post office account or have payments spread throughout the year. These last two methods are recommended if you spend a lot of time away from home or are a non-resident, as they will ensure that you won't be disconnected for non-payment. If you're a non-resident, you can have bills sent to an address outside France. If you pay your bills by direct debit, your invoice will specify the date of the debit from your account, usually around 20 days after receipt of the invoice. Contact your local France Télécom agent for information. FT are trying to encourage customers to pay by direct debit, telepayment by telephone or Minitel (see below), or by TIP (*Titre Interbancaire de Paiement*), whereby your bank account details are pre-printed on the pink part of the bill which you simply date and sign and return to France Télécom.

Minitel: Minitel (launched in 1985) is a computer-based videotex/teletext information system that can be linked to any telephone. For many years Minitel was in the vanguard of technology, although it's slowly but surely on its way out, having succumbed to the relentless march of the Internet. It is, however, still in widespread use and references to Minitel numbers are commonplace (even in this book). In order to access Minitel you need to buy or rent a terminal from France Télécom, who will happily advise you on the various options. They may, however, prefer to sell you their Internet service!

Internet: The Internet in France has got off to rather a slow start due to Minitel competition and the relative lack of computers. However, the government is keen to catch up with other European countries (such as Britain and Germany) and is injecting vast sums of money into the Internet. 'Internet Days' and venues are commonplace in large cities, where you can try the Internet free of charge. In 1998 there were less than two million Internet users in France (around 2 per cent of households), but predictions for 2002 run to over ten million users or some 20 per cent of households. This dramatic increase in the market has led to the prolific growth of servers (*fournisseurs d'accès/FAI*) with over 200 in early 1999 with a variety of products and prices. To find out which are the best you can consult the many computer magazines, some of which are dedicated to the Internet such as *Planète Internet* or *Démarrer sur Internet*. France Télécom offers *Wanadoo*, a package that includes e-mail, Minitel (of course) and on-line shopping. Vivendi AOL France and Compuserve are two other big Internet contenders. Between them, Wanadoo and AOL have some two-thirds of the market.

Fax: There has been a huge increase in the use of fax (facsimile) machines in France in the last decade, boosted by lower prices and the failings (and frequent strikes) of the French post office. Fax machines can be purchased (but not rented) from France Télécom and purchased or rented from private companies and shops. Shop around for the best price. Before bringing a fax machine to France, check that it will work there (i.e. is compatible or *agréé*) or that it can be modified. Note, however, that getting a fax machine repaired in France may be impossible unless the same machine is sold there. Public fax services (*Postéclair*) are provided by central post offices in most towns, although you can send faxes only and cannot receive them. The cost in France is 30F for the first page and 18F for subsequent pages. An international service is available to some 50 countries.

Mail Services: There's a post office (*la poste*) in almost every town and village in France, where in addition to the usual post office services, a range of other services are provided. These include telephone calls, telegrams, fax and telex transmissions, domestic and international cash transfers, payment of telephone and utility bills, and the distribution of mail-order catalogues. The post office also provides financial and banking services including cheque and savings accounts, mortgage and retirement plans, and share prices. Post offices usually have photocopy machines, telephone booths and Minitel terminals (see above).

Business hours for main post offices in towns and cities in France are usually from 0800 or 0900 to 1900, Mondays to Fridays and from 0800 or 0900 to noon on Saturdays. Main post offices in major towns don't close for lunch and may also provide limited services outside normal business hours. In small towns and villages post offices close for lunch, e.g. from noon to 1330. Post office opening hours in villages vary considerably and some open for just three hours a day from 0900 to noon Mondays to Saturdays, while others are open from 0800 to noon and 1330 to 1630 Mondays to Fridays and from 0800 to 1130 on Saturdays. In some villages opening hours are irregular, e.g. 0700 to 1030, 1345 to 1530 and 1630 to 1800 Mondays to Fridays, and 0700 to 1100 on Saturdays.

The French mail (*courrier*) delivery service has a reputation of being one of the slowest in Europe, although services have improved markedly in recent years. There are two categories of internal letter post in France and to French territories overseas (DOM-TOM), normal tariff (*service rapide*), which is supposed to ensure delivery the next working day, and reduced tariff (*service économique/ECOPLI*) for non-urgent letters, which take much longer. For elsewhere normal tariff (*service prioritaire*) and reduced tariff (*service économique*) exist. The maximum weight for domestic letter post is 3kg and for international letters it's 2kg. Domestic letters weighing up to 20 grammes cost 3F (2.70F reduced tariff) and airmail letters to EU countries 3F up to 20g (3.80F to other European destinations and 4.40 to North America).

The international postal identification for French zip or postcode (*code postal*) is 'F', which is placed before the code (although its use isn't mandatory). France uses an obligatory five-digit postcode, where the first two digits indicate the *département* and the last three the town or a district (*arrondissement*) in Paris, e.g. 75005 is the fifth *arrondissement*. Small villages often use the postcode of a nearby town and the village name should be included in the address before the postcode.

Courier Services: Express mail and courier services are provided by the post office, French railways (SNCF) and airlines, and international courier companies such as DHL and UPS. One of the most economical ways to send urgent international letters or parcels is via the post office's *Chronopost* express mail service serving around 160 countries. Within France packages up to 25kg are guaranteed to arrive at their destination within 24 hours, while mail sent to EU countries is guaranteed delivery within 24 or 48 hours (depending on the country), and mail sent to New York is guaranteed to arrive within 48 hours. The maximum time for delivery to any country is three or four days.

GETTING THERE

Although it isn't so important if you're planning to live permanently in France and stay put, one of the major considerations when buying a holiday home is the cost of getting to and from France. How long will it take to get to a home in France, taking into account journeys to and from airports, ports and railway stations? How frequent are flights, ferries or trains at the time(s) of year when you plan to travel? Are direct flights or trains available? Is it feasible to travel by car? What is the cost of travel from your home country to the region where you're planning to buy a home in France? Are off-season discounts or inexpensive charter flights available? If a long journey is involved, you should bear in mind that it may take you a day or two to recover, e.g. from jet-lag after a long flight. Obviously the travelling time and cost of travel to a home in France will be more critical if you're planning to spend frequent weekends there rather than a few long visits a year.

Airline Services: All major international airlines provide scheduled services to Paris and many also fly to other French cities such as Lyon, Nice and Marseille. The French national airline, Air France, is France's major international carrier, serving some 190 destinations in over 70 countries. It has a fleet of over 100 aircraft including seven Concordes (dubbed the world's fastest white elephant by jealous competitors) and carries some 16 million passengers annually. Air France operates main routes in Europe, North and South America and Japan, and has a majority stake in UTA, France's second international airline, which concentrates on serving the Ivory Coast, South Africa, Singapore and Australia. Air France provides a high standard of service and, as you would expect, provides excellent in-flight cuisine.

The main French gateway airports serving intercontinental flights are Paris Roissy-Charles-de-Gaulle, Paris Orly, Lyon-Satolas, Nice-Côte-d'Azur and Marseille-Provence. Paris (the only French transatlantic gateway) is served by direct flights from almost every major capital city in the world and there are direct flights from over 30 US and Canadian cities. Many of France's regional airports have flights to a number of European destinations, particularly London. Flights to North African countries are also common from regional airports, mainly to cater for migrant workers. Nice is France's busiest provincial airport with direct scheduled flights to around 80 cities worldwide, closely followed by Marseille serving around 70 international destinations. Among the many French cities and towns served by international flights are: Biarritz, Bordeaux, Brest, Brive La Gaillarde, Caen, Cherbourg, Clermont-Ferrand, Dijon, Fréjus, Grenoble, Hyères, Le Havre, Le Touquet, Lille, Lourdes, Lyon, Marseille, Montpellier, Mulhouse/Basel, Nancy-Metz, Nantes, Nice, Paris, Perpignan, Pontoise, Quimper, Rennes, Rouen, Strasbourg, Tarbes, Toulouse and Tours-Poitiers. There are also international flights to Ajaccio, Bastia, Calvi and Figari in Corsica.

Air France shares its monopoly on many international routes with just one foreign carrier and is thus able to charge high fares. The lack of competition means that international flights to and from most French airports, and French domestic flights, are among the world's most expensive (business fares are the biggest rip-off). However, some opposition is starting to appear and high fares on some routes, e.g. transatlantic flights, have been reduced in recent years by cut-price travel agents such as *Nouvelles Frontières* and cut-price, no-frills airlines such as EasyJet and Virgin Express. Competition on some routes from TGV trains (e.g. Paris-Lyon and Paris-London, the world's busiest international air corridor) has also helped reduce fares. Depending on your ultimate destination, it's sometimes cheaper or quicker to fly to an international airport outside France, such as Luxembourg for the northeast, Geneva (Switzerland) for the southeast (particularly Alpine ski resorts), and Barcelona or Gerona (Spain) for the southwest.

Train Services: There are direct trains to France from most major European cities including Amsterdam, Barcelona, Basle, Berlin, Brussels, Cologne, Florence, Frankfurt, Geneva, Hamburg, London, Madrid, Milan, Munich, Rome, Rotterdam, Venice, Vienna and Zurich. Some international services run at night only and daytime journeys may involve a change of train. Since the opening of the Channel Tunnel in 1994, Eurostar trains have operated from Paris to London taking around three hours (it would be faster, but French TGV trains must slow to a 'snail's' pace once they reach British soil).

Eurotunnel: Eurotunnel formally Le Shuttle) started operating its shuttle car train service from Coquelles (near Calais) to Folkestone (England) in 1995. It provides a 15-minute service during peak periods, taking just 35 minutes. Each train can carry around 180 cars. Fares are similar to ferries, e.g. a peak (summer) club class return costs around 3400F and an off-peak (January to March) return 1,700F for a vehicle and all passengers. It's advisable to book in advance, although you should note that reservations are for a particular day, not a particular train or time. Don't expect to get a place in summer on the 'turn up and go' service in the United Kingdom, particularly on Fridays, Saturdays and Sundays. Demand is usually lighter on services from France to Britain, when bookings may be unnecessary. Trains carry all 'vehicles' including cycles, motorcycles, cars, trucks, buses, caravans and motorhomes.

Motorail: Motorail is a European network of special trains, generally overnight, carrying passengers and their cars or motorbikes over distances of up to 1,500km (900mi). Caravans cannot be taken on car trains. SNCF provides an extensive motorail network of some 130 routes linking most regions of France. The principal internal Motorail routes are between Paris and Avignon, Biarritz, Bordeaux, Briançon, Brive, Evian, Fréjus-St. Raphaël, Gap, Grenoble, Lyon, Marseille, Narbonne, Nice, Nîmes, St. Gervais, Strasbourg, Tarbes, Toulon and Toulouse. The principal Motorail services from Britain operate from Calais and Dieppe to Avignon, Biarritz, Bordeaux, Brive, Fréjus-St. Raphaël, Narbonne, Nice, Moutiers and

Toulouse. Trains don't run every day and on most routes operate during peak months only.

Ferries: International services operate year round between France and Britain, Ireland and the Channel Islands. There's a wide choice of routes for travellers between France and Britain, depending on where you live, your ultimate destination and the best road connections. There are scheduled car ferry services from the French ports of Boulogne, Caen, Calais, Cherbourg, Dieppe, Le Havre, Roscoff, St. Malo to a number of British ports including Dover, Folkestone, Newhaven, Plymouth, Poole, Portsmouth and Weymouth, plus the Irish ports of Cork and Rosslare. There are also ferry services between St. Malo and the Channel Islands of Jersey, Guernsey and Sark (foot passengers only). The major ferry companies operating international services are P&O (which also operates as P&O Stena Line on some routes) and Brittany Ferries, which dominates the routes in the western Channel (from Caen, Cherbourg, Roscoff and St. Malo) with around 40 per cent of the market. Hoverspeed operates a hovercraft service between Calais and Dover and catamaran (Seacat) services on the same route plus Boulogne to Folkestone. A larger Hoverspeed superseacat service operates from Dieppe to Newhaven and Condor operate a fast service (five hours) from St. Malo to Weymouth.

Some ferry services operate during the summer months only, e.g. May to September, and the frequency of services varies from dozens a day on the busiest Calais-Dover route during the summer peak period, to one a week on longer routes. Services are less frequent during the winter months, when bad weather can also cause cancellations. Most Channel ferry services employ large super ferries with a capacity of up to 1,800 to 2,000 passengers and 700 cars. Ferries carry all vehicles, while hovercraft take all vehicles except HGVs, large trucks and buses. All operators except Hoverspeed offer night services, which may be cheaper. Berths, single cabins and pullman seats are usually available, and most ships have a restaurant, self-service cafeteria, a children's play area and duty-free shopping. Generally the longer the route, the better and wider the range of facilities provided, which often makes it worthwhile considering alternative routes to the Calais-Dover crossing. Although Calais-Dover is the shortest route and offers the most crossings, longer passages are generally less crowded and more relaxing.

Allow plenty of time to get to and from airports, ports and railway stations in France, particularly when travelling during peak hours when traffic congestion can be horrendous.

GETTING AROUND

Public transport (*transport public*) services in France vary considerably depending on where you live. Public transport is generally excellent in French cities, most of which have efficient local bus and rail services, many supplemented by *métro* (underground railway) and tram networks. French railways (SNCF) provide an excellent and fast rail service, particularly between cities served by the TGV, one of the world's fastest trains. It's a pleasure to

travel by train in France, particularly if you have plenty of time to enjoy the slow local trains that criss-cross the country. SNCF offer a range of special tickets and passes for commuters and travellers who book in advance. On the negative side, bus and rail services are poor or non-existent in rural areas and it's generally essential to have your own transport if you live in the country.

Paris has one of the most efficient, fully integrated and cheapest public transport systems of any major city in the world. In addition to its world-famous *métro*, public transport services include the RER express *métro*, an extensive suburban rail network and comprehensive bus services. The system is totally integrated and the same ticket can be used on all four services. Thanks to government subsidies, it's also inexpensive, although this doesn't stop the French from complaining about the cost (they have obviously never used British railways!). A range of commuter and visitors' tickets are available.

Bus: There are excellent bus services in Paris and other major cities, some of which also have trams or trolley buses. However, in rural areas, buses are few and far between, and the scant services that exist are usually designed to meet the needs of schoolchildren, workers and housewives on market days. This means that buses usually run early and late in the day with little or nothing in between, and services may cease altogether during the long summer school holiday period (July and August). Private bus services are often confusing and uncoordinated, and in cities may leave from different locations rather than a central bus station. Note that a city bus is generally called an *autobus* and a country bus a *car* or *autocar*. Smoking isn't permitted on buses. In rural areas, bus services are often operated by the SNCF and run between local towns and the railway station. An SNCF bus on which rail tickets and passes are valid is shown as an *Autocar* in rail timetables.

There are no national bus companies in France operating scheduled services, although many long-distance buses are operated by foreign companies such as Euroways/Eurolines, Riviera Express, Europabus, Miracle Bus and Grey-Green Coaches. Eurolines operate regular services from Britain to over 50 French cities including Bordeaux, Cannes, Lyon, Montpellier, Nice, Orléans, Paris, Perpignan, Reims, St. Malo and Strasbourg. Discounts are provided for students and youths on some routes. For information about internal inter-city services contact the *Fédération Nationale des Transports Routiers*, 6, rue Ampères, 75017 Paris (☎ 01.44.29.04.29).

Rail: The French railway network extends to every corner of France. French railways are operated by the state-owned SNCF (*Société Nationale des Chemins de fer Français*), which was formed in 1938 when the five major private railways were nationalised. The SNCF rail network is the largest in Western Europe with over 34,000km (21,100mi) of track, some 7,000 locomotives, around 15,000 passenger carriages (*voiture*) and 5,000 stations. It carries over 800 million passengers a year to over 6,000 destinations and has an excellent reputation for safety and punctuality. Most things in France start from or proceed via Paris and this is also true of the rail system. Paris and the Ile-de-France region provide SNCF with around two-thirds of its passengers (over 500 million a year) travelling on 5,000 trains a day. Note that there are few direct cross-country routes in France and it may be necessary to travel via Paris to reach your destination.

Air: There are a number of airlines offering domestic services including Air France, Air France Europe, UTA, TAT (Touraine Air Transport), Air Liberté (the latter two are owned by British Airways), Air Outre-Mer, Euralair, Aigle Azur, Air Littoral, Air Vendée and Europe Aero Service. Competition has intensified on

France's domestic routes in recent years where there has been a big improvement in regional services, partly as a result of a price war between airlines. Air Inter is France's largest domestic airline, operating 400 flights a day and carrying over 18 million passengers a year. It operates a comprehensive network of routes to around 40 regional airports and links regions both with Paris and with each other.

Air France also operates domestic services between major cities such as Paris, Bordeaux, Lyon, Marseille, Mulhouse/Basel, Nice, Strasbourg and Toulouse. Many domestic flights are timed to connect (*correspondance*) with international arrivals in Paris. Domestic air travel is being squeezed on some routes by TGV trains, although flying is sometimes cheaper than travelling by train and quicker on most routes. Any destination in France can be reached in less than 90 minutes (average one hour) by air and check-in times are just 15 to 30 minutes before departure. Private 24-hour air taxi services also operate from many French airports. Note that smoking is banned on French domestic flights and on Air France's international flights of less than two hours duration.

Road: France has an extensive motorway (*autoroute*) network of over 8,000km (some 5,000mi) supplemented by a comprehensive network (around 30,000km/ 18,500mi) of excellent trunk roads (*routes nationales*). French *autoroutes* are mostly toll roads built by private companies and are among Europe's finest. However, they are also among the world's most expensive and consequently main trunk roads (*routes nationales*) are jammed by drivers who are reluctant to pay or who cannot afford the high *autoroute* tolls. Driving is usually cheaper than taking the train, particularly when your car runs on diesel fuel, the costs are shared between a number of people *and* you avoid the *autoroutes*. However, if you're travelling long distances, you'll find it quicker and certainly less stressful to take a TGV train or fly. If you live in a city, particularly Paris, a car is usually a liability, while in rural areas it's a necessity. Driving is usually enjoyable in remote rural areas, particularly outside the tourist season, where it's possible to drive for miles without seeing another motorist (or a caravan). **Note, however, that the cost of motoring is high in France and it's an important consideration when buying a home there.**

Rush hours are from around 0630 to 0830 and 1630 to 1830, Mondays to Fridays, when town centres are best avoided. Paris is to be avoided by motorists at any time, where traffic moves at about the same speed as a hundred years ago (except for between 0200 and 0400). Friday afternoons are particularly busy on holiday weekends and also the period immediately before and after the lunch period, usually from around noon to 1500. Bottlenecks and traffic jams (*bouchons/embâcles*) are notorious at the start and end of holiday periods, particularly on roads out of Paris and other northern cities. Some areas and roads (particularly the *Autoroute du Soleil/de la Mort*) are to be avoided in July and August, when some six million Frenchmen and around over a million foreigners set off on their annual holidays. The most important days to stay at home are the first Saturday in August, when Parisians escape the city (*départ*) on their *grandes vacances*, and the last Sunday of August when they return (*la rentrée*). The 1st and 15th of July and the 15th August are also best avoided.

DRIVING

Like motorists in all countries, the French have their own idiosyncracies and customs, many of which are peculiar to a particular city or region. The personalities of most Frenchmen change the moment they get behind the wheel of a car, when even the most placid person can become an aggressive, impatient and intolerant homicidal maniac with a unshakable conviction in his own immortality. The French revere racing drivers (Alain Prost et al) and only the French could have invented the suicidal Paris-Dakar race (although it's a stroll compared with driving on French roads!). Some people (including a few foreigners) declare that the French aren't bad drivers at all, and simply innocent victims of a bad press and xenophobic foreigners (your own opinion will obviously depend on your personal experiences).

French drivers certainly aren't incompetent and must pass rigorous written and practical tests before they receive their licences. However, once they've discarded their '90' plates, the majority of French drivers are assailed by an uncontrollable urge to drive everywhere at maximum speed (young women often drive faster than men)

and they are among the world's most pathologically aggressive drivers. The French have a passion for fast cars (although their ardour doesn't extend to cleaning them) and abhor driving slowly and slow drivers. They are among the most impatient drivers in Europe and have no time for drivers who stick to speed limits, especially when driving through country towns. To a Frenchman, the racing line on a bend is *de rigueur* (which usually means driving on the wrong side of the road!) and overtaking is an obligation; me first (*moi d'abord*) is the Frenchman's motto.

You would think that with all the practice they get, the French would have mastered the art of overtaking safely. Unfortunately this isn't so. When it comes to reckless overtaking, France has some of the most dangerous drivers in Europe, who seem to use their brakes only when their horn doesn't work. They often hang out in the middle of the road, a few metres behind the vehicle they're planning to overtake and come perilously close to both the vehicle being overtaken and approaching vehicles – **BEWARE!** Foreigners (particularly *les rosbifs*) should be aware that many French drivers become apoplectic when overtaken by them.

When not overtaking, French drivers sit a few metres (centimetres) from your bumper trying to push you along irrespective of traffic density, road and weather conditions, or the prevailing speed limit. They are among Europe's worst tail-gaters and there's no solution short of moving out of their way or stopping, which is often impossible. Try to leave a large gap between your car and the one in front. This isn't just to give you more time to stop should the vehicles in front decide to get together, but also to give the inevitable tail-gater behind you more time to stop. **The closer the car is behind you, the further you should be from the vehicle in front.** On *autoroutes* and trunk roads, you must keep a safe distance (*distance de sécurité*) from the vehicle in front and you can be fined for not doing so. The safe distance on *autoroutes* is sometimes shown by arrows marked on the road surface.

The French have little respect for traffic rules, particularly anything to do with parking (in Paris, a car is a device used to create parking spaces). French drivers wear their dents with pride and there are many (many) dented cars in France (particularly in Paris, where the '75' registration number acts as a warning to other motorists). What makes driving in France even more of a lottery is that (apart from the unpredictability of French drivers) for many months of the year French roads are jammed with assorted foreigners. Their driving habits vary from exemplary to suicidal and include many (such as the British) who don't even know which side of the road to drive on! Beware of trucks on narrow roads, as truck drivers believe they have a divine right to three-quarters of the road and expect you to pull over. Don't, however, pull over too far, as many rural roads have soft verges and ditches.

If you drive in winter in areas that experience snow and ice – **take it easy!** In bad conditions you will notice that most French slow down considerably and even the habitual tail-gaters leave a larger gap than usual. Even a light snowfall can be treacherous, particularly on an icy road. When road conditions are bad, you should allow two to three times longer than usual to reach your destination (if you're wise, you'll stay at home). Note that many mountain passes are closed in winter (check with a French motoring organisation).

France has a good road system that includes everything from motorways (*autoroutes*) to forest dirt tracks. French *autoroutes* are excellent and most other main roads are also very good, although roads are generally poorer in the more remote departments with a low traffic density. Some 20 years ago France had fewer miles of motorways than many other western European countries. Since then there has been a huge investment in *autoroutes*, mainly by the private sector, and today France boasts one of the best motorway networks in Europe totalling over 8,000km (some 5,000mi). Because of the continuous expansion of the network, you shouldn't use a motoring atlas that's more than a few years out of date. A good guide to French *autoroutes* and their services is *Bonne Route!* by Anna Fitter (Anthony Nelson).

However, on the negative side, French *autoroutes* are toll roads (*autoroutes à péage*) and are among the most expensive in Europe. *Autoroute* travel costs an average of 0.40F per kilometre for a light car, e.g. 385F from Calais to Montpellier and 445F from Calais to Menton (not a great deal less than what it costs to fly with a budget airline from London to Nice!). A new system of tolls has been introduced in some areas with higher tolls during peak periods (an *autoroute tarifs* leaflet is available from the Association des Sociétés Françaises d'Autoroutes, 3 rue Edmond Valentin, 75007 Paris, ☎ 01.47.05.90.01). Goods vehicles over 7.5 tonnes are banned from roads between 1000 Saturday and 2200 Sunday, and from 2200 on the eve of a public holiday to 2200 on the day of the holiday. In Paris, goods vehicles aren't permitted to travel out of the city from 1600 to 1900 on Fridays to allow car drivers to get a head start for the weekend. However, although you may need to take out a second mortgage to drive on them, *autoroutes* are France's safest roads (e.g. you cannot get hit by a Frenchman overtaking on a blind bend).

For many Frenchmen, driving on *autoroutes* is a luxury and consequently they have the lowest traffic density of any European motorways. Unlike motorways in most other countries, French *autoroutes* have few access points and exits, which coupled with the high tolls, tends to discourage casual and local users. The same cannot be said of main trunk roads (*routes nationales*), which are jammed by drivers who are reluctant to pay or cannot afford the high *autoroute* tolls. If you must get from A to B in the shortest possible time, there's no alternative to the *autoroute* (apart from taking a plane or train). However, if you aren't in too much of a hurry, want to save money *and* wish to see something of France, you should avoid *autoroutes*. The money saved on tolls can pay for a good meal or an (inexpensive) hotel room and you'll arrive feeling much better. *Routes nationales* and other secondary roads are often straight (and dual carriageways) and you can usually make good time at (legal) speeds of between 80 and 110kph. Tolls are also levied to use the Mont Blanc (Chamonix-Entrèves, Italy, 11.6km/7.2mi), Fréjus (Modane-Bardonecchia, Italy, 12.8km/8mi) and Bielsa (Aragnouet-Bielsa, Spain, 3km/1.86mi) tunnels, and the Tancarville, St. Nazaire and Pont de Normandie bridges.

Driving in Paris is the motoring equivalent of hell – it's a beautiful city, but should be avoided at all costs when driving. If you cannot avoid driving in Paris, at least give the *Place Charles de Gaulle/Étoile (Arc de Triomphe)* a wide berth, which is one of the worst free-for-alls in the whole of Europe. This is a vast roundabout where 12 roads converge, all with (theoretical) *priorité à droite*. Because of the impossibility of apportioning blame in this circus, if you have an accident responsibility is automatically shared equally between the drivers concerned, irrespective of who had right of way (you have been warned!). The *Périphérique* is an eight lane race track around Paris, which although better than actually driving in Paris, is to be avoided if possible, particularly if you aren't sure which exit to take. Paris accommodates some three million vehicles a day, a third on the *Périphérique* ring road, although an advanced electronic traffic management system ensures that traffic keeps moving most of the time.

Anyone who has driven in France won't be surprised to learn that it has a high accident record, totalling some 8,000 to 9,000 deaths (16,000 in 1984!) and over 200,000 serious injuries a year – or around double that of Britain, Japan and the USA (in proportion to the number of vehicles). Given the Frenchman's *penchant* for a glass or two of *vin rouge* at lunchtime (or anytime), it isn't surprising that some 40 per cent of accidents involve drunken drivers (although the permitted alcohol level for motorists has been reduced).

Don't be too discouraged by the road hogs and tail-gaters. Driving in France can be a pleasant experience (Paris excepted), particularly when using country roads that are relatively traffic-free most of the time. If you come from a country where traffic drives on the left, most people quickly get used to driving on the 'wrong' side of the road. Just take it easy at first and bear in mind that there are other foreigners around just as confused as you are!

Driving Licences

The minimum age for driving in France is 18 for a motor car or motorcycle over 125cc and 14 for a motorcycle (moped) below 50cc. Holders of most foreign driving licences can drive in France for one year on a foreign or international driving licence from the date of receipt of their residence permit (*carte de séjour*). If you or any members of your family hold a foreign driving licence and intend to remain in France longer than one year, the procedure is as follows:

EU Members: The Second EU Driving Licence Directive provides, among other things, for the mutual recognition of driving licences issued by EU Member States. If EU citizens move from one Member State to another, it's no longer necessary to obtain a local driving licence after one year. **However, a resident who commits a motoring offence in France involving a loss of licence points (see below) is obliged to exchange his foreign licence for a French one so that the penalty may be applied.**

Non-EU Members: After residence of one year, a French driving licence is required by non-EU residents. You should expect the procedure to take at least two months and therefore should apply to the *Préfecture* or *Sous-préfecture* well before the year is up. You will need a valid, translated driver's licence; proof of domicile; your *carte de séjour*; two passport-size photographs; and the fee in the form of fiscal stamps (*timbre fiscal*). Some countries and some states within the United States have reciprocal agreements with France to waive the driving test, but applicants must take the written exam concerning rules of the road (including road sign recognition). If you need to take a driving test, it's advisable to take a course through a certified driving school, some of which have sections for English speakers. The French Highway Code (*Code de la Route*) is available at most bookshops. The French authorities will confiscate your foreign driving licence and return it to the country of issue or retain it and return it to you when you leave France permanently. It's advisable to make a copy of your foreign licence before surrendering it, as your French licence will show that you have been driving only since it was issued (which may make life difficult if you want to rent a car). A French driving licence is pink in colour and contains a photograph.

You can have your licence suspended in France for 7 to 28 days for minor offences and for up to six years or longer for manslaughter. Suspensions of a French driving licence for six months or longer are based on a controversial points system that came into effect on 1st December 1992. All drivers start with 12 licence points and from one to six points are deducted for offences, depending on their gravity. Typical offences are failing to dip headlights and minor speeding (one point, although speeding can 'earn' up to four points); parking on the hard shoulder of an *autoroute* or accelerating while being overtaken (two points); driving on the wrong side of the road (Britons beware!) and dangerous overtaking (three points); injuring somebody or failure to observe a stop sign or red light (four points); and for killing somebody or driving under the influence of alcohol (six points). The points system is explained in a booklet *permis à points* available from police stations.

When an offence is registered, you receive a letter of notification from the *préfecture* stating the number of points lost and the number remaining. All points are regained if no offences are committed within three years of your last conviction. When all 12 points have been lost, you receive a demand to hand over your licence within one week to your local *préfecture* and you're usually banned from driving for a minimum of six months. Depending on the circumstances, you may need to pass a written test, a practical driving test (e.g. drivers with less than three years experience) or a medical examination to regain your licence. If you lose your French driving licence or it's stolen, you must report it to the police. They will issue you with an acknowledgement (*récépissé de déclaration de perte ou de vol de pièces d'identité*) that's valid until a replacement is issued. Note that a replacement licence may cost twice as much as the original.

Car Insurance

Under French law, motor vehicles plus trailers and semi-trailers must be insured when entering France. However, it isn't mandatory for cars insured in most European countries to have an international insurance 'green' card (*carte internationale d'assurance automobile/carte verte*) in France. Motorists insured in an EU country or the Czech Republic, Hungary, Liechtenstein, Norway, the Slovak Republic and Switzerland are automatically covered for third party liability in France. If you arrive in France with a vehicle without valid insurance, you can buy a temporary policy valid for 8, 15 or 30 days from the vehicle insurance department of the French customs office at your point of entry. The following categories of car insurance are available in France:

Third Party (*responsabilité civile/minimale/tiers illimitée*): Third Party insurance is compulsory and includes unlimited medical costs and damage to third party property.

Third Party, Fire & Theft (*tiers personnes/restreinte/intermédiaire*): Third party, fire and theft (TPF&T) insurance, known in some countries as part comprehensive, includes cover against fire, natural hazards (e.g. rocks falling on your car), theft, broken glass (e.g. windscreen) and legal expenses (*défense-recours*). TPF&T includes damage (or theft) to contents and radio.

Multi-risk Collision (*multirisque collision*): Multi-risk collision covers all the risks listed under TPF&T plus damage caused to your own vehicle in the event of a collision with a person, vehicle, or animal belonging to an **identifiable person.**

Fully Comprehensive - all accidents (*multirisque tous accidents/tous risques*): Fully comprehensive insurance covers all the risks listed under TPF&T and multi-risk collision and includes damage to your vehicle however caused and **whether a third party can be identified or not.** Note, however, that illegally parked cars automatically lose their comprehensive cover. Fully comprehensive insurance is usually compulsory for lease and credit purchase contracts.

Driver protection (*protection du conducteur/assurance conducteur*) is usually optional in France and can be added to insurance policies. It enables the driver of a vehicle involved in an accident to claim for bodily injury to himself, including compensation for his incapacity to work or for his beneficiaries should he be killed.

Premiums: Insurance premiums are high in France – a reflection of the high accident rate and the large number of stolen cars. Premiums vary considerably depending on numerous factors including the type of insurance; your car, age and accident record; and the area where you live. Premiums are highest in Paris and other cities and lowest in rural areas. Premiums are lower for cars over three years old. Some premiums are based on the number of kilometres (*kilométrage*) driven annually. Shop around and obtain a number of quotations. Value added tax (TVA) is payable on insurance premiums in France.

You can reduce your premium by choosing to pay an excess (*franchise*), e.g. the first 2,000F to 5,000F of a claim. Special insurance can be purchased for contents and accessories such as an expensive car stereo system. A car with a value of over 100,000F must have an approved alarm installed and the registration number must be engraved on windows. A surcharge is made when a car isn't garaged over night. Drivers with less than three years experience usually pay a penalty (*malus*) and drivers under 25 pay higher premiums. However, the maximum penalty for young drivers due to their age is 100 per cent or double the normal premium. If you're convicted of drunken or dangerous driving, your premium will be increased considerably, e.g. by up to 150 per cent. It's possible to insure a vehicle for less than one year (e.g. three months) and you can also insure a vehicle for a single journey over 1,000km (621mi).

No-Claims: A foreign no-claims bonus is usually valid in France, but you must provide written evidence from your present or previous insurance company, not just an insurance renewal notice. You may also need an official French translation. You should insist on having your no-claims bonus recognised, even if you don't receive the same reduction as you received abroad (shop around!). If you haven't held car insurance for two years, you're usually no longer entitled to a no-claims bonus in France.

The no-claims bonus isn't as generous as in some other countries and is usually 5 per cent for each year's accident-free driving up to a maximum of 50 per cent after ten years. If you have an accident, you're usually required to pay a penalty (*malus*) or your bonus is reduced. Your premium will be increased by 25 per cent each time you're responsible for an accident or 12.5 per cent if you're partly to blame, up to a maximum penalty of 150 per cent after six accidents. However, if you have had the maximum bonus for three years, one accident won't reduce it. If you're only partly to blame for an accident, e.g. less than 50 per cent, your premium increase is reduced by half. There's no premium increase if your car is damaged while parked (although you must be able to prove it and identify the party responsible) or as a result of fire, theft, or glass breakage, and you should still receive your bonus for the current year.

Claims: In the event of an accident, claims are decided on the information provided in accident report forms (*Constat à l'Amiable/Constat Européen d'Accident*) completed by drivers, reports by insurance company experts and police reports. If you're judged to be less than 30 per cent responsible, you won't usually lose your no-claims bonus. You must notify your insurance company of a claim within a limited period, e.g. two to five days. If you have an accident, the damage must usually be inspected and the repair sanctioned by your insurance company's assessor, although sometimes an independent assessment may be permitted. For minor repairs, an inspection may be unnecessary. After reporting your car stolen, 30 days must elapse before an insurance company will consider a claim. Note that it often takes a long time to resolve claims in France and a number of years isn't unusual!

Cancellation: French insurance companies are forbidden by law to cancel third party cover after a claim, except in the case of drunken driving or when a driver is subsequently disqualified from driving for longer than one month. A company can, however, refuse to renew your policy at the end of the current period, although they must give you two months notice. If you have an accident while breaking the law, e.g. drunken driving or illegal parking, your comprehensive insurance may be automatically downgraded to third party only. This means that you must pay for your own repairs and medical expenses. If you find it difficult to obtain cover, the *Bureau Central de Tarification* can demand that the company of your choice provide you with cover, with the premium being fixed by the *Bureau*.

If you wish to cancel your car insurance at the end of the current term, you must notify your insurance company in writing by registered letter and give three months notice. You may cancel your insurance without notice if the premium is increased, the terms are altered, or your car has been declared a total loss or stolen. Policies can also be cancelled for certain personal reasons such as moving house, divorce or retirement.

Green Card: All French insurance companies and most other insurance companies in Western Europe provide an automatic 'green' card (yellow in France!), extending your normal insurance cover (e.g. fully comprehensive) to most other European countries. This doesn't, however, include cars insured in Britain, where most insurance companies (the Prudential Assurance Co. is one exception) usually provide a free green card for from 30 or 45 days to a maximum of three months a year. Nevertheless, you should shop around as some companies allow drivers a green card for up to six months a year. This is to discourage the British from driving on the continent, where they are a menace and a danger to other road users (most don't know their left from their right, particularly the politicians!). If you're British and have fully comprehensive insurance, it's wise to have a green card when visiting France.

If you drive a British-registered car and spend over six months a year on the continent, you may need to take out a special (i.e. expensive) European insurance policy or obtain insurance with a European company. Note that many French insurance companies will insure foreign-registered cars, although it may be for a limited period only. French regulations have traditionally required French-registered cars to be insured with a French insurance company. However, theoretically from 1st January 1993, EU residents can insure their cars in any EU country.

In France, an insurance certificate has a stick-on tab or vignette (*vignette d'assurance*) that must be displayed on your windscreen next to the road tax vignette. Driving without insurance is a serious offence, for which you can be fined up to 50,000F and imprisoned for up to six months. France has a national fund (*Fonds de garantie automobile*) that pays compensation to victims of hit-and-run drivers.

Car Crime

Car theft is rampant in France, which has one of the highest numbers of vehicle thefts in Europe (the thefts of contents or accessories from motor vehicles is even more commonplace). If you drive anything other than a worthless heap, you should have theft insurance that includes your car stereo and personal belongings. It's wise to have your car fitted with an alarm, an ignition disabling system or other anti-theft device, plus a visible deterrent, such as a steering or gear lock.

It's particularly important to protect your car if you own a model that's desirable to car thieves, e.g. most new sports and executive cars, which are often stolen to order by professional crooks. On the French Riviera stolen cars often find their way to Africa and may already be on a ferry by the time the owners report them stolen. A good security system won't stop someone breaking into your car (which usually takes most thieves a matter of seconds) and may not prevent your car being stolen, but it will at least make it more difficult and may persuade a thief to look for an easier target. Radios, tape and CD players attract a lot of the wrong attention in most French cities (especially Paris) and coastal resorts. If you buy an expensive stereo system, buy one with a removable unit or with a removable control panel that you can pop in a pocket. However, never forget to remove it, even when stopping for a few minutes. Some manufacturers provide stereo systems that won't work when they're removed from their original vehicles or are inoperable without a security code being entered.

When leaving your car unattended, store any valuables (including clothes) in the boot or out of sight. If you leave your car papers in your car, make sure you have a copy. If possible avoid parking in long-term car parks, as these are favourite hunting grounds for car thieves. Foreign-registered cars, particularly camper vans and mobile homes, are popular targets, particularly when parked in ports. When parking overnight or when it's dark, parking in a well-lit area may help deter car thieves. If your car is stolen or anything is stolen from it, report it to the police in the area where it was stolen. You can report it by telephone, but must go to the station to complete a report. Don't, however, expect the police to find it or even take any interest in your loss. Report a theft to your insurance company as soon as possible.

Highway Piracy: Highway piracy (*les pirates de la route*) is becoming an increasing problem in some areas, where foreign drivers are often the targets. Gangs deliberately bump or ram cars to get drivers to stop, usually late at night when there's little traffic about. A driver may also pose as a plain clothes policeman and try to get you to stop by flashing a 'badge' or setting up bogus road blocks. In the worst cases thieves take not just the car and its contents, but even the victims' clothes they are wearing. Travelling at night in France is becoming increasingly hazardous and should be avoided if possible.

General Road Rules

The following general road rules may help you adjust to driving in France. Don't, however, expect other motorists to adhere to them (many French drivers invent their own 'rules').

- You may have already noticed that the French drive on the right-hand side of the road (*serrez à droite*). It saves confusion if you do likewise! If you aren't used to driving on the right, take it easy until you're accustomed to it. Be particularly alert when leaving lay-bys, T-junctions, one-way streets, petrol stations and car parks, as it's easy to lapse into driving on the left. It's helpful to display a reminder (e.g. 'think right!') on your car's dashboard.

- Speed limits in France are 130/110kph (81/69mph) on *autoroutes*, 110/100kph (69/62mph) on dual carriageways, 90/80kph (56/50mph) on other rural roads, and 50kph (31mph) or as signposted (e.g. 40 or 45kph) in urban areas, towns and villages. Speed limits are reduced in rain (*par temps de pluie*), when the second limit shown above applies. In thick fog when visibility is less than 50 metres, speed limits are automatically reduced to 50kph on all roads.

- Alcohol is a major factor in some 30 to 40 per cent of France's road accidents. In 1995, the permitted blood alcohol concentration in France was lowered to 50mg of alcohol per 100ml of blood (it remains 80mg in Monaco), which is lower than most other European countries (although it's the proposed limit for the EU as a whole). Random breath tests (*alcooltest/dépistage*) can be carried out by the police at any time and motorists who are involved in accidents or who infringe motoring regulations are routinely breathalysed.

- All motorists must carry a red breakdown triangle and a full set of spare bulbs and fuses. It's advisable, but not mandatory, to carry a fire extinguisher and a first-aid kit.

- Most main roads are designated priority roads (*passages protégés*), indicated by one of three signs. The most common priority sign is a yellow diamond on a white background, in use throughout most of Europe. The end of priority is shown by the same sign with a black diagonal line through it. The other two signs are a triangular crossroad sign with the words *passage protégé* underneath and a triangular sign showing a broad vertical arrow with a thinner horizontal line through it. On secondary roads *without* priority signs and in built-up areas, you must give way to vehicles coming from your RIGHT. **Failure to observe this rule is the cause of many accidents.**
  The priority rule was fine when there was little traffic, but nowadays most countries (France included) realise the necessity of having 'stop' or 'give way' (*Cédez le Passage*) signs. Most French motorists no longer treat *priorité à droite* as a God-given right, although some still pull out without looking. The priority to the right rule usually also applies in car parks, but never when exiting *from* car parks or dirt tracks. If you're ever in doubt about who has the right of way, it's wise to give way (particularly to large trucks!).

- The wearing of seatbelts is *compulsory* in France and includes passengers in rear seats when seatbelts are fitted. Front belts are mandatory on cars registered after January 1965 and rear seatbelts on cars registered after October 1978. Children under the age of ten may ride in the front of a vehicle only when an approved seat is fitted (facing rearwards) or when a vehicle has no back seat. Children aged under ten riding in the rear must use a special seat or a safety belt suitable for children. A baby under nine months old must be strapped into a cot or special car seat on the rear seat and an infant from nine months to three years old must have an approved child safety seat. You can be fined up to 500F for not wearing a seatbelt. Note that if you have an accident and weren't wearing a seatbelt, your insurance company can refuse to pay a claim for personal injury.

- Don't drive in bus, taxi or cycle lanes (you can be fined for doing so) unless necessary to avoid a stationary vehicle or another obstruction. Bus drivers get irate if you drive in their lanes, identified by a continuous yellow line parallel to the kerb. Be sure to keep clear of tram lines and outside the restricted area, delineated by a line.

- The use of horns are forbidden in towns at night, when lights should be flashed to warn other motorists or pedestrians. In towns, horns should be used in emergencies only, day or night.

- The sequence of French traffic lights (*feux tricolores/feux de circulation*) is red, green, yellow (amber) and back to red. Yellow means stop at the stop line; you may proceed only if the yellow light appears after you have crossed the stop line or when stopping may cause an accident. Traffic lights are often suspended above the road, although most are on posts at the side, with smaller lights lower down at eye level for motorists who are too close to see the main lights (an excellent idea). In Paris and other cities there's a two-second delay after one set of lights change to red before the other set change to green, to allow time for those who don't care to stop at red lights or cannot tell the difference between red and green. You can be fined around 2,000F for running a red light, which also earns you four penalty points on your licence (or a ticket to the next life!).

- Always come to a complete stop when required at intersections and ensure that you stop behind the white line (intersections are a favourite spot for police patrols waiting for motorists to put a wheel a few centimetres over the line).

- White or yellow lines mark the separation of traffic lanes. A solid single line or two solid lines means no overtaking (*dépasser*) in either direction. A solid line to the right of the centre line, i.e. on your side of the road, means that overtaking is prohibited in your direction. You may overtake only when there's a single broken line in the middle of the road or double lines with a broken line on your side of the road. No overtaking may also be shown by the international sign of two cars side by side (one red and one black). Processions, funerals or foot soldiers mustn't be overtaken at more than 30kph (18mph).

  Always check your rear view and wing mirrors carefully before overtaking as French motorists seem to appear from nowhere and zoom past at a 'zillion' miles an hour, especially on country roads. If you drive a right-hand drive (RHD) car, take extra care when overtaking – the most dangerous manoeuvre in motoring. It's wise to have a special 'overtaking mirror' fitted to a RHD car.

- Many motorists seem to have an aversion to driving in the right-hand lane on a three-lane *autoroute*, in effect reducing it to two lanes. It's illegal to overtake on an inside lane unless traffic is being channelled in a different direction. Motorists must indicate before overtaking *and* when moving back into an inside lane after overtaking, e.g. on an *autoroute*.

- Studded tyres may be used from 1st November to 31st March (although this can be extended in bad weather conditions) on vehicles weighing under 3.5 tonnes. Vehicles fitted with studded tyres or snow chains are restricted to a maximum speed of 90kph (56mph) and a '90' disc must be affixed to the rear. Note that you can be fined for not having snow chains (in your car) in winter in mountain areas, even when there's no snow!

- Take care when crossing railway lines, particularly at crossings with no barriers, which can be *very* dangerous. Approach a railway level crossing slowly and **STOP**:

  - as soon as the barrier or half-barrier starts to fall;
  - as soon as the red warning lights are illuminated or flashing, or the warning bell is ringing;
  - when a train approaches!

  Your new car may be built like a tank, but it won't look so smart after a scrap with a 70-tonne locomotive.

- Be particularly wary of moped (*vélomoteur*) riders and cyclists. It isn't always easy to see them, particularly when they're hidden by the blind spots of a car or are riding at night without lights. Many young moped riders seem to have a death wish and tragically hundreds lose their lives each year in France (maybe 14 years of age is too young to let them loose on the roads!). They are constantly pulling out into traffic or turning without looking or signalling. **Follow the example set by French motorists, who, when overtaking mopeds and cyclists, ALWAYS give them a wide . . . . WIDE berth.** If you knock them off their bikes you may have a difficult time convincing the police that it wasn't your fault; far better to avoid them (and the police).

● An 'F' nationality plate (*plaque de nationalité*) must be affixed to the rear of a French-registered car when motoring abroad and drivers of foreign registered cars in France must have the appropriate nationality plate affixed to the rear of their cars. You can be fined on the spot for not displaying it, although it isn't often enforced judging by the number of cars without them.

● Cars mustn't be overloaded, particularly roofracks, and luggage weight shouldn't exceed that recommended in manufacturers' handbooks. Note that carrying bicycles on the back of a car is illegal if they obscure the rear lights or the registration number. French police make spot checks and fine offenders around 500F on the spot. If you want to transport bikes in France you should have a roof-mounted rack and (if necessary) a boot rack for transportation on a ferry.

● Be careful where you park, particularly in cities where your car can be clamped or towed away in a flash. *Never* park across entrances, at bus stops or taxi ranks, in front of fire and ambulance stations and schools (which may be indicated by yellow kerbstones) or near pedestrian crossings. No parking may be shown by a *Stationnement Gênant* sign (with a picture of a truck towing away a vehicle) or a *Stationnement Interdit* sign, which means parking is forbidden, and may be accompanied by the sign of a 'P' with a line through it. Read all parking signs carefully and look for kerb markings (ask someone if you aren't sure whether parking is permitted).

● The maximum dimensions for caravans or trailers are 2.5m (8.2ft) wide and 11m (36ft) long, or a combined length of 18m (59ft) for car and caravan/trailer combined. No passengers may be carried in a moving caravan. On narrow roads, drivers towing a caravan or trailer are (where possible) required to slow or pull into the side of the road to allow faster vehicles to overtake (although they rarely do). The speed limits for a towing car depends on the weight of the trailer or caravan.

● All motorists in France must be familiar with the French highway code (*Code de la Route*), available from bookshops throughout France.

Car Rental

Car rental companies such as Avis, Budget, Citer, Eurodollar, Europcar, Hertz, Solvet and Thrifty have offices in most large towns and major airports. Look under *location de voitures* in your local Yellow Pages. If you're a visitor, it's advisable to reserve a rental car before arriving in France. Fly-drive deals are available through most airlines and travel agents. French railways (SNCF) offer inclusive train and car rental deals and their *France Vacances Pass* provides car rental. You can rent an Avis car from some 200 SNCF stations and leave it at any station operating the scheme (*Train + auto* leaflets are available at SNCF stations and include a map of participating stations).

Car rental in France is expensive, particularly for short periods, and includes value added tax (TVA) at 20.6 per cent. For example Budget charge around 600F (including optional insurances and taxes, plus almost 3F per km above 100km a day) for a one day rental of their cheapest models, e.g. Peugeot 106 KID or Renault Clio.

Rates reduce considerably over long periods, e.g. a week or a month. Note that a diesel car is much cheaper to run than a petrol-engined car. Special rates are available for weekends, usually from noon on Fridays to 0900 on Mondays. Local rental companies are usually cheaper than the nationals, although cars must be returned to the pick-up point. Car rental rates usually include Collision Damage Waiver (CDW) and Personal Accident Insurance (PAI). If required, check in advance that you're permitted to take a car out of France (usually prohibited).

To hire a car in France you must be a minimum of 18 years old, although most companies have increased this to 21 (e.g. Budget, although drivers under 25 must pay an extra 100F per day of rental) or even 25 (e.g. Hertz). For certain categories of car the limit is 25. Drivers must have held a full licence for a minimum of one year and most companies have an upper age limit of 60 or 65. International companies require payment by credit card, although local firms may allow you to pay a cash deposit of 1,000F to 2,000F (although the whole rental period may need to be paid in advance). You may also require a residence permit (*permis de séjour*) and an identification check will be made.

Rental cars can be ordered with a portable telephone, a luggage rack, snow chains and child seats can be fitted for an extra charge. You can also hire a 4-wheel drive car, station wagon, minibus, luxury car, armoured limousine or a convertible, possibly with a choice of manual or automatic gearbox. Minibuses accessible to wheelchairs can also be hired, e.g. from Hertz. Older cars can be hired from many garages at lower rates than those charged by the national car-hire companies. Vans and pick-ups are available from the major rental companies by the hour, half-day or day, or from smaller local companies (which, once again, are cheaper).

Note that cars can be rented in France through major international rental companies such as Alamo (☎ USA 800-327-9633), Avis (☎ USA 800-331-1212), Budget (☎ USA 800-527-0700) and Hertz (☎ USA 800-654-3131) by booking through their American offices and paying by credit card. This is a legitimate practice and can save 50 per cent or more on local hire rates. At present the car hire companies have no way of knowing where the calls were made and therefore cannot prevent this practice. Toll-free (800) numbers of other US-based rental companies can be obtained from international directory enquiries, although you pay international rates when phoning from abroad.

2.

FURTHER CONSIDERATIONS

This chapter contains important considerations for most people planning to buy a home in France, particularly those planning to live there permanently or semi-permanently. It contains information about the climate, geography, health, insurance, shopping, pets, television and radio, learning French and crime.

CLIMATE

France is the only country in Europe that experiences three distinct climates: continental, maritime and Mediterranean. It isn't easy to generalise about French weather (*temps*), as many regions and areas of France are influenced by surrounding mountains, forests and other geographical features, and have their own micro-climates. If you're planning to live in France and don't know whether the climate in a particular region will suit you, it's advisable to rent accommodation until you're absolutely sure, as the extremes of hot and cold in some areas are too much for some people. If you're seeking 'guaranteed' sun you need to head south. Generally the Loire river is considered to be the point where the cooler northern European climate gradually begins to change to the warmer southern climate. Spring and autumn are usually fine throughout France, although the length of the seasons vary depending on the region and altitude. In Paris, it's rare for the temperature to fall below minus 5°C (41°F) in winter or to rise above 30°C (86°F) in summer. However, Paris gets its fair share of rain. The expression 'raining cats and dogs' (*il pleut chats et chiens*) was coined here, when during periods of heavy rainfall, dead cats and dogs were flushed out of the sewers into the streets!

The west and northwest (e.g. Brittany and Normandy) have a maritime climate tempered by the Atlantic and the Gulf Stream, with mild winters and warm summers, and most rainfall in spring and autumn. The area around La Rochelle in the west enjoys a pleasant micro-climate and is the second sunniest area of France after the French Riviera. Many people consider the western Atlantic coast has the best summer climate in France, with the heat tempered by cool sea breezes. The Massif Central (which acts as a weather barrier between north and south) and eastern France have a moderate continental climate with cold winters and hot and stormy summers. However, the centre and eastern upland areas have an extreme continental climate with freezing winters and sweltering summers. The northern Massif is prone to huge variations in temperature and it was here that an amazing 41°C (106°F) minimum/maximum temperature difference was recorded **in one day** (on 10th August 1885).

The Midi, stretching from the Pyrénées to the Alps, is hot and dry except for early spring, when there's usually heavy rainfall; the Cévennes region is the wettest in France with some 200cm (79in) of rain a year. Languedoc has hot dry summers and much colder winters than the French Riviera, with snow often remaining until May in the mountainous inland areas. The Riviera enjoys a Mediterranean climate of mild winters, daytime temperatures rarely dropping below 10°C (50°F), and humid and very hot summers, with the temperature often rising above 30°C (86°F). The average sunshine on the French Riviera is five hours in January and 12 hours in July. Note, however, that it isn't always warm and sunny on the Riviera and it can get quite cold and wet in some areas in winter.

The higher you go, the colder it gets, therefore if you don't like cold and snow, don't live up a mountain, e.g. in the Alps, Pyrénées, Vosges, Auvergne or Jura mountains. The mountains of the Alps and Pyrénées experience extremes of weather with heavy snow in winter and hot summers, although the western Pyrénées have surprisingly mild winters. The natural barrier of the Alps disrupts normal weather patterns and there are often significant local climatic variations. Central and eastern France have the coldest winters and consequently the highest heating bills. One of the most unpleasant aspects of very cold winters is motoring. If you need to commute in winter, bear in mind that roads are inevitably treacherous at times and can be frightening if you aren't used to driving on ice and snow (fog is also a particular hazard).

France occasionally experiences extreme and unpredictable weather (it's all the fault of the politicians), which has become a favourite topic of conversation in some areas. Freak conditions combined to create violent storms in the south of France in recent years, e.g. in 1992 winds of 150km (93mph) an hour and flash floods resulted in over 40 deaths, and 63 communes being declared disaster areas. They were the worst storms in living memory and of a ferocity experienced only once every 50 years. In some areas 30cm (12in) of rain fell in three hours and half the annual rainfall for the region fell in just ten hours. Wherever you live in France, if you're anywhere near a waterway you should ensure that you have insurance against floods.

France experiences many violent cold and dry winds (*vent violent*) including the *Mistral* and the *Tramontane*. The *Mistral* is a bitterly cold wind that blows down the southern end of the Rhône valley into the Camargue and Marseille. The *Tramontane* affects the coastal region from Perpignan, near the Pyrénées, to Narbonne. Corsica is buffeted by many winds including the two aforementioned plus the *Mezzogiorno* and *Scirocco*.

Average daily maximum/minimum temperatures for selected cities in Centigrade and Fahrenheit (in brackets) are:

Location	Spring	Summer	Autumn	Winter
Bordeaux	17/6 (63/43)	25/14 (77/57)	18/8 (64/46)	9/2 (48/36)
Boulogne	12/6 (54/43)	20/14 (68/57)	14/10 (57/50)	6/2 (43/36)
Lyon	16/6 (61/43)	27/15 (81/59)	16/7 (61/45)	5/-1 (41/30)
Nantes	15/6 (59/43)	24/14 (75/57)	16/8 (61/46)	8/2 (46/36)
Nice	17/9 (63/48)	27/18 (81/64)	21/12 (70/54)	13/4 (55/39)
Paris	16/6 (61/43)	25/15 (77/59)	16/6 (57/43)	6/1 (43/34)
Strasbourg	16/5 (61/41)	25/13 (77/55)	14/6 (57/43)	1/-2 (37/28)

A quick way to make a *rough* conversion from Centigrade to Fahrenheit is to multiply by two and add 30. Weather forecasts (*météo*) are broadcast on TV and radio stations and published in daily newspapers. You can obtain the weather forecast for a particular department by telephoning 08.36.68.02 followed by the department number, e.g. 24 for Dordogne. Forecasts are also available via Minitel (3615 *météo*) and the Internet.

GEOGRAPHY

France, often referred to as *l'héxagone* due to its hexagonal shape, is the third largest country in Western Europe after Russia and the re-unified Germany. It covers an area of almost 550,000km² (213,000mi²), stretching 1,050km (650mi) from north to south and almost the same distance from west to east (from the tip of Britanny to Strasbourg). Its land and sea border extends for 4,800km (around 3,000mi) and includes 2,700km (1,677mi) of sea coast. France also incorporates the Mediterranean island of Corsica (*Corse*) situated 160km (99mi) from France and 80km (50mi) from Italy, covering 8,721km² (3,367mi²) and with a coastline of 1,000km (620mi). France is bordered by Andorra, Belgium, Germany, Italy, Luxembourg, Spain and Switzerland, and the opening of the Channel Tunnel in 1994 connected it with Britain (although only by rail). Its borders are largely delimited by geographical barriers including the English Channel (*la Manche*) in the north, the Atlantic Ocean in the west, the Pyrénées and the Mediterranean in the south, and the Alps and the Rhine in the east.

The north and west of France is mostly low-lying. The Paris basin in the centre of the country occupies a third of France's land area and is one of Europe's most fertile agricultural regions. The Massif Central in the centre of France is noted for its extinct volcanoes, hot springs and many rivers. In general the south and southeast of France are mountainous, although despite its many mountain ranges (Alps, Auvergne, Jura, Massif Central, Pyrénées and Vosges), France is largely a lowland country with most of its area less than 200 metres above sea level. Almost 90 per cent of the land is productive, with around one-third cultivated, one-quarter pasture and one-quarter forest.

France has a comprehensive network of rivers and canals comprising some 40 per cent of European waterways, including the Garonne, Loire, Rhine, Rhône and the Seine. The Loire, 1,020km (634mi) in length, is France's longest river. The Massif Central has many peaks rising above 1,500m (5,000ft) and Europe's highest mountain, Mont Blanc (4,810m/15,781ft), is situated in the French Alps.

France also has a number of overseas territories, four of which are classified as overseas departments: Guadaloupe, Guyane, Martinique and Réunion. Although situated within France, Monaco is an independent principality and isn't governed by France. France has 22 regions and 95 *départements*, shown on the map in **Appendix C**. A map of France showing the major cities and geographical features is shown on page 6.

HEALTH

One of the most important aspects of living in France (or anywhere else for that matter) is maintaining good health. The quality of health care and health care facilities in France are excellent and rate among the best in the world. There are virtually no waiting lists for operations or hospital beds and the standard of hospital treatment is second to none. Public and private medicine operate alongside one another and there's no difference in the quality of treatment provided by public hospitals and private establishments. However, local hospital services, particularly hospitals with casualty departments, are limited in rural areas.

France has an excellent, although expensive, national health system, providing free or low cost health care for all those who contribute to French social security, plus their families and retirees (including those from other European Union countries). Those who don't automatically qualify for health care under the French national health system can contribute voluntarily or take out private health insurance. The French spend around 10 per cent of their national income on health care and are the world's second largest spenders after the USA. However, funding of the public health service is spiralling out of control and spending could increase to 20 per cent of GDP in a decade if it isn't checked. In France there's a cosy relationship between the doctors and unions, who between them control health spending, with the state's role being simply to cover the deficit. France needs to drastically reform its health care system and cut some 50,000 hospital beds. However, while most people recognise the need for reform, they are reluctant to lose hospitals, unlimited second opinions and an endless supply of free pills.

France devotes a greater proportion of its GDP to health than to defence or education, the lion's share being spent on medicines and drugs rather than hospitals. It has long been a nation of hypochondriacs and the French visit their doctors more often than most other Europeans and buy large quantities of medicines, health foods and vitamin pills. In general, French medicine places the emphasis on preventive medicine, rather than treating sickness. Alternative medicine is popular (*médecine douce*), particularly acupuncture and homeopathy. These treatments are recognised by France's medical council (*Ordre des Médecins*) and reimbursed by social security when prescribed by a doctor. France is the world leader in homeopathy and some 15 per cent of the population regularly consults homeopathic doctors.

Despite the common stereotype of the French as wine-swilling gourmets stuffing themselves with rich foods, many have become health freaks in recent years. Fitness and health centres flourish in most towns and even jogging has become fashionable in recent years. Smoking has declined considerably and is now a minority habit, although higher than in many other European countries. Air pollution (caused by vehicles not smokers!) is an increasing problem in Paris and other French cities such as Grenoble, Lyon and Strasbourg, where it's blamed for a sharp rise in asthma cases. There's also a high and increasing rate of stress in French cities. The average life expectancy is 81 for women (the highest in Europe) and 73 for men.

The incidence of heart disease in France is among the lowest in the world, a fact that has recently been officially contributed in part to their (largely Mediterranean) diet and high consumption of red wine. They do, however, have a high incidence of cirrhosis of the liver and other problems associated with excess alcohol. Among expatriates, sunstroke, change of diet, too much rich food and (surprise, surprise) too much alcohol are the most common causes of health problems. When you have had too much of *la bonne vie* you can take yourself off to a French spa for a few weeks to rejuvenate your system (in preparation for another bout of over indulgence). Among the most popular treatments offered is thalassotherapy, a sea water 'cure' recommended for arthritis, circulation problems, depression and fatigue.

Pre-Departure Check: If you're planning to take up residence in France, even if for part of the year only, it's wise to have a health check (medical or screening, eyes, teeth, etc.) before your arrival, particularly if you have a record of poor health or are elderly. If you're already taking regular medication, you should note that the brand names of drugs and medicines vary from country to country and you should ask your doctor for the generic name. If you wish to match medication prescribed abroad, you will need a current prescription with the medication's trade name, the manufacturer's name, the chemical name and the dosage. Most drugs have an equivalent in other countries, although particular brands may be difficult or impossible to obtain in France.

It's possible to have medication sent from abroad, when no import duty or value added tax is usually payable. If you're visiting a holiday home in France for a limited period, you should take sufficient medication to cover your stay. In an emergency a local doctor will write a prescription that can be filled at a local pharmacy or a hospital may refill a prescription from its own pharmacy. It's also advisable to take some of your favourite non-prescription drugs with you (e.g. aspirins, cold and flu remedies, creams, etc.) as they may be difficult or impossible to obtain in France or may be much more expensive. If applicable, you should also take a spare pair of spectacles, contact lenses, dentures or a hearing aid.

You can safely drink the water in France unless it's labelled as non-drinking (*eau non-potable*), but the wine (especially the 1973 Château Mouton Rothschild) and beer are more enjoyable. *Santé!*

INSURANCE

An important aspect of owning a home in France is insurance, not only for your home and its contents, but also for your family when visiting. If you live in France permanently you will require additional insurance. It's unnecessary to spend half your income insuring yourself against every eventuality from the common cold to being sued for your last *centime*, but it's important to insure against any event that could precipitate a major financial disaster, such as a serious accident or your house being demolished by a storm. The cost of being uninsured or under-insured can be astronomical.

As with anything connected with finance, it's important to shop around when buying insurance. Simply collecting a few brochures from insurance agents or making a few telephone calls can save you a lot of money. Note, however, that not all insurance companies are equally reliable or have the same financial stability, and it may be better to insure with a large international company with a good reputation than with a small local company, even if this means paying a higher premium. Read all insurance contracts carefully and make sure that you understand the terms and the cover provided before signing them. Some insurance companies will do almost anything to avoid paying out on claims and will use any available legal loophole, therefore it pays to deal only with reputable companies (not that this provides a foolproof guarantee). Policies often contain traps and legal loopholes in the small print and it's sometimes advisable to obtain legal advice before signing a contract.

In matters regarding insurance, you're responsible for ensuring that you and your family are legally insured in France. Regrettably you cannot insure yourself against being uninsured or sue your insurance agent for giving you bad advice! Bear in mind that if you wish to make a claim on an insurance policy, you may be required to report an incident to the police within 24 hours (this may also be a legal requirement). The law in France may differ considerably from that in your home country or your previous country of residence and you should *never* assume that it's the same. If you're unsure of your rights, you're advised to obtain legal advice for anything other than a minor claim. Under EU regulations, insurance companies can sell their policies in any EU member country, although under French law contracts covering property or persons in France must be drawn up in French (although this is being challenged by the European Commission).

This section contains information about health insurance, household insurance, third party liability insurance and travel insurance. See also **Car Insurance** on page 37.

Health Insurance

If you're visiting, living or working in France, it's extremely risky not to have health insurance for your family, as if you're uninsured or under-insured you could be faced with some very high medical bills. When deciding on the type and extent of health insurance, make sure that it covers *all* your family's present and future health requirements in France before you receive a large bill. A health insurance policy should cover you for *all* essential health care whatever the reason, including accidents (e.g. sports accidents) and injuries, whether they occur in your home, at your place of work or while travelling. Don't take anything for granted, but check in advance.

If you're planning to take up residence in France and will be contributing to French social security (*sécurité sociale*), you and your family will be entitled to subsidised or (in certain cases) free medical and dental treatment. Most residents also subscribe to a complementary health insurance fund, called a *mutuelle*, that pays the portion of medical bills that isn't paid by social security. Residents who don't contribute to social security should have private health insurance, which is mandatory for non-EU residents when applying for a visa or residence permit (*carte de séjour*). Note that some foreign insurance companies don't provide sufficient cover to satisfy French regulations, therefore you should check the minimum cover necessary with a French consulate in your country of residence.

Students over 26 are required to take out health insurance in their country of origin or insurance under the French social security system on arrival in France. Long stay visitors should have travel or long stay health insurance or an international health policy (see **Health Insurance for Visitors** on page 56). If your stay in France is limited, you may be covered by a reciprocal agreement between your home country and France (see page 57). When travelling in France, you should carry proof of your health insurance with you.

Health Insurance for Residents

If you contribute to French social security (*sécurité sociale*), you and your family are entitled to subsidised or (in certain cases) free medical and dental treatment. Benefits include general and specialist care, hospitalisation, laboratory services, drugs and medicines, dental care, maternity care, appliances and transportation. To qualify for health benefits under social security, you must have been employed in France for 600 hours during the last six months or for six months at the minimum wage, or for 200 hours in the last quarter or 120 hours in the last month. When a person no longer meets these qualifying conditions, benefits are extended for a maximum of one year from the applicable date. Benefits are extended indefinitely for the long-term unemployed providing they are actively seeking employment. Retirees living in France and receiving a state pension from another EU country are entitled to free health benefits.

Under the social security health system, health treatment is assigned a basic monetary value (*tarif de convention*), of which social security pays a proportion (see the table below). The actual amount paid depends on your social security status, the kind of treatment received and whether the practitioner is approved (*agréé*) by social security. Most people are reimbursed for doctors' bills at 75 per cent, although the self-employed receive 50 per cent only. Certain patients are classified as needing serious long-term treatment, e.g. diabetic, cancer and cardiac patients, and receive 100 per cent reimbursement. The balance of medical bills, called the *ticket modérateur*, is usually paid by a complementary health insurance (*mutuelle*) scheme to which most people belong. The standard social security reimbursements are as follows (n.b. these are intended only as a guide and should be confirmed with social security and practitioners):

Reimbursement	Practitioner/Treatment
100 per cent	Maternity-related care
80 per cent	Hospitalisation
75 per cent	Doctors, dentists and midwife services; consultations as an out-patient; basic dental care
70 per cent	Miscellaneous items, e.g. laboratory work, apparatus, spectacles, ambulance services
65 per cent	medical auxiliaries, e.g. nurses, chiropodists, masseurs, therapists
35 to 100 per cent*	drugs and medicines

* The level of reimbursement for medicines is usually 65 per cent, although medicines for 'common' ailments are reimbursed at 35 per cent and certain essential medication at 100 per cent, e.g. insulin or heart pills.

When choosing a medical practitioner, e.g. a doctor or dentist, it's important to verify whether he has an agreement (*convention*) with social security. If he has an agreement he's known as *conventionné* and will charge a fixed amount for treatment as specified under the *tarif de convention*. If he *hasn't* signed an agreement with social security he's termed *non-conventionné* and the bill may be two to five times that set by the *tarif de convention*. Note that some *non-conventionné* practitioners are approved (*agréé*) by social security, but only a small proportion of fees are reimbursed. The reimbursement you receive applies only to the standard medical charges (*tarif de convention*). For example if a blood test costs 500F and the *tarif de convention* is 400F, you would pay the difference of 100F plus 30 per cent of 400F (120F) after social security has refunded its 70 per cent (280F), leaving you with a total bill of 220F. You can, however, take out insurance to pay the portion that isn't paid by social security.

There are also special classes of medical professionals classified as *conventionné honoraires libres*, who although they are *conventionné*, are permitted to charge higher fees than the standard rates. These include practitioners who perform special services (*dépassement exceptionnel*) and those with a special title or expertise (*dépassement permanent*). If you're in any doubt, you should ask exactly what the fee is for a consultation or treatment and what percentage will be reimbursed by social security.

Medical treatment must usually be paid for in advance and a claim for reimbursement made to social security and your *mutuelle* later. When paying bills, cash is preferred to cheques, particularly when dealing with non-resident foreigners, although cheques drawn on a French bank are acceptable. One benefit of the payment in advance system, is that it reduces the number of time wasters and hypochondriacs (*malades imaginaires*). If you're unable to pay your portion of the bill (the *ticket modérateur*), you can apply to your social security payment centre (*Caisse Primaire d'Assurance Maladie*) for a waiver (*prise en charge*). In the case of urgent or necessary treatment, approval is a formality.

Changing Employers or Insurance Companies: When changing employers or leaving France, you should ensure that you have continuous health insurance. If you and your family are covered by a company health plan, your insurance will probably cease after your last official day of employment. **If you're planning to change your health insurance company, you should ensure that no important benefits are lost, e.g. existing medical conditions won't usually be covered by a new insurer.** When changing health insurance companies, it's advisable to inform your old company if you have any outstanding bills for which they are liable.

Complementary Health Insurance: Most residents subscribe to a complementary health insurance fund (*assurance complémentaire maladie*), commonly called a *mutuelle*, that pays the portion of medical bills that isn't paid by social security (the *ticket modérateur*). A *mutuelle* scheme may also provide a supplementary pension. Almost every trade or occupation has its own *mutuelle* and in many cases it's obligatory for employees to join. Many *mutuelles* base their reimbursements on those of social security (see above) and reimburse a patient only after social security has paid a proportion of a fee. Therefore in a case where social security doesn't contribute, e.g. when a medical practitioner isn't approved by social security (*non-conventionné, non-agréé*), a *mutuelle* may also pay nothing. However, some *mutuelles* pay the whole cost or part of the cost for wholly private treatment and for treatment or items that aren't covered or barely covered by social security, such as false teeth and spectacles.

If you aren't covered by French social security you should take out private health insurance. It's an advantage to be insured with a company that will pay large medical bills directly, because if you're required to pay bills and claim reimbursement from the insurance company, it can take you several months to receive your money. All French health insurance companies pay hospital bills directly, unlike some foreign companies such as the American Blue Cross (although Blue Cross *will* pay the American Hospital of Paris and some medical practitioners directly). Most private health insurance policies don't pay family doctors' fees or pay for medication that isn't provided in a hospital or there's a high 'excess', e.g. you must pay the first 500F of a claim, which often exceeds the cost of treatment. Most will, however, pay for 100 per cent of specialist fees and hospital treatment in the best French hospitals. Note that a French insurance company cannot cancel your policy or increase your premiums if your health deteriorates with advancing years and increasing needs, providing you have been insured with the same company for at least two years. If you already have private health insurance in another country, it may be possible to extend it to cover you in France.

Health Insurance for Visitors

Visitors spending short periods in France (e.g. up to a month) should have a travel health insurance policy (see page 59), particularly if they aren't covered by an international health policy. If you plan to spend up to six months in France you should take out a travel or special long-stay health policy or have an annual international health policy. Premiums vary considerably and it's important to shop around. Most international health policies include repatriation or evacuation (although it may be optional), which may also include shipment (by air) of the body of a person who dies abroad to his home country for burial. An international policy also allows you to choose to have non-urgent medical treatment in the country of your choice.

Most international insurance companies offer health policies for different areas, e.g. Europe, worldwide excluding North America, and worldwide including North America. Most companies offer different levels of cover, for example basic, standard, comprehensive and prestige. There's always an annual limit on the total annual medical costs, which should be at least 2½ million francs (although many provide cover of up to ten million francs) and some companies also limit the charges for specific treatment or care such as specialists' fees, operations and hospital accommodation. A medical examination isn't usually required for international health policies, although pre-existing health problems are excluded for a period, e.g. one or two years.

Claims are usually settled in most major currencies and large claims are usually settled directly by insurance companies (although your choice of hospitals may be limited). Check whether an insurance company will settle large medical bills directly,

as if you're required to pay bills and claim reimbursement from an insurance company it can take several months before you receive your money (some companies are slow to pay). It isn't usually necessary to translate bills into English or another language, although you should check a company's policy. Most international health insurance companies provide emergency telephone assistance.

The cost of international health insurance varies considerably depending on your age and the extent of cover. Note that with most international insurance policies, you must enrol before you reach a certain age, usually between 60 and 75, to be guaranteed continuous cover in your old age. Premiums can sometimes be paid monthly, quarterly or annually, although some companies insist on payment annually in advance. When comparing policies, carefully check the extent of cover and exactly what's included and excluded from a policy (often indicated only in the *very* small print), in addition to premiums and excess charges. In some countries, premium increases are limited by law, although this may apply only to residents in the country where a company is registered and not to overseas policyholders. Although there may be significant differences in premiums, generally you get what you pay for and can tailor premiums to your requirements. The most important questions to ask yourself are: does the policy provide the cover required and is it good value for money? If you're in good health and are able to pay for your own out-patient treatment, such as visits to your family doctor and prescriptions, the best value is usually a policy covering specialist and hospital treatment only.

Reciprocal Health Agreements: If you're entitled to social security health benefits in another EU country or in a country with a reciprocal health agreement with France, you will receive free or reduced cost medical treatment in France. You should apply for a certificate of entitlement to treatment (form E111) from your local social security office (or a post office in Britain) at least three weeks before you plan to travel to France. An E111 is open-ended and valid for life. However, you must continue to make social security contributions in the country where it was issued and if you become a resident in another country (e.g. in France) it becomes invalid. It covers emergency hospital treatment but doesn't include prescribed medicines, special examinations, X-rays, laboratory tests, physiotherapy and dental treatment. If you use the E111 in France, you must apply for reimbursement to French social security (instructions are provided with the form), which can take months. **Note, however, that you can still receive a large bill from a French hospital, as your local health authority assumes only a percentage of the cost!**

Participating countries include EU member states and most other European countries, **excluding** Albania, Switzerland and Turkey. The USA doesn't have a reciprocal health agreement with France and therefore American students and other Americans who aren't covered by French social security *must* have private health insurance in France. British visitors or Britons planning to live in France can obtain information about reciprocal health treatment in France from the Department of Social Security, Overseas Branch, Newcastle-upon-Tyne, NE98 1YX, UK.

Household Insurance

Household insurance in France generally includes third party liability, building and contents insurance, all of which are usually contained in a multi-risk household insurance policy (*assurance multirisques habitation*).

Third Party Liability (*responsabilité civile propriétaire*): It's a legal requirement in France that property is insured for third party liability at all times or when building work starts on a new home (so that your neighbour can sue you when your chimney stack falls on his head). It's common for a buyer to take over the insurance of the vendor of a property and under French law, third party liability insurance automatically transfers to the new owner unless he takes out new insurance. The insurance must be transferred to the new owner's name on completion or be cancelled. One of the duties of the notary (*notaire*) is to check that a buyer has third party insurance. If you take over the existing insurance you should ensure that it provides adequate cover (many French tend to under-insure) and isn't too expensive.

Building (*bâtiment*): Although it isn't compulsory for owners, it's advisable to take out property insurance covering damage to the building due to fire, water, explosion, storm, freezing, snow, theft, malicious damage, acts of terrorism, broken windows and natural catastrophes. Property insurance is based on the cost of rebuilding your home and is increased annually in line with an industry agreed inflation figure. It also covers you against third party liability to guests and visitors on your property (*responsabilité civile vie privée*). **Make sure that you insure your property for the true cost of rebuilding.**

Contents (*contenu*): Contents are usually insured for the same risks as a building (see above) and are insured for their replacement value. Items of high value must usually be itemised and photographs and documentation (e.g. a valuation) provided. When claiming for contents, you should produce the original bills if possible (keep bills for expensive items) and bear in mind that replacing imported items may be much more expensive than buying them abroad. Note that contents' policies usually contain security clauses and if you don't adhere to them a claim won't be considered.

Apartments: If you own an apartment as a *copropriétaire*, building insurance is included in your service charges, although you should check exactly what's covered. You must, however, still be insured for third party risks in the event that you cause damage to neighbouring apartments, e.g. through flooding or fire.

Holiday Homes: Premiums are generally higher for holiday homes, due to their high vulnerability, particularly to burglaries, and are usually based on the number of days a year a property is inhabited and the interval between periods of occupancy. Cover for theft, storm, flood and malicious damage may be suspended when a property is left empty for more than three weeks at a time (or if there's no visible forced entry). It's possible to negotiate cover for periods of absence for a hefty surcharge, although valuable items are usually excluded. If you're absent from your property for long periods, e.g. more than 60 days a year, you may also be required to pay an excess (e.g. 1,500F) on a claim arising from an occurrence that takes place during your absence (and theft may be excluded). You should read all small print in policies. **Note that, where applicable, it's important to ensure that a policy specifies a holiday home and not a principal home.**

In areas with a high risk of theft (e.g. some parts of Paris and the French Riviera), you may be required to fit extra locks (e.g. two locks on external doors, one of a deadlock type) and internal-locking shutters or security bars on windows. A policy may specify that all forms of protection on doors must be employed whenever a property is unoccupied, and that all other forms (e.g. shutters) must also be used after 2200 and when a property is left empty for two or more days. Some companies may not insure holiday homes in high risk areas. It's unwise to leave valuable or irreplaceable items in a holiday home or a home that will be vacant for long periods. **Note that some insurance companies will do their utmost to find a loophole which makes you negligent and relieves them of their liability.** While it may be cheaper or more convenient to take out contents insurance abroad, you should be aware that this can lead to conflicts when the building is insured with a French company, e.g. in France door locks are part of the contents and in Britain they constitute part of the building.

Rented Property: Your landlord will usually insist that you have third party liability insurance. A lease requires you to insure against 'tenant's risks', including damage you may make to a rental property and to other properties if you live in an apartment, e.g. due to floods, fire or explosion. You can choose your own insurance company and aren't required to use one recommended by your landlord.

Premiums: Premiums are usually calculated on the size of the property, either the habitable area in square metres or the number of rooms, rather than its value. Usually the sum insured (house and contents) is unlimited, providing the property doesn't exceed a certain size, e.g. 1,200m², and is under a certain age, e.g. 200 years old. However, some companies restrict home insurance to properties with a maximum number of rooms (e.g. seven) and/or a maximum value of contents. e.g. 400,000F. The cost of multi-risk property insurance in a *low-risk* area is around 700F to 800F a year for a property with one or two bedrooms, 1,200F to 1,400F for three or four bedrooms and around 1,500F to 1,700F to a year for five or six bedrooms. Premiums are much higher in high risk areas and increase annually. If you have an index linked policy, your cover is increased annually in line with inflation.

It's possible to take out building and contents insurance in another country for a property in France, although the policy is usually written under French law. The advantage is that you will have a policy you can understand and you will be able to handle claims in your own language. This is usually a good option for the owner of a holiday home in France, although it can be much more expensive than insuring with a French company, so it pays to compare premiums. Carefully check that the details (*conditions particulières*) listed on a policy are correct, otherwise your policy could be void.

Claims: If you wish to make a claim you must usually inform your insurance company in writing (by registered letter) within two to five days of the incident or 24 hours in the case of theft. Thefts should also be reported to the local police within 24 hours as the police statement (*déclaration de vol/plainte*), of which you receive a copy for your insurance company, usually constitutes irrefutable evidence of your claim. Check whether you're covered for damage or thefts that occur while you're away from the property and are therefore unable to inform the insurance company immediately.

Note that in certain cases, claims for damaged property aren't considered unless the government declares the situation a natural catastrophe or Act of God, as has happened with floods in southern France in recent years. Even so, many people found after the floods that their household insurance didn't cover them for water coming in from ground level, only for water seeping in through the roof. Read the small print, and if floods are one of your concerns, make sure that you're covered. It's particularly important to have insurance for storm damage in France, which can be severe in some areas. Note, however, that if you live in an area that's hit by a succession of natural disasters (such as floods), your household insurance may be cancelled. Household insurance is often combined with third party liability insurance.

Holiday & Travel Insurance

Holiday and travel insurance (*assurance voyage*) is recommended for all those who don't wish to risk having their holiday or travel spoilt by financial problems or to arrive home broke. As you're no doubt already aware, anything can and often does go wrong with a holiday, sometimes before you even reach the airport or port, particularly when you *don't* have insurance. The following information applies equally to both residents and non-residents, whether they are travelling to or from

France or within France. Nobody should visit France without travel (and health) insurance!

Travel insurance is available from many sources including travel agents, insurance agents, motoring organisations, transport companies and direct from insurance companies. Package holiday companies also offer insurance policies, **most of which don't provide adequate cover.** You can also buy 24-hour accident and flight insurance at major airports, although it's expensive and doesn't offer the best cover. Before taking out travel insurance, carefully consider the level of cover you require and compare policies. Short-term holiday and travel insurance policies may include cover for holiday cancellation or interruption; missed flights; departure delay at both the start *and* end of a holiday (a common occurrence); delayed, lost or damaged baggage; personal effects and money; medical expenses and accidents (including evacuation home); flight insurance; personal liability and legal expenses; and default or bankruptcy insurance, e.g. a tour operator or airline going bust.

Health Cover: Medical expenses are an important aspect of travel insurance and you shouldn't rely on reciprocal health arrangements (see page 57), charge and credit card companies, household policies or private medical insurance (unless it's an international policy), none of which usually provide adequate cover (although you should take advantage of what they offer). The minimum medical insurance recommended by experts is 2½ million francs in France and the rest of Europe, and five to ten million francs in North America and some other destinations, e.g. Japan (many policies have limits of between 15 to 50 million francs). If applicable, check whether pregnancy related claims are covered and whether there are any restrictions for those over a certain age, e.g. 65 or 70 (travel insurance is becoming increasingly more expensive for those aged over 65).

Check any exclusion clauses in contracts by obtaining a copy of the full policy document (all relevant information isn't included in the insurance leaflet). Skiing and other winter sports should be specifically covered and *listed* in your travel insurance policy. Special winter sports policies are available and are more expensive than normal holiday insurance ('dangerous' sports are excluded from most standard policies). Third party liability cover should be around ten million francs in Europe and 20 million in North America. **Note that this doesn't cover you when you're using a car or other mechanically propelled vehicle.**

Visitors: Travel insurance for visitors to France should include personal liability and repatriation expenses. If your travel insurance expires while you're visiting France, you can buy further insurance from an insurance agent, although this won't include repatriation expenses. Flight insurance and comprehensive travel insurance is available from insurance desks at most airports, including travel accident, personal accident, worldwide medical expenses and in-transit baggage.

Cost: The cost of travel insurance varies considerably, depending on where you buy it, how long you intend to stay in France and your age. Generally the longer the period covered, the cheaper the daily cost, although the maximum period covered is usually limited, e.g. six months. With some policies a deductible (excess) must be paid for each claim. As a rough guide, travel insurance for France (and most other European countries) costs from around 200F for one week, 300F for two weeks and 400F for a month for a family of four (two adults and two children under 16). Premiums may be higher for those aged over 65 or 70.

Annual Policies: For people who travel abroad frequently, whether on business or pleasure, an annual travel policy usually provides the best value, but carefully check exactly what it includes. Many insurance companies (e.g. Europ Assistance) offer annual travel policies for a premium of around 1,000F for an individual (the equivalent of around three months insurance with a standard travel insurance policy), which are excellent value for frequent travellers. Some insurance companies also offer an 'emergency travel policy' for holiday home owners who need to travel abroad at short notice to inspect a property, e.g. after a severe storm. The cost of an annual policy may depend on the area covered, e.g. Europe, worldwide (excluding North America) and worldwide (including North America), although it doesn't usually cover travel within your country of residence. There's also a limit on the number of trips a year and the duration of each trip, e.g. 90 or 120 days. An annual policy is usually a good choice for owners of a holiday home in France who travel there frequently for relatively short periods. **However, carefully check exactly what's covered (or omitted) as an annual policy may not provide adequate cover.**

Claims: If you need to make a claim, you should provide as much documentary evidence as possible to support it. Travel insurance companies gladly take your money, but they aren't always so keen to pay claims and you may need to persevere before they pay up. Be persistent and make a claim *irrespective* of any small print, as this may be unreasonable and therefore invalid in law. Insurance companies usually require you to report a loss (or any incident for which you intend to make a claim) to the local police or carriers within 24 hours and obtain a written report. Failure to do so may mean that a claim won't be considered.

SHOPPING

France is one of Europe's great shopping countries and French shops are designed to seduce you with their artful displays of beautiful and exotic merchandise. Paris is a shoppers' paradise, where even the shop windows are a delight, although it isn't the best place to find bargains and is generally no place for budget shoppers. Nevertheless, Paris attracts an army of foreign shoppers keen to pay for top quality French labels such as Chanel, Dior, Hermès and Louis Vuitton. French products are distinguished by their attention to detail, elegance, flair and quality, particularly good clothes (not to mention their high prices). However, unless you have money to burn, don't even think about buying imported branded goods in France!

Most French towns of any size have a supermarket or two and on the outskirts of large towns there are huge shopping centres with hypermarkets, do-it-yourself stores and furniture warehouses (there's a constant battle between town centres and out-of-town shopping centres). In many city centres there are pedestrian streets (*rues piétonnes*) where you can walk and shop without fear of being run down by a speeding motorist. French retailers are among the world's most competitive and have smaller profit margins than many other countries. Price fixing isn't permitted in France, with the exception of books, where the price is fixed to protect small bookshops from 'unfair' competition from large retailers. Many retailers do, however, accept recommended prices as a condition of supply by manufacturers and the price of bread and pharmaceuticals are controlled by the government.

As in most countries, it's important to shop around and compare prices, which can vary considerably (not only between small shops and hypermarkets, but also between different supermarkets and hypermarkets in the same town). Note, however, that price differences usually reflect different quality, so make sure that you're comparing similar products. Some products are particularly expensive in France and are worth importing. These include electronic and audio equipment, cameras, cosmetics, furniture, books and almost anything that's imported from outside the EU. Among the best buys in France are pottery, decorative glass, kitchenware, quality clothes (including children's), fashion accessories, toys, domestic electrical equipment, wines, liquors, luxury foods, perfumes and handicrafts.

You should beware of fake goods as some 70 per cent of fake products are copies of French brands (perfumes are a favourite target). Even French truffles, which cost around 7,000F a kilo for the black variety, have been substituted by inferior Chinese truffles in recent years! You should also be aware that bringing counterfeited goods into France is now a criminal offence. In theory having a pirated Cartier watch or fake Louis Vuitton handbag can result in a jail sentence, although in practice it will usually just be confiscated. Having more than one item, however, carries a fine of up to one million francs and two years in prison!

Hard-hit Parisian department stores have held early sales in recent years in a bid to attract reluctant shoppers and sales and special offers are commonplace. In general, French shops are limited to just two sales (*soldes/fins de série*) a year, each for a maximum of two months duration. Items sold in sales must show the lowest price offered during the previous month and the sale price. Note that a *liquidation totale* isn't a closing down sale, but a clearance sale. The main sales are held in the first two weeks of January and July. It's also possible to buy goods direct from factories in France, with discounts of between 30 and 70 per cent, although factory shops aren't nearly as common as in the USA. Keen bargain hunters may be interested in *The Factory Shop Guide for Northern France*, Gillian Cutress & Rolf Stricker (1 Rosebery Mews, Rosebery Road, London SW2 4DQ, UK). Other books of interest to shopaholics are Frommer's *Born to Shop France* by Suzy Gershman and *Paris Pas Cher* (Flammarion).

French shopkeepers are usually honest and won't try to rob you, although you should check your change. In some stores you don't pay the person serving you but a cashier, who may be the owner. The French don't usually make good servants and store staff are often surly and unhelpful. Rude sales staff are commonplace, particularly in department stores, where you can wait ages to be served while staff chat among themselves and ignore customers (in France the customer often comes last). French stores rarely allow customers to exchange unwanted goods or offer a money-back guarantee. If you break something in a store, you're legally liable to pay for it, although the shopkeeper may not wish to enforce the law. In Paris and other cities, or anywhere there are lots of tourists, you *must* be wary of pickpockets and bag-snatchers. *Never* tempt fate with an exposed wallet or purse, or by flashing your money around.

Furniture & Furnishings

Furniture (*meubles*) is generally good value in France, although more expensive than in some other European countries. The choice is often between relatively inexpensive budget furniture and high quality expensive furniture, with little in between. Exclusive modern and traditional furniture is available everywhere, although not everyone can afford the exclusive prices, including bizarre pieces from designers such as Gaultier for those with money to burn. Many regions of France have a reputation for quality handmade furniture. If you're buying a large quantity of furniture, don't be reluctant to ask for a reduction as many stores will give you a discount.

Modern furniture is popular in France and is often sold in huge stores located in commercial centres. Inexpensive chain stores include But, Conforama, Fly and Monsieur Meuble, most of which also loan or hire self-drive vans to customers at reasonable rates. Good basic furniture (including garden furniture) can be purchased inexpensively at hypermarkets, all of which have special offers throughout the year (ask about special offers even if none are advertised). Pine furniture is inexpensive and popular. Beware of buying complicated home-assembled furniture with indecipherable French instructions and too few screws. If you want reasonably priced, good quality, modern furniture, you need look no farther than Ikea, a Swedish company manufacturing furniture for home assembly with a 14-day money-back guarantee (note that the price of Ikea furniture varies depending on the country and most items are much cheaper in France than, for example, in Britain).

Apart from genuine antiques, secondhand furniture is usually good value for money in France, particularly solid (*massif*) traditional furniture. You can pick up bargains at *magasins d'occasion* (literally 'opportunity shops'), a *troc* ('swap shop') such as the *Troc de l'Isle* chain (around 75 outlets), and possibly at a *brocante,* although these aren't usually much cheaper than antique shops. You can also buy good secondhand and antique furniture at bargain prices from a *dépôt-vente*, where people sell their old furniture and repossessed household goods are sold. Look under *Dépôts-vente ameublement et divers* in your local Yellow Pages.

Brocante fairs, held annually or biannually throughout France, are good for antique furniture at affordable prices. However, you must usually drive a hard bargain as the asking prices can be a joke. Markets are also good for fabric (e.g. for curtains) bed linen and wallpaper. Note, however, that summer markets are often geared to the tourist trade and you're likely to find better buys in spring or autumn. Charity shops such as Emmäus are an Aladdin's cave of household goods and furniture (they also hold periodic sales). A *friperie* is a shop selling secondhand clothing, bedding and bed linen.

The kind of furniture you buy for your French home will depend on a number of factors including the style and size of your home, whether it's a permanent or holiday home, your budget, the local climate, and not least, your personal taste. If you intend to furnish a holiday home with antiques or expensive modern furniture, bear in mind that you will need good security and comprehensive insurance. If you own a holiday home in France, it's usually worthwhile shipping surplus items of furniture you have in your home abroad. If you intend to move permanently to France in a number of years and already have a house full of good furniture abroad, there's little point in buying expensive furniture in France. It may be worthwhile comparing the cost of furniture in a neighbouring country with that in France, although it usually doesn't pay to buy new furniture abroad to furnish a French home (particularly as you must usually add shipping costs).

Household Goods

Household goods in France are generally of good quality with a large choice. Prices compare favourably with other European countries and bargains can be found at supermarkets and hypermarkets such as Auchan, Carrefour, Mammouth and Rallye. Apart from hypermarkets, one of the best stores for household appliances is Darty, which has outlets in most towns. Not surprisingly for a nation that spends much of its time in the kitchen (the rest is spent eating!), French kitchenware, crockery, cutlery and glasses can all be purchased cheaply in France and the quality is usually excellent.

It's advisable to buy white goods (such as refrigerators and washing machines) in France, as imported appliances may not function properly due to differences in the electrical supply (and they may also be difficult to get repaired). Note also that the standard size of kitchen appliances and cupboard units in France *isn't* the same as in other countries, and it may be difficult to fit an imported dishwasher or washing machine into a French kitchen. Check the size *and* the latest French safety regulations before shipping these items to France or buying them abroad, as they may need expensive modifications. Appliances such as refrigerators, freezers, cookers and washing machines can often be purchased cheaply from bankrupt stock shops in many towns. If you're looking for bargains, don't neglect the many French secondhand shops (see under **Furniture & Furnishings** on page 63).

If you already own small household appliances, it's worth bringing them to France, as usually all that's required is a change of plug. Bear in mind when importing household goods that aren't sold in France that it may be difficult or impossible to get them repaired or serviced locally. If you bring appliances with you, don't forget to bring a supply of spares and refills such as bulbs for a refrigerator or sewing machine, and spare bags for a vacuum cleaner. If you're coming from a country with a 110/115V electricity supply, such as the USA, you'll need a lot of expensive transformers and it's usually better to buy new appliances in France. Small appliances such as vacuum cleaners, grills, toasters and electric irons aren't expensive in France and are of good quality. Don't bring a TV without checking its compatibility first, as TVs from many countries won't work in France (see page 69).

If you need kitchen measuring equipment and cannot cope with decimal measures, you will need to bring your own measuring scales, jugs, cups and thermometers. Foreign pillow sizes (e.g. American and British) aren't the same as in France and the French use duvets and not blankets to keep warm in winter (besides more 'natural' methods!).

Shopping Abroad

Shopping abroad makes a pleasant change from all those 'boring' French shops full of tempting and expensive luxuries (although the information in this section applies equally to foreign residents shopping in France as it does to French residents shopping abroad). It can also save you money and makes a pleasant day out for the family. Don't forget your passports or identity cards, car papers, dog's vaccination papers and foreign currency. Most shops in border towns eagerly accept French francs, but will usually give you a lower exchange rate than a bank. Many families, particularly those living in border areas, take advantage of lower prices outside France, particularly when it comes to buying alcohol (e.g. in Andorra, Belgium and Italy). Whatever you're looking for, compare prices and quality before buying. Bear in mind that if you buy goods that are faulty or need repair, you may need to return them to the place of purchase.

From 1993 there have been no cross-border shopping restrictions within the European Union for goods purchased duty and tax paid, providing goods are for personal consumption or use and not for resale. Although there are no restrictions, there are 'indicative levels' for certain items, above which goods may be classified as commercial quantities. For example, persons entering Britain aged 17 or over may import the following amounts of alcohol and tobacco without question:

- 10 litres of spirits (over 22° proof);

- 20 litres of sherry or fortified wine (under 22° proof);

- 90 litres of wine (or 120 x 0.75 litre bottles/ten cases) of which a maximum of 60 litres may be sparkling wine;

- 110 litres of beer;

- 800 cigarettes and 400 cigarillos and 200 cigars and 1kg of smoking tobacco.

There's no limit on perfume or toilet water. If you exceed the above amounts you may have to convince the customs authorities that you aren't planning to sell the goods. Thousands of Britons have got into the habit of popping across the Channel to do some shopping in the last few years, particularly for alcohol and tobacco. The vast complex *Cité Europe*, situated just two minutes from Eurotunnel's terminal is one of Europe's biggest shopping centres with more than 150 shops and restaurants (attracting over 17 million visitors a year). A number of books have also been published on the subject including *The Cross-Channel Drinks Guide* by Tom Stevenson (Absolute Press); *A Bootful of Wine* by Alec King (Mandarin); and *The Calais Beer, Wine & Tobacco Directory* by Alan Kelly and Kim Whitaker (Euro Publishing). The huge difference in the price of alcohol and tobacco between Britain and France has been called 'a bootleggers' charter', although there are huge fines for anyone caught selling duty-paid alcohol and tobacco in Britain, which is classed as smuggling.

Never attempt to import illegal goods into France and don't agree to bring a parcel into France or deliver a parcel in another country without knowing exactly what it contains. A popular confidence trick is to ask someone to post a parcel in France (usually to a *poste restante* address) or to leave a parcel at a railway station or restaurant. **THE PARCEL USUALLY CONTAINS DRUGS!**

Duty-Free Allowances

Duty-free (*hors-taxe*) shopping within the EU is due to be abolished on the 30th June 1999, although it will still be available when travelling further afield. Duty-free allowances are the same whether or not you're travelling within the EU or from a country outside the EU. From 1st January 1993, for each journey to another EU member state travellers aged 17 or over (unless otherwise stated) are entitled to import the following goods purchased duty-free:

- one litre of spirits (over 22° proof) *or* two litres of fortified wine (under 22° proof) *or* two litres of wine;
- two litres of still table wine;
- 200 cigarettes *or* 100 cigarillos *or* 50 cigars *or* 250g of tobacco;
- 60ml of perfume;
- 250ml of toilet water;
- 500g of coffee (*or* 200g coffee extract) and 100g tea (*or* 40g tea extract) for persons aged 15 or over;
- other goods including gifts and souvenirs to the value of 300F (150F for those aged under 15).

Duty-free allowances apply to both outward and return journeys, even if both are made on the same day, and the combined total (i.e. double the above limits) can be imported into your 'home' country. Since 1993, duty-free sales have been 'vendor-controlled', meaning that vendors are responsible for ensuring that the amount of duty-free goods sold to individuals doesn't exceed their entitlement. Duty-free goods purchased on board ships and ferries are noted on boarding cards that must be presented with each purchase. Ferry companies usually have a number of special offers providing additional savings.

If you live outside the EU you can obtain a VAT refund on purchases if the total value (excluding books, food, services and some other items) amounts to 2,000F or more. Large department stores, particularly in Paris, often have a special counter where non-EU shoppers can arrange for the shipment of duty-free goods. An export sales invoice (*bordereau pour détaxe*) is provided by retailers, listing all purchases and comprising three pages (each of which must be signed), two pink and one green. When you leave France your purchases must be validated by a customs officer who will retain the two pink pages and return a copy to the vendor responsible for reimbursing the VAT. The third (green page) is stamped and returned to you and is your receipt. At major airports (e.g. in Paris) there are special *douane de détaxe* offices where you can obtain a VAT refund on the spot, but you must show your purchases so don't pack them in your checked baggage. Note that French bureaucracy ensures that the process takes at least an hour to complete. If the refund is made by the vendor it can take up to six months.

PETS

If you plan to take a pet (*animal domestique*) to France, it's important to ascertain the latest regulations. Make sure that you have the correct papers, not only for France, but for all the countries you will pass through to reach France. Particular consideration must be given before exporting a pet from a country with strict quarantine regulations, such as Britain. If you need to return prematurely, even after a few hours or days in France, your pet must go into quarantine, e.g. for six months in Britain, which apart from the expense is distressing for both pets and owners. Norway and Sweden abolished quarantine on 1st May 1994 and Britain plans to replace quarantine in 1999 or 2000 with a new system under which animals must be microchipped and have a 'passport' listing their vaccinations. It will be restricted to animals imported from rabies-free countries and countries where rabies is under control (e.g. Western Europe and possibly North America), but the quarantine law will remain in place for pets coming from Eastern Europe, Africa, Asia and South America. The new regulations are expected to initially cost pet owners GB£150 a year plus GB£60 a year for follow-up vaccinations and around GB£20 for a border check.

You can take up to three animals into France at any one time, one of which may be a puppy (three to six months old), although no dogs or cats under three months of age may be imported. Two parrot-like (psittacidae) birds can be imported into France and up to ten smaller species; all require health certificates issued within five days of departure. Other animals require special import permits from the French Ministry of Agriculture. There's generally no quarantine period for animals in France. However, there are strict vaccination requirements for dogs, although France has almost eradicated rabies in the last 20 years by vaccinating foxes and it could disappear in the next few years.

If you're importing a dog into France, it must be vaccinated against rabies and have a certificate (*certificat contre la rage*) or have a health certificate (*certificat de bonne santé*) signed by an approved veterinary surgeon issued no more than five days before your arrival. British owners must complete an *Application for a Ministry Export Certificate for dogs, cats and rabies susceptible animals* (form EXA1), available from the Ministry of Agriculture, Fisheries & Food (☎ 0181-330 4411). A health inspection must be performed by a licensed veterinary officer before you're issued with an export health certificate. If you're transporting a pet to France by ship or ferry, you should notify the ferry company. Some companies insist that pets are left in vehicles (if applicable), while others allow pets to be kept in cabins. If your pet is of nervous disposition or unused to travelling, it's best to tranquillise it on a long sea crossing. Pets can also be transported by air.

For visitors with pets, a rabies vaccination is compulsory only for animals entering Corsica, being taken to campsites or holiday parks, or participating in shows in a rabies-affected area. Where applicable, the rabies vaccination must have been given between 30 days and less than a year before arrival in France. If you intend to live permanently in France, most vets recommend that you have a dog vaccinated against rabies before your arrival, which saves you having to get your dog vaccinated on arrival in France. Resident dogs must also be vaccinated against distemper and hardpad and need an annual rabies booster. Cats aren't required to have regular rabies vaccinations, although if you let your cat roam free outside your home it's advisable to have it vaccinated annually. Cats must, however, be vaccinated against feline gastro-enteritis and typhus. All vaccinations must be registered with your veterinary surgeon (*vétérinaire*) and be listed on your pet's vaccination card or health certificate.

All dogs in France must be tattooed with an identity number inside one of their ears, enabling owners to quickly find lost pets and also preventing a rabies or other vaccination certificate from being used for more than one dog. Tattooing is done by vets and costs around 250F. The identity numbers are kept in a central computer controlled by the French Society for the Protection of Animals (*Société Protectrice des Animaux/SPA*). Contact the nearest SPA office if you lose your pet. Dogs and cats don't wear identification discs in France and there's no system of licensing.

Veterinary surgeons are well trained in France, where it's a highly popular and well paid profession. Emergency veterinary care is available in major cities, where there are also animal hospitals (*hôpital pour animaux*) and vets on 24-hour call for emergencies. A visit to a vet usually costs 150F to 200F. Some vets also make house calls, for which there's a minimum charge of 400F to 500F. Taxi and ambulance services are also provided for pets. Health insurance for pets is available from a number of insurance companies and it's common practice in France to have third party insurance in case your pet bites someone or causes an accident. This is usually included in general third party liability insurance. Dogs must be kept on leads in most public parks and gardens in France and there are large fines for dog owners who don't comply. Dogs are forbidden in some parks, even when on leads. On public transport, small pets must usually be carried in a basket or cage if a fare is to be avoided (the SNCF charges half 2nd class fare for uncaged dogs weighing over 6kg).

The unpleasant aspect of France's vast dog population is abundantly evident on the streets of French towns and cities every day, where dogs routinely leave their 'calling cards'. You must *always* watch where you walk in France. Most dog owners don't take their pets on long country walks, but just to a local park or car park or simply let them loose in the streets to do their business. In Paris, there are laws against fouling footpaths, although most French ignore the 'pooper-scooper' law requiring them to clean up after their dogs. At the very least owners are required to take their pets to the kerb to relieve themselves (you're reminded by dog silhouettes on the footpath in Paris and other cities). Signs also encourage owners to teach their dogs to use gutters (*Apprenez-lui le caniveau*), which are regularly cleaned and disinfected. There are dog toilet areas in Paris and some other French cities. In Paris and some other towns there are patrolmen on motorised pooper-scoopers (*caninettes*), a motorbike-cum-vacuum cleaner equipped with suction tubes, brushes and disinfectant (they pick up four tonnes of doggy-do from the streets of Paris alone, every single day). Although it's of little consolation, it's supposedly good luck to tread in something unpleasant!

If you want to take your pet from France to a country without rabies, it may need to go into quarantine for a period. This applies, for example, to Australia, Britain and Ireland. Check with the authorities of the country concerned. For the latest regulations regarding the importation and keeping of pets in France contact *Sous Direction de la Santé et de la Protection Animales*, 175, rue du Chevaleret, 75646 Paris Cedex 13 (☎ 01.45.84.13.13). If you wish to import an exotic pet or more pets than the standard quota, contact the *Direction Générale des Douanes*, 23bis, rue de l'Université, 75007 Paris.

TELEVISION & RADIO

Until 1974, all French television (TV) and radio stations were state-owned and under the tight control of the government. However, there has been a minor revolution in the last few decades, particularly since 1981 when the Socialists came to power, although two of the three principal TV stations remain under government control.

Cable TV is available in the main French cities and towns, although it's less common in France than in many other western European countries. Satellite TV is largely ignored by the French and is mainly watched by expatriates. Almost every French household has a TV and there are some 20 million in France, most of which are colour.

The French complain endlessly about their TV, particularly its lack of quality, surfeit of advertising, dependence on trashy foreign programmes, moronic game shows and endless repeats, although it's generally no worse than most other European countries. Although France prides itself on its culture, this isn't evident from its TV programmes (at least they were spared *A Year in Provence!*). Many Frenchmen prefer to listen to the radio rather than watch TV, particularly the educated middle classes, many of whom don't watch TV at all. The most popular TV programmes include films, sport, theatre, variety, serials and game shows in that order. The daily TV viewing time in France is about average for Western Europe.

TV and radio programmes are listed in daily newspapers, some of which provide free weekly programme guides with reviews and comments (e.g. the Saturday edition of *Le Figaro* and the Sunday edition of *Le Monde*). Weekly TV magazines include *Télé 7 Jours*, *Télé Loisirs*, *Télé Poche*, *Télé Star* and *Télé Z*, published two weeks in advance.

Standards: The standards for TV reception in France **aren't the same as in some other countries**. Due to the differences in transmission standards, TVs and video recorders operating on the PAL system or the North American NTSC system won't function in France. Most European countries use the PAL B/G standard, except for Britain, which uses a modified PAL-I system that's incompatible with other European countries. Naturally France has its own standard called SECAM-L, which is different from the SECAM standard used elsewhere in the world, e.g. SECAM B/G in the Middle East and North African countries, and SECAM D/K in eastern European and many African countries.

If you want a TV that will work in France and other European countries, and a VCR that will play back both PAL and SECAM videos, you must buy a multi-standard TV and VCR. These are widely available in France and contain automatic circuitry that can switch from PAL-I (Britain), to PAL-B/G (rest of Europe) to SECAM-L (France). Some multi-standard TVs also handle the North American NTSC standard and have an NTSC-in jack plug connection allowing you to play American videos. If you have a PAL TV, it's also possible to buy a SECAM to PAL transcoder that converts SECAM signals to PAL. Some people opt for two TVs, one to receive French TV programmes and another (i.e. PAL or NTSC) to play their favourite videos. A British or US video recorder won't work with a French TV unless it's dual-standard (with SECAM). Although you can play back a SECAM video on a PAL VCR, the picture will be in black and white. Most video machines sold in France are multi-standard PAL and SECAM. Video recordings can be converted from PAL to SECAM or vice versa, although the cost is prohibitive.

If you decide to buy a TV in France, you will find it advantageous to buy one with teletext, which apart from allowing you to display programme schedules, also provides a wealth of useful and interesting information. A portable colour TV can be purchased in France from around 1,200F for a 36cm (14in) with remote control. A 55cm (21in) TV costs between 3,000F and 4,500F depending on the make and features, and a 70cm (27in) model 5,000F to 6,500F. Special offers can be up to 50 per cent cheaper than the prices quoted, particularly at hypermarkets such as But, Cora, Mammouth and Rallye.

Stations: France has six terrestrial stations broadcasting throughout the country: TF1, France 2, France 3, Canal Plus, M6 and Arte. Reception is poor in some areas, particularly if you're in a valley or surrounded by tower blocks. There's advertising (*publicité* or *pub*) on all French channels, although the public channels aren't permitted to raise more than 25 per cent of their revenue from advertising. Limits are imposed on the amount of TV advertising permitted, which may not average more than six minutes per hour per day, with a maximum of 12 minutes in any single hour. The public channels France 2 and France 3 are permitted to show advertisements between programmes only, whereas private channels (TF1, Canal-Plus, M6 and Arte) may have an advertising break during films and other major programmes.

The two main TV stations, TF1 and France 2, broadcast their main evening news at 2000 for half an hour. Newsreaders are huge celebrities in France and receive vast salaries. They are chosen for their intelligence, personality and in some cases their good looks. Some TV weathermen are incredible and speak faster than DJs – perhaps they are allocated a 1-minute slot to give a 2-minute weather report! News is followed by a film on most channels starting between 2030 and 2100 (the highlight of the evening's viewing). One of the aims of the 1982 broadcasting law was to encourage the production of French programmes, thus reducing the reliance on foreign, particularly American, imports. However, there remain a large number of American films and other programmes, many very old. French TV has a huge number of talk shows, probably because they are inexpensive to produce.

Cable TV: Cable TV is available only in large towns and cities in France although the number of subscribers increases annually. The percentage of homes with cable TV in France is low compared with some 95 per cent in Belgium, 85 per cent in the Netherlands and over 40 per cent in Germany. Most of Paris is covered by cable TV and some towns or areas have their own local cable TV network. If your locality is cabled, Reseau Cable de France (RSF) offer over 30 different channels (mostly in French) for 132F a month for the basic option and 242F a month for full access. Foreign channels such as Sky, CNN, BBC, Eurovision and MTV are also available. Programme listings for the most popular French cable stations are included in French TV guides.

Satellite TV: There are a number of satellites positioned over Europe carrying over 200 stations broadcasting in a variety of languages. Satellite TV has been growing apace in France in recent years and there are now around one million homes with satellite TV, many owned by expatriates. Although it wasn't the first in Europe (which was Eutelsat), the European satellite revolution really took off with the launch of the Astra 1A satellite in 1988 (operated by the Luxembourg-based *Société Européenne des Satellites* or SES), positioned 36,000km (22,300mi) above the earth. TV addicts (easily recognised by their antennae and square eyes) are offered a huge choice of English and foreign-language stations which can be received throughout France with a 60 or 85cm dish. Since 1988 a number of additional Astra satellites have been launched, increasing the number of available channels to 64 (or over 200 with digital TV). An added bonus is the availability of radio stations via satellite, including all the national BBC stations (see **Satellite Radio** on page 74).

Among the many English-language stations available on Astra are Sky One, Movimax, Sky Premier, Sky Cinema, Film Four, Sky News, Sky Sports (three channels), UK Gold, Channel 5, Granada Plus, TNT, Eurosport, CNN, CNBC Europe, UK Style, UK Horizons, The Disney Channel and the Discovery Channel. Other stations broadcast in Dutch, German, Japanese, Swedish and various Indian languages. The signal from many stations is scrambled (the decoder is usually built into the receiver) and viewers must pay a monthly subscription fee to receive programmes. You can buy pirate decoders for some channels. The best served by clear (unscrambled) stations are German-speakers (most German stations on Astra are clear).

BSkyB Television: You must buy a receiver with a Videocrypt decoder and pay a monthly subscription to receive BSkyB or Sky stations except Sky News, which isn't scrambled. Various packages are available costing from around GB£12 to GB£30 a month for the premium package offering all movie channels plus Sky Sports. To receive scrambled channels such as Movimax and Sky Sports you need an address in Britain. Subscribers are sent a coded 'smart' card (similar to a credit card) that must be inserted in the decoder to switch it on (cards are updated every few years to thwart counterfeiters). Sky won't send smart cards to overseas viewers as they have the copyright for a British-based audience only, and overseas homeowners need to obtain a card through a friend or relative in Britain. However, a number of satellite companies in France (some of which advertise in the expatriate press) supply BSkyB cards.

Digital Television: Digital TV was launched on 1st October 1998 by BSkyB in the UK. The benefits include a superior picture, better (CD) quality sound, widescreen cinema format and access to many more stations. To watch digital TV you require a Digibox and a (digital) Minidish, which in 1998 could be purchased at a subsidised price by existing Sky customers in the UK. Customers had to sign up for a 12-month subscription and agree to have the connection via a phone line (to allow for future interactive services). In addition to the usual analogue channels (see above), digital TV offers BBC 1, BBC 2 and Channel 4 (but not ITV or ITV2), plus many new digital channels (a total of 200 with up to 500 possible later). ONdigital launched a rival digital service on 15th November 1998, which although it's cheaper, provides a total of just 30 channels (15 free and 15 subscription) including BBC 1 and 2, ITV, ITV2, Channel 4 and Channel 5. Widescreen digital TVs cost around GB£1,000, but will inevitably become cheaper as more models become available and the demand increases. At the time of writing, digital satellite TV wasn't officially available in France, although it's offered by some expatriate satellite companies.

Eutelsat: Eutelsat was the first company to introduce satellite TV to Europe (in 1983) and it now runs a fleet of communications satellites carrying TV stations to over 50 million homes. Until 1995 they had broadcast primarily advertising-based, clear-access cable channels. Following the launch in March 1995 of their Hot Bird satellite, Eutelsat hoped to become a major competitor to Astra, although its channels are mostly non-English. The English-language stations on Eutelsat include Eurosport, BBC World and CNBC Europe. Other channels broadcast in Arabic, French, German, Hungarian, Italian, Polish, Portuguese, Spanish and Turkish.

BBC Worldwide Television: The BBC's commercial subsidiary, BBC Worldwide Television, broadcasts two 24-hour channels: BBC Prime (general entertainment) and BBC World (24-hour news and information). BBC World is free-to-air and is transmitted via the Eutelsat Hot Bird satellite, while BBC Prime is encrypted and transmitted via the Intelsat satellite. BBC Prime requires a D2-MAC decoder and a smartcard costing around GB£25 and an annual GB£75 subscription fee (plus VAT). Smartcards are available from TV Extra, PO Box 304, 59124 Motala, Sweden (☎ 46-141-56060). For more information and a programming guide contact BBC Worldwide Television, Woodlands, 80 Wood Lane, London W12 0TT, UK (☎ 0181-576 2555). The BBC publishes a monthly magazine, *BBC On Air*, giving comprehensive information about BBC Worldwide Television programmes. A programme guide is also listed on the Internet (www.bbc.co.uk/schedules) and both BBC World and BBC Prime have their own websites (www.bbcworld.com and www.bbcprime.com). When accessing them, you need to enter the name of the country (e.g. France) so that schedules appear in local time.

French Satellite TV: There are no French-language channels on Astra. If you wish to receive French satellite TV you need to tune in to French satellites such as the Télécom 2A and 2B satellites, which between them carry around 20 French-language stations. A SECAM standard TV isn't required to receive most French satellite broadcasts, which are different from terrestrial broadcasts, but a decoder (e.g. Syster) is required to unscramble most signals.

Equipment: A satellite receiver should have a built-in Videocrypt decoder (and others such as Eurocrypt, Syster or SECAM if required) and be capable of receiving satellite stereo radio. A 60cm dish (to receive Astra stations) costs from around 2,000F plus the cost of installation (which may be included in the price). Shop around as prices vary enormously. You can also install a motorised 1.2 or 1.5 metre dish and receive hundreds of stations in a multitude of languages from around the world. If you wish to receive satellite TV on two or more TVs, you can buy a system with two or more receptors. To receive stations from two or more satellites simultaneously, you need a motorised dish or a dish with a double feed (dual LNBs) antenna. **When buying a system, ensure that it can receive programmes from all existing and planned satellites.**

Location: To receive programmes from any satellite, there must be no obstacles between the satellite and your dish, i.e. no trees, buildings or mountains must obstruct the signal, so check before renting or buying a home. Before buying or erecting a satellite dish, check whether you need permission from your landlord or the local authorities. France has strict laws regarding the positioning of antennas in urban areas, although in rural areas they are more relaxed. Dishes can be mounted in a variety of unobtrusive positions and can be painted or patterned to blend in with the background.

Programme Guides: Many satellite stations provide teletext information, which includes programme schedules. Satellite programme listings are provided in a number of British publications such as *What Satellite, Satellite Times* and *Satellite TV* (the best), available on subscription and from some international news kiosks in France. The annual *World Radio and TV Handbook* (Billboard) contains over 600 pages of information and the frequencies of radio and TV stations worldwide.

Radio: Radio was deregulated in France in the '80s, since when there have been commercial local radio (*radio libre*) stations. Deregulation led to scores of radio stations springing up overnight, representing diverse ethnic groups, lifestyles and communities. Consequently the wavebands were flooded with stations and the only ones that could be received clearly were the large commercial stations with powerful transmitters such as NRJ, Radio Luxembourg and Radio Monte Carlo. This led to the introduction of new regulations, although less stringent than in the '70s. Local radio stations (*Radio Locales Privées*) often have limited audiences due to their small catchment areas and low transmitting power, and many have been grouped together into national networks. The largest is operated by NRJ, a popular Paris music station. With an estimated 35 million radios in France (plus ten million car radios) embracing some 99 per cent of the population, France has one of Europe's largest radio markets and it's much more popular than TV. A radio licence isn't required in France.

Music Stations: There's a wealth of excellent FM stations in Paris and other cities, although in some rural areas you may be lucky to receive a few FM stations clearly, e.g. one chat show and one playing nothing but folk music! French radio stations are often original and progressive, particularly in Paris, and play a wide variety of music. Among the most popular FM stations are Kiss FM (89.0), France Info (105.5), Radio Classique (101.1), RTL (104.3) and Europe 1 (104.7). Radio Classique is also available throughout France on other wavelengths. France has many excellent music stations, which previously played mostly American and British pop songs. However, from the 1st January 1996 at least 40 per cent of radio musical broadcasts have had to consist of songs sung in French. Stations that don't comply can be fined or even closed. This has led to talk shows replacing the 40 per cent French music, as in the words of one French DJ, 'no-one wants to listen to 40 per cent of Sacha Distel'!

Radio France: Radio France public radio is divided into three networks: France-Inter, France-Musique and France-Culture. France-Inter is the main channel and broadcasts news bulletins, current events, magazine programmes, discussions, light music and plays (many foreigners tune in to improve their French). During the summer it broadcasts news bulletins in English (at 0900 and 1600). France-Musique broadcasts mostly classical music with some jazz and contemporary music. Much of France-Culture's output is highbrow and somewhat pretentious and includes talks, debates and interviews on arts and literature.

Other Stations: Many French people tune into foreign radio stations such as Europe One, Radio Luxembourg (RTL), Radio Monte-Carlo and Radio Sud, all broadcasting from outside French territory, having been established many years ago to circumvent the earlier French government monopoly on radio stations. Together they have a larger audience than Radio France. Other popular stations include France Info, a continuous news channel available throughout France, Radio Bleue, targeted at mature listeners, and Fun Radio, part of a new wave of youth-oriented radio stations that have saturated French airwaves in recent years. Radio France International (RFI) is France's world service station, broadcasting 24 hours a day in some 15 languages. There are also a number of expatriate English-language radio stations in France, such as Riviera Radio (FM stereo 106.3 and 106.5) in the south of France.

BBC: The BBC World Service is broadcast on short wave on several frequencies (e.g. 12095, 9410, 7325, 6195, 3955, 648 and 198khz) simultaneously and you can usually receive a good signal on one of them. The signal strength varies depending on where you live in France, the time of day and year, the power and positioning of your receiver, and atmospheric conditions. You can also receive BBC radio stations in some northern and western areas of France. All BBC radio stations, including the World Service, are also available on the Astra satellite (see below). The BBC publish a monthly magazine, *BBC On Air*, containing comprehensive information about BBC World Service radio and TV programmes. For a free copy and frequency information write to BBC On Air, Room 205 NW, Bush House, Strand, London WC2B 4PH, UK (☎ 0171-240 3456).

Satellite Radio: If you have satellite TV, you can also receive many radio stations via your satellite link. For example, BBC Radio 1, 2, 3, 4 and 5, BBC World Service, Sky Radio, Virgin 1215 and many foreign-language stations are broadcast via the Astra satellites. Satellite radio stations are listed in British satellite TV magazines such as the *Satellite Times*. If you're interested in receiving radio stations from further afield you should obtain a copy of the *World Radio TV Handbook* (Billboard).

LEARNING FRENCH

If you don't speak French fluently, you may wish to enrol in a language course. If you want to make the most of the French way of life and your time in France, it's absolutely essential to learn French as soon as possible. For people living in France permanently, learning French isn't an option, but a necessity. Although it isn't easy, even the most non-linguistic person can acquire a working knowledge of French. All that's required is a little hard work, some help and perseverance, particularly if you have only English-speaking colleagues and friends. **Note that your business and social enjoyment and success in France will be directly related to the degree to which you master French.**

Most people can teach themselves a great deal through the use of books, tapes, videos and even computer-based courses. However, even the best students require some help. Teaching French is big business in France, with classes offered by language schools, French and foreign colleges and universities, private and international schools, foreign and international organisations (such as the British Institute in Paris), local associations and clubs, and private teachers. Tuition ranges from language courses for complete beginners, through specialised business or cultural courses to university-level courses leading to recognised diplomas. Most French universities provide language courses and many organisations offer holiday courses year-round, particularly for children and young adults (it's best to stay with a local French family). If you already speak French but need conversational practice, you may prefer to enrol in an art or craft course at a local institute or club. You can also learn French via a telephone language course, which is particularly practical for busy executives and those who don't live near a language school.

There are many language schools (*écoles de langues*) in French cities and large towns. Most schools run various classes depending on your language ability, how many hours you wish to study a week, how much money you want to spend and how quickly you wish to learn. For those for whom money is no object (hopefully your employer!), there are total immersion courses where you study for up to nine hours a day, five days a week. The cost for a one-week (45 hours) total immersion course is usually between 15,000F and 20,000F depending on the school. Rates vary so shop around. Language classes generally fall into the following categories:

extensive	4 to 10	hours per week
intensive	15 to 20	"
total immersion	20 to 40+	"

Don't expect to become fluent in a short time unless you have a particular flair for languages or already have a good command of French. Unless you desperately need to learn French quickly, it's better to arrange your lessons over a long period. However, don't commit yourself to a long course of study, particularly an expensive one, before ensuring that it's the right course. Most schools offer free tests to help you find your appropriate level and a free introductory lesson.

You may prefer to have private lessons, which are a faster, although more expensive way of learning a language. The main advantage of private lessons is that you learn at your own speed and aren't held back by slow learners or left floundering in the wake of the class genius. You can advertise for a teacher in your local newspapers, on shopping centre/supermarket bulletin boards, university notice boards, and through your or your spouse's employer. Don't forget to ask your friends, neighbours and colleagues if they can recommend a private teacher. Private lessons by the hour cost from around 350F at a school or 100F to 200F with a private tutor. In some areas a *Centre Culturel* provides free French lessons to foreigners. If you're officially registered as unemployed and have a residence permit (*carte séjour*), you can obtain free French lessons (*prefectionnement de la langue Française*), although complete beginners don't qualify (contact your local ANPE office for information).

One of the most famous French language teaching organisations is the *Alliance Française*, 101, boulevard Raspail, 75270 Paris Cedex 06 (☎ 01.45.44.38.28), a state-approved, non-profit organisation with centres in over 100 countries and throughout France. *Alliance Française* run general, special and intensive courses, and can also arrange a homestay in France with a host family. Another non-profit organisation is *Centre d'Échanges Internationaux* (104, rue de Vaugirard, 75006 Paris, ☎ 01.45.49.26.25), offering intensive French language courses for juniors (13 to 18 years) and adults throughout France. Courses include accommodation in their own international centres, with a French family, or a hotel, bed and breakfast, or self-catering studio. Junior courses can be combined with tuition in a variety of sports and other activities including horse riding, tennis, windsurfing, canoe-kayak, diving and dancing.

Parents with young children who are planning to move to France may be interested in *En Famille International,* an exchange organisation founded in the late '70s by Frenchman Jacques Pinault. It specialises in six-month exchange visits for children aged 9 to 13 between European countries and France. Children stay with a French family, attend a French school and return speaking fluent French. One of the most important aspects of the scheme is that children must be enthusiastic about the exchange. It can take up to a year to match two families, so you should make enquiries as early as possible. For further information contact Jacques and Katherine Pinault, 'Savarias', Salignac, 33240 St André de Cubzac (☎ 05.57.43.52.48).

A comprehensive list of schools, institutions and organisations providing French language courses throughout France is contained in a booklet, *Cours de français langue étrangère et stages pédagogie du français langue étrangère en France.* It includes information about the type of course, organisation, dates, costs and other practical information, and is available from French consulates or from the ADPF, 9, rue Anatole de la Forge, 75017 Paris (☎ 01.44.09.27.40). A useful book for anyone wishing to visit France to study the French language and culture is *Study Holidays* (Central Bureau for Educational Visits & Exchanges, c/o British Council, 10 Spring Gardens, London SW1A 2BN, UK, ☎ 0171-389 4383) containing practical information on accommodation, travel, and sources of bursaries, grants and scholarships.

CRIME

France has a similar crime rate to most other European countries and in common with them crime has increased considerably in recent years. Stiffer sentences have failed to stem the spiralling crime rate and the prison population in France has doubled to some 60,000 in the past decade, creating a crisis in the overcrowded jails. Although most crimes are against property, violent crime is increasing, particularly in Paris. Mugging is on the increase throughout France, although it's still relatively rare in most cities. In some towns in southern France pensioners have been the target of muggers and even truffle hunters have been robbed of their harvest at gun point. Sexual harassment (or worse) is common in France and women should take particular care late at night and never hitchhike alone. Some 'experts' recommend that women carry a tear gas aerosol, although it's officially illegal.

Thefts are soaring and housebreaking and burglary have reached epidemic proportions in some areas ('holiday' or second homes are a popular target). Many people keep dogs as a protection or warning against burglars (*attention: chien méchant*) and have triple-locked and steel-reinforced doors. However, crime in rural areas remains relatively low and it's still common for people in villages and small towns not to lock their homes and cars. Car theft and theft from cars is rife in Paris and other cities. Foreign-registered cars are a popular target, particularly expensive models, which are often stolen to order and spirited abroad.

Pickpockets and bag-snatchers have long been a plague in Paris, where the 'charming' street urchins (often gypsies) are a highly organised and trained bunch of pickpockets. They try to surround and distract you, and when your attention is diverted pick you clean without you noticing. Keep them at arm's length, if necessary by force, and keep a firm grip on your valuables. Remain vigilant in tourist haunts, queues and on the *métro*. *Never* tempt fate with an exposed wallet or purse or by flashing your money around and hang on tight to your shoulder bag. One of the most effective methods of protecting your passport, money, traveller's cheques and credit cards, is with an old-fashioned money belt. Tourists and travellers are the targets of some of France's most enterprising criminals, including highwaymen and train robbers.

The worst area for crime is the Mediterranean coast (one of the most corrupt and crime-ridden regions in Europe), particularly around Marseille and Nice, where most crime is attributable to the vicious underworld (*Milieu*) of the Côte d'Azur racketeers and drug dealers. Marseille is notorious for its links with organised crime such as drug-trafficking (the *French Connection*), money-laundering, robbery and prostitution. There's a growing use of guns in urban crime and gang killings are fairly frequent in Marseille and Corsica, where separatist groups such as the *Front Libéral National Corse (FLNC)*, *Cuncolta Naziunalist* and the *Mouvement pour l'Autodétermination (MPA)* have become increasingly violent in recent years. In Paris there's a threat from bombs planted by Algerian Islamic militants, which have killed a number of people in the last few years.

Although the increase in crime isn't encouraging, the crime rate in France is relatively low, particularly violent crime. This means that you can usually safely walk almost anywhere at any time of day or night and there's usually no need for anxiety or paranoia about crime. However, you should be 'street-wise' and take certain elementary precautions. These include avoiding high-risk areas at night, particularly those frequented by drug addicts, prostitutes and pickpockets. Street people (*clochards*) in Paris and other cities may occasionally harass you, but they are generally harmless. You can safely travel on the Paris *métro* (and other *métros* in France) at any time, although some stations are best avoided late at night. When you're in an unfamiliar city, ask a policeman, taxi driver or other local person whether there are any unsafe neighbourhoods – and avoid them! See also **Car Crime** on page 40, **Home Security** on page 178 and **Household Insurance** on page 57.

3.

FINANCE

One of the most important aspects of buying a home in France and living there (even for relatively brief periods) is finance, which includes everything from transferring and changing money to mortgages and taxes. If you're planning to invest in a property or a business in France financed with imported funds, it's important to consider both the present and possible future exchange rates. On the other hand, if you live and work in France and are paid in French francs, this may affect your financial commitments abroad. **Bear in mind that if your income is paid in a currency other than French francs (or Euros) it can be exposed to risks beyond your control when you live in France, particularly regarding inflation and exchange rate fluctuations.**

If you own a home in France you can employ a French accountant or tax adviser to look after your financial affairs there and declare and pay your local taxes. You can also have your financial representative receive your bank statements, ensure that your bank is paying your standing orders (e.g. for utilities and property taxes) and that you have sufficient funds to pay them. If you let a home in France through a French company, they may perform the above tasks as part of their services.

Although the French prefer to pay cash rather than use credit or charge cards, it's wise to have at least one credit card when visiting or living in France (Visa is the most widely accepted). Even if you don't like credit cards and shun any form of credit, they do have their uses, for example no-deposit car rentals, no pre-paying hotel bills (plus guaranteed bookings), obtaining cash 24-hours a day, simple telephone and mail-order payments, greater security than cash and, above all, convenience. Note, however, that not all French businesses accept credit cards.

Wealth Warning: If you plan to live in France you must ensure that your income is (and will remain) sufficient to live on, bearing in mind devaluations (if your income isn't paid in French francs), rises in the cost of living (see page 109), and unforeseen expenses such as medical bills or anything else that may reduce your income (such as stock market crashes and recessions!). Foreigners, particularly retirees, often under-estimate the cost of living in France and many are forced to return to their home countries after a year or two. Note also that France is one of the highest taxed countries in the European Union, when both direct and indirect taxes (including social security) are taken into consideration.

This section includes information on importing and exporting money; banking; mortgages; taxes (property, income, capital gains, inheritance, gift and sales); wills; and the cost of living.

FRENCH CURRENCY

On 1st January 1999 the Euro (€) was introduced in France (plus Austria, Belgium, Finland, Germany, Ireland, Italy, Luxembourg, the Netherlands, Portugal and Spain) and will eventually become the country's currency. The currencies of all 11 Euro countries are locked into a fixed exchange rate (set by the European Central Bank) with the Euro and consequently with each other. Euro notes and coins will become legal tender on 1st January 2002 and for six months will circulate alongside the French franc, which will then be withdrawn (Euro coins and notes will be introduced earlier in some countries and will circulate alongside the national currency, but they won't become legal currency until 2002). Companies and banks already use Euros for trading, accounts, statements and receipts, and shops, supermarkets and restaurants produce bills in both currencies. Several towns in France have had 'Euro Days', when the new currency is temporarily the only legal tender and (in general) enthusiasm for the Euro among the French is high.

Until the Euro is officially introduced, the French unit of currency remains the French franc, introduced by King Jean le Bon in 1360 to show that his part of France was free of the English, *franc des anglais*. The franc is also the official currency in Monaco, French overseas territories, such as Guadeloupe and Martinique, and many former French colonies. The French franc is divided into 100 centimes and French coins are minted in coins of 5, 10, 20 and 50 centimes and 1, 2, 5, 10 and 20 (introduced in 1993) francs. The 5, 10 and 20 centime coins are copper coloured (*pièces jaunes*) and the 50 centime, 1, 2, and 5 franc coins are silver coloured. Some old French coins are mostly silver and worth a lot more than their face value. The 10F and 20F coins are small silver-centred coins with a copper rim. Note that money is *argent* in French and small change is called *monnaie* (also currency).

French banknotes (*billets*) depict famous Frenchmen and are printed in denominations of 20 (depicting Debussy), 50 (Antoine de St.-Exupéry), 100 (Cézanne), 200 (Gustave Eiffel) and 500 (Marie and Pierre Curie) francs. The size of notes increases with their value (who said size doesn't matter!). **Beware of counterfeit notes, some of which are made with sophisticated colour laser copiers.** However, new notes have been introduced in recent years containing many new anti-counterfeit measures, including a special strip which is reproduced as black if a banknote is photocopied.

The franc is usually written as F, used in this book, or FF. When writing figures, a period (.) is used to separate units of millions and thousands and a comma is used to denote centimes, e.g. 1.500.485,34 is one million, five hundred thousand, four hundred and eighty five francs and 34 centimes (a nice healthy bank balance!). Store and market prices are written with an F after the figure, e.g. 5,50F is five francs 50 centimes. Values below one franc are written with zero francs, e.g. 0,75F is seventy five centimes.

It's advisable to obtain some French coins and banknotes before arriving in France and to familiarise yourself with them. You should have some French francs in cash, e.g. 500F to 1,000F in small notes, when you arrive. It's best to avoid 500F notes, which sometimes aren't accepted, particularly for small purchases or on public transport! This will save you having to queue to change money on arrival at a French airport, although you should avoid carrying a lot of cash.

IMPORTING & EXPORTING MONEY

Exchange controls in France were abolished on 1st January 1990 and there are no restrictions on the import or export of funds. A French resident is permitted to open a bank account in any country and to export an unlimited amount of money from France. However, if you're a French resident, you must inform the French tax authorities of any new foreign account in your annual tax return. Sums in excess of 50,000F deposited abroad, other than by regular bank transfers, must be reported to the Banque de France. If you send or receive any amount above 10,000F by post, it must be declared to customs. Similarly if you enter or leave France with 50,000F or more in French or foreign banknotes or securities (e.g. traveller's cheques, letters of credit, bills of exchange, bearer bonds, giro cheques, stocks and share certificates, bullion, and gold or silver coins quoted on the official exchange), you must declare it to French customs. **Note that if you exceed the 50,000F limit and are found out,** you can be fined an extortionate 10,000F or more (a number of people fall foul of this legalised form of highway robbery each year, which almost certainly contravenes EU law).

When transferring or sending money to (or from) France you should be aware of the alternatives. One way to do this is via a bank draft (*chèque de banque*), which should be sent by registered mail. Note, however, that in the unlikely event that it's lost or stolen, it's impossible to stop payment and you must wait six months before a new draft can be issued. Bank drafts aren't treated as cash in France and must be cleared, as with personal cheques. One of the safest and fastest methods of transferring money is to make a direct transfer (*transfert*) or a telex or electronic transfer (e.g. via the SWIFT system in Europe) between banks. A 'normal' transfer should take three to seven days, but in reality it usually takes much longer and an international bank transfer between non-affiliated banks can take weeks! A SWIFT telex transfer *should* be completed in a few hours, with funds being available within 24 hours. The cost of transfers vary considerably, not only commission and exchange rates, but also transfer charges (such as the telex charge for a SWIFT transfer). Note that it's usually faster and cheaper to transfer funds between branches of the same bank than between non-affiliated banks.

When you have money transferred to a bank in France, ensure that you give the name, account number, branch number (*code agence*) and the bank code (*clé rib*). If money is 'lost' while being transferred to or from a French bank account, it can take weeks to locate it. If you plan to send a large amount of money to France or abroad for a business transaction such as buying property, you should ensure you receive the commercial rate of exchange rather than the tourist rate. Check charges and rates in advance and agree them with your bank (you may be able to negotiate a lower charge or a better exchange rate).

You can also send money by international money order from a post office or a telegraphic transfer, e.g. via Western Union, the fastest and safest method, but also the most expensive. Money can be sent via American Express offices by Amex card holders. It's also possible to send cheques drawn on personal accounts and Eurocheques, although both of these take a long time to clear (usually a number of weeks) and fees are high. Postcheques can be cashed at any post office in France and most credit and charge cards can be used to obtain cash advances.

Most banks in major cities have foreign exchange windows and there are banks or exchange bureaux with extended opening hours at airports, major railway stations in Paris and in all major cities. Here you can buy or sell foreign currencies, buy and cash traveller's cheques, cash eurocheques, and obtain a cash advance on credit and charge cards. Note, however, that some French banks refuse to cash traveller's cheques or eurocheques. At airports and in tourist areas in major cities, there are automatic change machines accepting up to 15 currencies including US$, £Sterling, Deutschmarks and Swiss francs.

There are many private *bureaux de change* in Paris and other major cities, with longer business hours than banks, particularly at weekends. Most offer competitive exchange rates and low or no commission (but check). They are easier to deal with than banks and if you're changing a lot of money you can also usually negotiate a better exchange rate. Never use unofficial money changers, who are likely to short change you or leave you with worthless foreign notes rather than French francs. The best exchange rate is usually provided by banks (Banque Nationale de Paris has a reputation for offering the best exchange rate and charging the lowest commission).

The French franc exchange rate (*cours de change*) for most European and major international currencies is listed in banks and daily newspapers, and is also given on Minitel (see page 27).

If you're visiting France, it's safer to carry traveller's cheques (*chèques de voyage*) than cash. It's best to buy traveller's cheques in French francs when visiting France, although they aren't as easy to cash as in some other countries, e.g. the USA. They aren't usually accepted as cash by businesses, except perhaps in Parisian hotels, restaurants and shops, all of which usually offer a poor exchange rate. You can buy traveller's cheques from any French bank, usually for a service charge of 1 per cent of the face value. There should be no commission charge when cashing French franc traveller's cheques at any bank in France (you must show your passport). However, charges and rates can vary considerably on traveller's cheques in foreign currencies. Banks usually offer a better exchange rate for traveller's cheques than for banknotes, although they often levy a high commission, e.g. between 20F and 30F per cheque.

Keep a separate record of cheque numbers and note where and when they were cashed. American Express provides a free, 24-hour replacement service for lost or stolen traveller's cheques at any of their offices worldwide, providing you know the serial numbers of the lost cheques. Without the serial numbers, replacement can take three days or longer. All companies provide local numbers for reporting lost or stolen traveller's cheques.

One thing to bear in mind when travelling anywhere isn't to rely on one source of funds only.

BANKS

There are two main kinds of banks in France: commercial and co-operative. The largest commercial banks have branches in most large towns and cities and include Crédit Lyonnais, Banque Nationale de Paris (BNP) and Société Générale. All three have now been privatised and in order to compete with other larger European banks, are intent on merging, the latest being a union between BNP and Société Générale. The top four French banks (Crédit Agricole, Crédit Lyonnais, Société Générale and BNP) are among the world's top ten banks. Note that as in many other European countries, the post office serves as the largest banking facility in France.

The largest co-operative banks are Crédit Agricole, Crédit Mutuel and Banque Populaire. They began life as regional, community-based institutions working for the mutual benefit of their clients, although most are now represented nationally and offer a full range of banking services. Unlike commercial banks, each branch office of a co-operative bank is independent and issues its own shares. Anyone can become a member and invest in their shares, which is usually mandatory if you wish to take out a mortgage or loan but isn't necessary to open a current cheque account. Crédit Agricole is the largest co-operative bank and is also the biggest landholder in France. It's the largest retail bank in Europe with around 10,000 branches and some 17 million customers.

There are also savings banks in France such as Caisses d'Épargne with a network of over 400 regional institutions, although they offer a limited range of services compared with commercial and co-operative banks. Foreign-owned banks in France number some 175, more than in any other European country except Britain, although they have a small market share. However, competition from foreign banks is set to increase, as EU regulations allow any bank trading legitimately in one EU country to trade in another. All banks, including foreign banks, are listed in the Yellow Pages under *Banques*.

Most major foreign banks are present in Paris, but branches are rare in the provinces. In many small villages there are often tiny bank offices (*permanences*) which usually open one morning a week only. Among foreigners in France, the British are best served by their national banks, both in Paris and in the provinces, particularly the French Riviera. The most prominent British bank is Barclays with around 100 branches, including at least one in major cities. If you do a lot of travelling abroad or carry out international business transactions, you may find that the services provided by a foreign bank are more suited to your needs. They are also more likely to have staff who speak English and other foreign languages. Note, however, that many foreign banks and some French banks such as Banque Paribas, handle mainly corporate clients and don't provide banking services for individuals.

Although banking has become highly automated in recent years, French banks still lag behind banks in many other European countries (notably Britain, Germany, the Netherlands and Switzerland) in terms of efficiency and the range and quality of services provided. Decisions regarding loans and other transactions often aren't made by managers at local level and must be referred to a regional head office.

You must usually press a bell to gain access to a French bank. After deciding that you aren't a robber a staff member presses a button to open the outer door. For security purposes, most banks have two entrance doors, the second of which is opened only after the first has closed (intended to trap potential robbers as they attempt to flee with their booty). French banks usually have a more casual air than banks in many other countries and most use open counters rather than protected teller windows.

Opening an Account

You can open a bank account in France whether you're a resident or a non-resident, although a bank can refuse to open an account. However, if you have been refused by two banks, the third must open an account for you (you must obtain proof of refusals in writing). It's best to open a French bank account in person, rather than by correspondence from abroad. Ask your friends, neighbours or colleagues for their recommendations and just go along to the bank of your choice and introduce yourself. You must be aged at least 18 and provide proof of identity, e.g. a passport (be prepared to produce other forms of identification), and your address in France (an EDF bill usually suffices).

If you wish to open an account with a French bank while you're abroad, you must first obtain an application form, available from overseas branches of French banks. You need to select a branch from the list provided, which should be close to where you will be living in France. If you open an account by correspondence you must provide a reference from your current bank, including a certificate of signature or a signature witnessed by a lawyer. You also need a photocopy of the relevant pages of your passport and a French franc draft to open the account.

Non-Residents: If you're a non-resident, you're entitled to open a non-resident account (*compte non-résident*) only. A non-resident account previously had many restrictions, including limiting account holders to making deposits from outside France only, although this is no longer the case. There's little difference between non-resident and resident accounts for deposits up to 50,000F, and you can deposit and withdraw funds in any currency without limit. Non-resident accounts have a ban on ordinary overdrafts (*découverts*), although loans for a car or house purchase are possible. If you're a non-resident with a second home in France it's possible to survive without a French account by using eurocheques, traveller's cheques and credit cards, although this isn't wise and is an expensive option. If you're a non-resident you can have documentation (e.g. cheque books, statements, etc.) sent to an address abroad.

Residents: You're considered to be a resident of France if you have your main centre of interest there, i.e. you live or work there more or less permanently. To open a resident account you must usually have a residence permit (*carte de séjour*) or evidence that you have a job in France.

Note that it isn't advisable to close your bank accounts abroad, unless you're certain that you won't need them in the future. Even when resident in France, it's cheaper to keep money in local currency in an account in a country that you visit regularly, rather than pay commission to convert French francs. Many foreigners living in France maintain at least two accounts, a foreign bank account for international transactions and a local account with a French bank for day-to-day business.

Cheque Accounts

The normal bank account for day-to-day transactions in France is a cheque or current account (*compte de chèque*). When opening a cheque account, you should request a *carte bleue* debit card, which can be used to pay bills throughout France. You will receive a cheque book (*chéquier/carnet de chèques*) and your *carte bleue* around two to three weeks after opening an account (although some banks don't issue a cheque book until it has been operated for at least two months). You must usually collect your cheque book and *carte bleue* in person from your branch, although it can be sent to you abroad by registered post at your expense. Note that it usually takes weeks to obtain a new cheque book, so you should keep a spare one. Many French employers pay their employees' salaries into a bank or post office account by direct transfer (*virement*), so make sure that you give your employer your account details.

It's illegal for banks in France to pay interest on current accounts. Most French people deposit their 'rainy day' money in a savings account. However, most banks will transfer funds above a certain sum from a cheque account into an interest-bearing savings account. There are no monthly charges on a cheque account and no charges for transactions such as direct debits or (usually) standing orders, except when made overseas. You may withdraw any amount up to the balance (*solde*) of your account by cashing a cheque (*encaisser un chèque*) at the branch where you have your account. At any other branch of your bank, you can usually withdraw up to 3,000F per week and must provide identification and your cheque book. If the branch has a computer link to your branch, you may withdraw any amount up to the balance of your account. When withdrawing cash from a French bank, you may need to go to one counter (*guichet*) for the transaction and then to the cashier (*caisse*) to collect your money (the system was invented by bureaucrats!).

Personal cheques (*chèques*) are widely accepted throughout France and many people use them to buy everything from petrol to food, from restaurant meals to travel tickets. All stores accept cheques. There are no cheque guarantee cards in France and therefore you're usually asked to produce identification, e.g. a passport or *carte de séjour*, when paying by cheque. Usually cheques are crossed (*chèques barrés*) and personal cheques aren't negotiable, i.e. they cannot be signed and endorsed for payment to a third party. They can be paid into an account in the name of the payee only (who must sign the back). This means you cannot cash a cheque unless you have your own bank account. It's possible to obtain 'open' uncrossed cheques (*chèques non-barrés*), although your bank is required to notify the French tax authorities of any uncrossed cheques issued. Because of this rule, few people request uncrossed cheques as they attract the (very) unwelcome attention of the tax inspectors. The main reason that cheques are crossed and cannot be endorsed is to discourage tax evasion, a national sport in France.

The design of a French cheque may be different from what you're used to and looks as if it was designed by a committee! In the top right-hand corner is a box or line where the value of the cheque is written in numerals. The line *payez contre ce chèque* is where the value of the cheque is written in words. Write the name of the payee next to the line marked *à l'ordre de* (or *moi-même* when writing a cheque for cash). The date line is in the lower right-hand corner above the signature position and is preceded by the town where the cheque was written (*lieu de création*). It isn't possible to post-date a cheque in France, as cheques are payable on the date presented irrespective of the date written on them and are valid for one year and one day after this date. At the bottom of the cheque is your name and address.

When writing figures in France, or anywhere on the continent of Europe, the number seven should be crossed ($\digamma$) to avoid confusion with the number one, written with a tail and looking like an uncrossed seven ($\mathcal{1}$) to many foreigners. The date is written in the standard European style, for example 10th September 1999 is written: 10.9.99, not as in the USA, 9.10.99. If there's a difference between the amount written in figures and the amount in words, the amount written in words is assumed to be correct. Most banks supply a specimen cheque showing how it's written.

Cheque clearing takes longer in France than it does in most other countries. Under the French system, a cheque paid into your account will show on your account balance the day it's deposited (using the 'value date' or *date de valeur* system), **although it won't have been cleared**. Two dates are usually shown, the date a transaction is recorded and the date it's credited or debited to your account. Make sure that cheques, including bank drafts (which *aren't* treated as cash in France), have been cleared before making a withdrawal against them. The time needed to clear a cheque depends on whether it's drawn on a bank in the same town (*sur place*) or in another town (*hors place*). A cheque drawn on a different bank in another town may take up to 12 days to clear. Note also that some people are slow to pay in cheques that you have written. When making payments into an account, a distinction is made between cash (*espèces*) and cheques, which must be listed (*versement de chèques*) on the paying-in form.

You should **NEVER** go overdrawn or write 'rubber' cheques in France (called a *chèque en bois* in French, literally a wooden cheque, or *chèque sans provision*). Writing rubber cheques is a criminal offence and there are no cheque cards in France to guarantee them. If you illegally overdraw your account (*en découvert*), your bank will send you a registered letter demanding that the necessary funds be paid into the account within 30 days. You will also be 'fined' around 200F to 300F. In the meantime you mustn't write any more cheques. If the funds aren't deposited within 30 days or if you overdraw your account twice within a 12-month period, your account will be closed! You must return your cheque book to your bank and also cheque books for other bank accounts in France.

Your name will also be entered on a blacklist (*interdit bancaire*) maintained by the Banque de France. You will be unable to operate a cheque account at any bank in France for one year and your name will remain on the blacklist for three years. If you're blacklisted it can make life difficult and can make obtaining a French mortgage or loan impossible for years afterwards. Around one cheque in every 1,500 'bounces' in France and some 750,000 people are forbidden to operate bank accounts. If you can prove that overdrawing your account was due to the fault of another party, you can avoid being blacklisted. Persistent cheque bouncers can be fined from 3,000F to 250,000F and receive prison sentences of from one to five years.

Account statements (*relevés*) are usually sent monthly, although you can usually choose to receive them weekly or quarterly. Your account details (*relevés d'identité bancaire*) such as your bank, branch and account number are printed at the top of statements. This information is required when payments are to be made directly to or from your account, e.g. when electricity and telephone bills are paid by direct debit.

Offshore Banking

If you have a sum of money to invest or wish to protect your inheritance from the tax man, it may be worthwhile looking into the accounts and other services (such as pensions and trusts) provided by banks in offshore tax havens such as the Channel Islands (Guernsey and Jersey), Gibraltar and the Isle of Man (around 50 locations worldwide are officially classified as tax havens). The big attraction of offshore banking is that money can be deposited in a wide range of currencies, customers are usually guaranteed complete anonymity, there are no double-taxation agreements, no withholding tax is payable and interest is paid tax-free. Many offshore banks also offer telephone banking (usually seven days a week).

A large number of American, British and other European banks and financial institutions provide offshore banking facilities in one or more locations. Most institutions offer high-interest deposit accounts for long-term savings and investment portfolios, in which funds can be deposited in any major currency. Many people living abroad keep a local account for everyday business and maintain an offshore account for international transactions and investment purposes. However, most financial experts advise investors never to rush into the expatriate life and invest their life savings in an offshore tax haven until they know what their long-term plans are.

Accounts have minimum deposits levels which usually range from the equivalent of around 5,000F to 100,000F (i.e. GB£500 to GB£10,000), with some as high as one million francs (GB£100,000). In addition to large minimum balances, accounts may also have stringent terms and conditions, such as restrictions on withdrawals or high early withdrawal penalties. You can deposit funds on call (instant access) or for a fixed period, e.g. from 90 days to one year (usually for larger sums). Interest is usually paid monthly or annually; monthly interest payments are slightly lower than annual payments, although they have the advantage of providing a regular income. There are usually no charges providing a specified minimum balance is maintained. Many accounts offer a cash card (usually aligned with Mastercard or Visa) that can be used to obtain money from cash machines throughout the world.

When selecting a financial institution and offshore banking centre, your first priority should be for the safety of your money. In some offshore banking centres bank deposits are guaranteed up to a maximum amount (e.g. GB£100,000) under a deposit protection scheme should a financial institution go to the wall (the Isle of Man, Guernsey and Jersey all have such schemes). Unless you're planning to bank with a major international bank (which is only likely to fold the day after the end of the world!), you should check the credit rating of a financial institution before depositing any money, particularly if it doesn't provide deposit insurance. All banks have a credit rating (the highest is 'AAA') and a bank with a high rating will be happy to tell you (but get it in writing). You can also check the rating of an international bank or financial organisation with Moodys Investor Service. You should be wary of institutions offering higher than average interest rates, as if it looks too good to be true it probably will be – like the Bank of International Commerce and Credit (BICC) which went bust in 1992.

MORTGAGES

Mortgages (home loans) are available from major French banks (both for residents and non-residents) and many foreign banks. Most French banks offer French franc mortgages on French property through foreign branches in European Union and other countries. Crédit Agricole is the largest French lender, with a 25 per cent share of the French mortgage market. Most financial advisers advise lenders to borrow from a large reputable bank rather than a small one. French law doesn't permit French banks to offer mortgages or other loans where repayments are more than 30 per cent of your net income. Joint incomes and liabilities are included when assessing a couple's borrowing limit (usually a French bank will lend to up to three joint borrowers). The 30 per cent of income includes existing mortgage or rental payments, both in France and abroad. If the total sum exceeds 30 per cent of your income, French banks aren't permitted to extend further credit. Should they attempt to do so, the law allows a borrower to avoid liability for payment.

Both French and foreign lenders have tightened their lending criteria in the last few years due to the repayment problems experienced by many recession-hit borrowers in the early '90s. Some foreign lenders apply stricter rules than French lenders regarding income, employment and the type of property on which they will lend, although some are willing to lend more than a French lender. It can take some foreigners a long time to obtain a mortgage in France, particularly if you have neither a regular income or assets there. If you have difficulty you should try a bank that's experienced in dealing with foreigners such as the Bank Transatlantique in Paris.

To calculate how much you can borrow in France, multiply your total net monthly earnings by 30 per cent and deduct your monthly mortgage, rent and other regular payments. Note that earned income isn't included if you're aged over 65. The remainder is the maximum amount you can repay each month on a French mortgage. For example:

monthly net income	30,000F
multiplied by 30 per cent	9,000F
less monthly deductions	4,000F
maximum monthly repayments	5,000F

As a rough guide, repayments on a 400,000F mortgage are around 4,000F a month at 6 per cent over 15 years. There are special low mortgage rates for low-income property buyers in some departments.

Mortgages can be obtained for any period from two to 20 years, although the usual term in France is 15 years (some banks won't lend for longer than this). In certain cases mortgages can be arranged over terms of up to 25 years, although interest rates are higher. Generally the shorter the period of a loan, the lower the interest rate. All lenders set minimum loans, e.g. 100,000F to 200,000F, and some set minimum purchase prices. Usually there's no maximum loan amount, which is subject to status and possibly valuation (usually required by non-French lenders).

French mortgages are usually limited to 70 or 80 per cent of a property's value (although some lenders limit loans to just 50 per cent). A mortgage can include renovation work, when written quotations must be provided with a mortgage application. Note that you must add expenses and fees totalling around 10 to 15 per cent of the purchase price on an 'old' property, i.e. one over five years old. For example if you're buying a property for 500,000F and obtain an 80 per cent mortgage, you must pay 20 per cent deposit (100,000F) plus 10 to 15 per cent fees (50,000F to 75,000F), making a total of 150,000F to 175,000F.

Note that when buying a property in France, the deposit paid when signing the preliminary contract (*compromis de vente*) is automatically protected under French law should you fail to obtain a mortgage. Some lenders will provide a mortgage offer within a few weeks of an application. It's possible to obtain a mortgage guarantee or certificate from most lenders, valid for from two to four months, during which period a lender will guarantee you a mortgage, perhaps subject to valuation of the property. There may be a commitment fee of around 1,000F (banks charge fees for everything).

Once a loan has been agreed, a French bank will send you a conditional offer of a loan (*offre préalable*), outlining the terms. In accordance with French law, the offer cannot be accepted until after a 'cooling off' period of ten days. The borrower usually has 30 days to accept the loan and return the signed agreement to the lender. The loan is held available for four months and can be used over a longer period if it's for a building project.

To obtain a mortgage from a French bank, you must provide proof of your monthly income and out-goings such as mortgage payments, rent and other loans or commitments. Proof of income includes three months pay slips for employees, confirmation of income from your employer and tax returns. If you're self-employed you require an audited copy of your balance sheets and trading accounts for the past three years, plus your last tax return. French banks aren't particularly impressed with accountants' (*expert comptable/conseiller fiscal*) letters. If you want a French mortgage to buy a property for commercial purposes, you must provide a detailed business plan (in French).

There are various fees associated with mortgages. All lenders charge an arrangement fee (*frais de dossier*) for setting up a loan, usually 1 per cent of the loan amount. There's usually a minimum fee, e.g. 2,500F (plus TVA) and there may also be a maximum. Many lenders impose an administration fee of around 1 per cent of the loan with minimum (e.g. 500F) and maximum (e.g. 3,500F) fees. Although it's unusual to have a survey in France, foreign lenders usually insist on a 'valuation survey' (costing around 1,500F) for French properties before they grant a loan. Using the above examples, these fees add another 9,000F to the cost of a 400,000F loan.

It's customary in France for a property to be held as security for a loan taken out on it, i.e. the lender takes a charge on the property. If a loan is obtained using a French property as security, additional fees and registration costs are payable to the notary (*notaire*) for registering the charge against the property. Note that some foreign banks won't lend on the security of a French property. If you live in France and borrow from the Crédit Agricole or another co-operative bank, you're obliged to subscribe to the capital of the local bank. The amount (number of shares) is decided by the board of directors and you will be sent share certificates (*certificat nominatif de parts sociales*) for that value. The payment is usually deducted from your account at the same time as the first mortgage repayment. When the loan has been repaid, the shares are reimbursed (if required).

If you're buying a new property off-plan, when payments are made in stages, a bank will provide a 'staggered' loan, where the loan amount is advanced in instalments as required by the *contrat de réservation*. During the period before completion (*période d'anticipation*), interest is payable on a monthly basis on the amount advanced by the bank (plus insurance). When the final payment has been made and the loan is fully drawn, the mortgage enters its amortisation period (*période d'amortissement*).

If you fail to maintain your mortgage repayments, your property can be repossessed and sold at auction (as many foreign homeowners have found to their cost in the last few years). However, this rarely happens as most lenders are willing to arrange lower repayments when borrowers get into financial difficulties

Types of Mortgages

All French mortgages are repaid using the capital and interest method (repayment), and endowment and pension-linked mortgages aren't offered. As a condition of a French mortgage, you must take out a life (usually plus health and disability) insurance policy equal to 120 per cent of the amount borrowed. The premiums are included in mortgage payments. An existing insurance policy may be accepted, although it must be assigned to the lender. A medical examination may be required, although this isn't usual if you're under 50 years of age. Note that in France, a borrower is responsible for obtaining building insurance (see page 57) on a property and must provide the lender with a certificate of insurance.

French loans can be arranged with a fixed or variable rate. When comparing rates, the fixed rate is higher than the variable rate to reflect the increased risk to the lender. The advantage of a fixed rate is that you know exactly how much you must pay over the whole term. Variable rate loans may be fixed for the first two or more years, after which they are adjusted up or down on an annual basis in line with prevailing interest rates, but usually within a pre-arranged limit, e.g. 3 per cent of the original rate. You can usually convert a variable rate mortgage to a fixed rate mortgage at any time. There's normally a redemption penalty, e.g. 3 per cent of the outstanding capital, for early repayment of a fixed rate mortgage, although that isn't usual for variable rate mortgages. If you think you may want to repay early, you should try to have the redemption penalty waived or reduced before signing the agreement. In France, a mortgage cannot be transferred from one person to another, as is possible in some countries.

Mortgages for Second Homes

If you have spare equity in an existing property, either in France or abroad, it may be more cost effective to remortgage (or take out a second mortgage) on that property, rather than take out a new mortgage for a second home. It involves less paperwork and therefore lower legal fees, and a plan can be tailored to meet your individual requirements. Depending on the equity in your existing property and the cost of a French property, this may enable you to pay cash for a second home. The disadvantage of remortgaging or a second mortgage is that you reduce the amount of equity available in the property. When a mortgage is taken out on a French property, it's based on that property, which could be important if you get into repayment difficulties. Note that French lenders are usually reluctant to remortgage.

It's also possible to obtain a foreign currency mortgage, other than in French francs, e.g. £Sterling, Swiss francs, $US, Deutschmarks, Dutch guilders or Euros. However, you should be extremely wary before taking out a foreign currency mortgage, as interest rate gains can be wiped out overnight by currency swings and devaluations. It's generally recognised that you should take out a loan in the currency in which you're paid or in the currency of the country where a property is situated, i.e. French francs. In this case, if the foreign currency is devalued you will have the consolation of knowing that the value of your French property will ('theoretically') have increased by the same percentage, when converted back into the foreign currency. When choosing between a French franc loan and a foreign currency loan, be sure to take into account all costs, fees, interest rates and possible currency fluctuations. However you finance the purchase of a second home in France, you should obtain professional advice from your bank manager and accountant.

Note that if you have a foreign currency mortgage or are a non-resident with a French franc mortgage, you must usually pay commission charges each time you make a mortgage payment or remit money to France. However, some lenders will transfer mortgage payments to France each month free of charge or for a nominal amount. If you let a second home, you can offset the interest on your mortgage against rental income, but pro rata only. For example if you let a French property for three months of the year, you can offset a quarter of your annual mortgage interest against your rental income.

INCOME TAX

Generally speaking, income tax (*impôt sur le revenu*) in France is below average for EU countries, particularly for large families, and accounts for some 20 per cent of government revenue only. However, when income tax is added to the crippling social security contributions, regarded as a form of tax in France, and other indirect taxes, French taxes are among the highest in the industrialised world (around 50 per cent). Unlike many other countries, employees' income tax *isn't* deducted at source (i.e. pay as you earn) by employers in France, where individuals are responsible for paying their own income tax. Most taxpayers pay their tax a year in arrears in three instalments, although it can be paid in ten monthly instalments. However, tax is withheld at flat rates and at source for non-residents who receive income from employment and professional activities in France. Non-residents who receive income from a French source must file a statement with the *Centre des Impôts de Non-Résidents* (9, rue d'Uzès, 75094 Paris Cedex 02) annually.

The French have a pathological hatred of paying taxes and tax evasion is a national sport (most Frenchmen don't consider cheating the 'tax man' a crime). It's estimated that around one-third of non-salaried taxpayers don't declare a substantial part of their income. Consequently, if your tax affairs are investigated the authorities often take a hard line if they find you have been 'cheating', even if you made an 'innocent' mistake. If your perceived standard of living is higher than would be expected on your declared income, the tax authorities may suspect you of fraud, so contrive to appear poor (not difficult for struggling authors!). In extreme circumstances, income tax or a higher rate of tax can be arbitrarily imposed by tax inspectors (*régime d'imposition forfaitaire*). The tax authorities maintain details of tax declarations, employers and bank accounts on computers to help them expose fraud, and can now use social security numbers and access other government computer systems to identify residents and their circumstances.

As you would expect in a country with a 'billion' bureaucrats, the French tax system is inordinately complicated and most Frenchmen don't understand it. It's difficult to obtain accurate information from the tax authorities and errors in tax assessments are commonplace. Unless your tax affairs are simple, it's prudent to employ an accountant to complete your tax return and ensure that you're correctly assessed. The information below applies only to personal income tax (*Impôt sur le Revenu des Personnes Physiques/IRPP*) and not to companies.

Many books are available to help you understand and save taxes and income tax guides are published each January including *VO Impôts* and the *Guide Practique du Contribuable*. You can obtain tax information and calculate your tax using Minitel (3615 IR SERVICE) if you're very smart! You will, however, need to understand French perfectly (and then some) to complete your own tax return.

Liability

Your liability for French taxes depends on where you're domiciled. Your domicile is normally the country you regard as your permanent home and where you live most of the year. A foreigner working in France for a French company who has taken up residency in France and has no income tax liability abroad, is considered to have his tax domicile (*domicile fiscal*) in France. A person can be resident in more than one country at any given time, but can be domiciled only in one country. The domicile of a married woman isn't necessarily the same as her husband's, but is determined using the same criteria as anyone capable of having an independent domicile. Your country of domicile is particularly important regarding inheritance tax (see page 104).

Under the French tax code, domicile is decided under the 'tax home test' (*foyer fiscal*) or the 183-day rule. You're considered to be a French resident and liable to French tax if any of the following apply:

- your permanent home, i.e. family or principal residence, is in France;

- you spend over 183 days in France during any calendar year;

- you carry out paid professional activities or employment in France, except when secondary to business activities conducted in another country;

- your centre of vital economic interest, e.g. investments or business, is in France.

If you intend to live permanently in France, you should notify the tax authorities in your present country (you will be asked to complete a form, e.g. a form P85 in Britain). You may be entitled to a tax refund if you depart during the tax year, which usually necessitates the completion of a tax return. The tax authorities may require evidence that you're leaving the country, e.g. evidence of a job in France or of having bought or rented a property there. If you move to France to take up a job or start a business, you must register with the local tax authorities (*Centre des Impôts*) soon after your arrival.

Double-Taxation: French residents are taxed on their worldwide income, subject to certain treaty exceptions (non-residents are taxed only on income arising in France). Citizens of most countries are exempt from paying taxes in their home country when they spend a minimum period abroad, e.g. one year. France has double-taxation treaties with over 70 countries including all members of the EU, Australia, Canada, China, India, Israel, Japan, Malaysia, New Zealand, Pakistan, the Philippines, Singapore, Sri Lanka, Switzerland and the USA.

Treaties are designed to ensure that income that has already been taxed in one treaty country isn't taxed again in another treaty country. The treaty establishes a tax credit or exemption on certain kinds of income, either in the country of residence or the country where the income is earned. Where applicable, a double-taxation treaty prevails over domestic law. Many people living abroad switch their investments to offshore holdings to circumvent the often complicated double-taxation agreements. If you're in doubt about your tax liability in your home country, contact your nearest embassy or consulate in France. The USA is the only country that taxes its non-resident citizens on income earned abroad.

Leaving France: Before leaving France, foreigners must pay any tax due for the previous year and the year of departure by applying for a tax clearance (*quitus fiscal*). A tax return must be filed prior to departure and should include your income and deductions from 1st January of the departure year up to the date of departure. The local tax inspector will calculate the tax due and provide a written statement. When departure is made before 31st December, the previous year's taxes are applied. If this results in overpayment, a claim must be made for a refund. A French removal company isn't supposed to export your household belongings without a 'tax clearance statement' (*bordereau de situation*) from the tax authorities stating that all taxes have been paid.

Note that moving to France (or another country) may offer considerable opportunities for 'favourable tax planning', i.e. tax avoidance, rather than tax evasion. To take the maximum advantage of your situation, you should obtain professional advice from a tax adviser who's familiar with both the French tax system and that of your present country of residence.

Allowances

Before you're liable for income tax, you can deduct social security payments and certain allowances. The resultant figure is your taxable income. Income tax is calculated upon both earned income (*impôt sur le revenu*) and unearned income (*impôt des revenus de capitaux*). If you have an average income and receive interest on bank deposits only, tax on unearned income won't apply as it's deducted from bank interest before you receive it. Taxable income includes base pay; overseas and cost of living allowances; contributions to profit sharing plans; bonuses (annual, performance, etc.); storage and relocation allowances; language lessons provided for a spouse; personal company car; payments in kind (such as free accommodation or meals); stock options; home leave or vacations (paid by your employer); children's education; and property and investment income (dividends and interest).

Although the tax percentage rates in France are high, your taxable income is considerably reduced by allowances. Note that social security payments *aren't* taxable and are deducted from your gross income before your allowances are applied. Some income such as certain social security benefits, e.g. family and maternity allowances, aren't subject to income tax. Everyone is entitled to a 10 per cent allowance (*déduction forfaitaire normale*) for 'professional' or 'notional' expenses which is a minimum of 2,230F and a maximum of 74,590F. A general allowance of 20 per cent is deducted from the balance of income after deduction of the 10 per cent allowance. It also applies to everyone and is deductible on taxable income up to 680,000F. This is reduced to 10 per cent for the portion of your salary above 478,000F if you own over 35 per cent of the share capital of the company paying your salary.

There are also allowances for pension contributions (up to a maximum amount); major property repairs for your principal French residence; alimony and child support payments; certain support payments to parents and descendants; child-minding costs; life insurance premiums; mortgage interest payments; certain investments in rented property; gifts and subscriptions to charitable, educational, scientific, social and cultural organisations; and certain foreign-source income such as dividends, interest and royalties. Further supplementary allowances of up to 40 per cent are granted to around 100 professions including artists, actors, journalists, models, photographers, travelling sales people, radio hosts, commercial pilots, stewardesses, weavers and certain categories of civil servants. Note that anyone can itemise their actual expenses and claim additional deductions if these exceed their standard deductions.

Calculation

The tax year in France runs for a calendar year from 1st January to 31st December. Families are taxed as a single entity, thus a father's return normally includes his wife's and children's income, although he can elect for a dependant child's income to be taxed separately if this is advantageous. A wife may be taxed separately if she's separated from her husband. The French income tax system favours the family, as the amount of income tax paid is directly related to the number of dependant children.

French tax rates are based on a system of coefficients or parts, reflecting the family status of the taxpayer and the number of dependant children under the age of 18, or handicapped dependants of any age, as shown below:

| No. Of Children | Parts | |
	Married/Widow(er)	Single/Divorced/Separated
0	2 (1 or 1.5*)	1 or 1.5*
1	2.5	2
2	3	2.5
3	4	3.5
4	5	4.5
5	6	5.5
+1	+1	+1

* 1 or 1.5 parts apply to widows and widowers with no dependants and ex-servicemen over the age of 75 (who are allowed an extra 0.5 part).

Dependant children are classified as those aged under 18 years and unmarried or handicapped children of any age. However, if children are unmarried and aged under 21, in full-time education and aged under 25, or any age and doing military service, they can be claimed as dependants. A form requesting dependant status must be signed by the child and must be sent with the parents' tax return. All income of dependant children must be included in the parents' tax return.

The income tax rates for a single person (1 part) for 1999 income (2000 tax return) are shown in the table below. Note that taxable income, is income after the deduction of social security contributions and various allowances (listed above). Tax is calculated by multiplying the taxable income within a particular bracket by the tax rate, e.g. 51,340 – 26,100 = 25,240 x 10.5 per cent = 2,651.20.

Taxable Income (F)	Rate (%)	Portion	Aggregate
below 26,100	0	0.00	0.00
between 26,100 and 51,340	10.5	2,524.00	2,524.00
" 51,340 and 90,370	24	9,367.20	11,891.20
" 90,370 and 146,320	33	18,463.50	30,354.70
" 146,320 and 238,080	43	39,456.80	69,811.50
" 238,080 and 293,600	48	26,649.60	96,461.10
above 293,600	54		

The tax rate for other taxpayers can be calculated using the above table by multiplying the taxable income by the number of parts. For example if you're a married couple with no children (2 parts) simply double the taxable income amounts shown; if you're a married couple with two children (3 parts) treble the taxable income shown (and so on). The following table shows the amount of tax payable for selected taxable incomes from 50,000F to 300,000F (1999 income):

Taxable Income	1	1.5	2	2.5	3	3.5	4	4.5	5
50,000F	2510	0	0	0	0	0	0	0	0
75,000F	8328	3764	2394	1024	346	0	0	0	0
100,000F	15195	9492	5019	3649	2278	908	0	0	0
150,000F	32062	22794	21907	11821	7528	6158	4788	3418	2047
200,000F	53562	39294	35640	17196	25016	14150	10038	8668	7297
300,000F	100043	80346	58826	54488	45585	38150	33313	28479	23643

The following table shows a simple tax calculation:

Item	Sum (F)
gross annual salary	300,000
minus social security payments	(31,000)
minus 1st standard allowance (10%)	269,000
	(26,900)
minus 2nd standard allowance (20%)	242,100
	(48,420)
	193,680
minus other allowances	(25,000)
Taxable income	**168,680F**

Examples of tax payable (1999 income):

- single person (1 part)   39,750F
- couple (2 parts)   20,980F
- couple with two children (3 parts)   11,305F

Self-Employed

Those who qualify as self-employed in France include artisans or craftsmen (*professions artisanales*) such as builders, plumbers and electricians. Others include those involved in trading activities such as shopkeepers, anyone buying and selling goods, agents, brokers and property dealers. There are three ways in which a self-employed person or sole trader can be taxed in France, depending upon his income or turnover: a flat rate tax (*forfait*), simplified accounts (*bénéfice réel simplifié*) or through regular accounts (*bénéfice réel normal*).

Flat rate tax (*forfait*) is limited to anyone earning less than 500,000F a year. Accounts don't need to be submitted in the usual way and the tax assessment is a flat rate based on the normal net earnings for the type of business. This represents a saving in administration fees for both the taxpayer and tax officials. This arrangement is, however, limited to a maximum of two years with a possible extension for a further year.

Simplified accounts (*bénéfice réel simplifié*) are a compromise between flat rate tax and regular accounts. Businesses that qualify for simplified accounts are those with earnings between 500,000F and 1,500,000F a year. Only simple accounts need be kept, such as a cash book recording receipts and outgoings. All expenditure must, however, be supported by a receipt or an invoice.

Regular accounts (*bénéfice réel normal*) must be submitted by those with earnings in excess of 1,500,000F a year and those who choose not to use the simplified accounts procedure.

Professionals: If you're a professional such as an accountant, doctor or lawyer or a freelance worker such as an artist or writer, you're classified as a *profession libérale* or a *travailleur indépendant*. There are two ways in which you can file your income tax return. You can choose the *déclaration contrôlée* system requiring you to keep accounts of income and expenses, including all related receipts and documents. The second option is the *évaluation administrative* scheme, whereby you must keep a ledger of all income, but the tax department takes care of deductions.

MICRO-BIC & BNC: If you earn less than 120,000F from a commercial but non-salaried source, you can declare it as 'MICRO-BIC' income on your tax return and receive a 50 per cent allowance before paying income tax. The same applies to small earnings from a non-commercial organisation such as a charity, which is declared under the BNC (i.e. non-commercial, micro-earnings regime) and attracts a 25 per cent reduction before tax. If after deducting the allowance your income is below the tax threshold, you will pay no income tax.

Taxation of Property Income

Income tax is payable in France on rental income from a French property, even if you live abroad and the money is paid there. All rental income must be declared to the French tax authorities whether you let a property for a few weeks to a friend or 52 weeks a year on a commercial basis. Furnished property lettings are exempt from value added tax (TVA), although you may need to charge clients TVA if you offer services such as bed and breakfast, a daily maid, linen or a reception service.

You're eligible for deductions such as repairs and maintenance; security; cleaning costs; mortgage interest (French loans only); management and letting expenses (e.g. advertising); local taxes; and an allowance to cover depreciation and insurance. You should seek professional advice to ensure that you're claiming everything to which you're entitled. If you receive less than 30,000F a year in income you can choose to pay tax on the income received less a reduction of one-third to cover expenses. Property rental qualifies as a small business and the method used to determine the taxable income varies depending on the annual turnover. If turnover is less than 100,000F, 50 per cent can be deducted for expenses and when it's between 100,000F and 500,000F the 'flat rate' tax regime (*forfait*) applies. For incomes above 500,000F the simplified accounts regime is used (see above). Most people earning less than 100,000F a year find that there's little tax to pay after deducting their expenses. National taxes such as *Doit de Bail* and *Taxe Additionnelle* are also payable on income from the seasonal letting of furnished property. You should contact your local tax office to clarify your position (don't rely on your accountant).

Non-resident property owners who receive an income from a French source must file a tax return, *Déclaration des Revenus* (Cerfa 2042N/2044), available from local tax offices in France or French consulates abroad. Completed forms must be sent to the *Centre des Impôts de Non-Résidents* (9, rue d'Uzès, 75094 Paris Cedex 02) before 30th April each year. It's advisable to keep a copy of your return and send it by registered letter (so that there's no dispute over whether it was received). Some months after filing you will receive a tax assessment detailing the tax due. There are penalties for late filing and non-declaration, which can result in fines, high interest charges and even imprisonment. The tax authorities have many ways of detecting people letting homes and not paying tax and have been clamping down on tax evaders in recent years.

Non-residents must also declare any income received in France on their tax return in their country of residence, although tax on French letting income is normally paid only in France. However, if you pay less tax in France than you would have paid in your home country, you must usually pay the difference. On the other hand, if you pay more tax in France than you would have paid on the income in your home country, you aren't entitled to a refund.

Note that if you're a non-resident of France for tax purposes and own residential property there that's available for your use, you're liable for French income tax on the basis of a deemed rental income equal to three times the real rental value of the property (usually calculated to be 5 per cent of its capital value). There are, however, exceptions such as if you have French source income that exceeds this level or when you're protected by a double-taxation treaty (which applies to all EU countries). Consult a tax accountant to clarify your position.

Income Tax Returns

You're sent an annual tax return (*déclaration des revenus*) by the tax authorities around March of each year. If you aren't sent a form you can obtain one from your local town hall or tax office. The standard return is the 2042N, although there's a simplified form (2042S) for those with uncomplicated tax affairs. There are supplementary forms for non-commercial profits (forms 2035, 2037); property income (2044); foreign source income such as a pension or dividends (2047); capital gains on financial investments (2074); and other capital gains (2049).

The head of a household usually completes the tax return for the whole family's income (*quotient familial*), including his or her spouse and dependant children. There's no independent taxation of married women in France, where taxation is based on the family unit. An unmarried couple living together have a legal status called *concubinage*, providing certain tax advantages. A tax return can be completed by either the husband or wife but must be signed by both, making both jointly responsible for any errors (this also means that both partners know exactly what the other earns!).

A wife living apart from her husband who isn't married in 'community of property' can choose to be assessed separately. A wife's income is assessed separately in the first year of marriage from 1st January to the date of her marriage. It's possible for children under 18 with their own income, e.g. income from an inheritance or their own earnings, to be independently assessed.

The tax return must be filed by 28th February (29th February in a leap year) and is for the current year. Income tax is based on the preceding year's income, taking into account any deductible allowances. For example the return filed in February 1999 was for the calendar year 1998. Late filing, even by one day, attracts a penalty of 10 per cent of the amount due.

French tax returns are complicated, despite attempts to simplify them in recent years. The language used is particularly difficult to understand for foreigners (and many French) and is quite complex. Local tax offices (*bureau des impôts/Hôtel d'Impôts*) are usually helpful and will help you complete your tax return. You can make an appointment for a free consultation with your local tax inspector at your town hall. However, if your French isn't excellent you will need to take someone with you who's fluent. Alternatively you can employ a tax accountant (*expert-comptable/conseiller fiscal*).

If you pay income tax abroad, you must return the form uncompleted with evidence that you're domiciled abroad. Around one month later you should receive a statement from the French tax authorities stating that you have no tax to pay (*vous n'avez pas d'impôt à payer*). The French tax authorities may request copies of foreign tax returns.

Changes in your tax liability may be made by the tax authorities up to three years after the end of the tax year to which the liability relates. Therefore you should retain all records relating to the income and expenses reported in your tax returns, until the expiration of this period, even if you have left France. Penalties for undeclared or understated income and unjustified deductions range from 40 per cent for 'bad faith' errors to 80 per cent for fraud, plus interest on the amount owed.

Tax Bills

Sometime between September and December you will receive a tax bill (*avis d'imposition*) for the current tax year, based on your income tax return for the previous year, e.g. in September 1999 you will receive your tax bill for 1999 based on your 1998 income. There are two methods of paying your tax bill in France: in three instalments (*tiers provisionnels*) or in ten equal monthly instalments (*mensualisation*).

Three Instalments: The most common method of payment is by three instalments. The first two payments, each comprising around one-third (*tiers*) of the previous year's tax liability, are provisional (*acompte provisionnel*) and are payable on 15th February and 15th May each year. For example in 1999, these payments each represent around a third of your total tax bill for 1998. The third and final instalment, the balance of your tax bill, is payable by 15th September. The tax authorities adjust your third payment to take into account your actual income for the previous year. To take a simple example, if you paid 120,000F in income tax in 1997, your first two payments in 1999 (for tax year 1998) would each be for 40,000F, i.e. one-third of your previous bill. If your actual tax liability for 1998 was 150,000F, you would pay the balance of 70,000F (150,000F minus the 80,000F already paid) in September 1999 as a final payment.

Payment dates are officially 31st January, 30th April and 31st August, but the tax authorities allow you an extra two weeks (or 15 days) to pay bills. If you pay your tax bill late, you must pay a penalty equal to 10 per cent of your annual tax bill. The following schedule shows the tax payment for a new arrival in France:

Year   Tax Return/Bill

1st   (arrival in France) no tax payable

2nd   **28th February** - file tax return for 1st year's income

          15th September - pay entire tax bill for 1st year

3rd   **15th February** - pay first instalment of 2nd year's tax

          28th February - file tax return for 2nd year's income

          15th May - pay second instalment of 2nd year's tax

          15th September - pay final instalment of 2nd year's tax

4th   as for 3rd year

During your first year in France you won't have a previous year's tax liability (in France). Therefore the income tax computed with the information contained in the tax return filed on 28th February of your second year is payable in full on 15th September of the same year. In the following year, the normal procedure is applied. Note that if you arrive in France in, for example, September 1999, you won't start paying tax until September 2000. Even then you will only have been resident in France for less than four months of your first tax year (1999) and will pay little or no tax in the year 2000 and won't need to pay any significant income tax until two years after your arrival, i.e. September 2001.

Monthly Instalments: You can choose to pay your tax in ten equal monthly instalments (*Mensualisation*) by direct debit from a bank or post office account. Under this system you pay one tenth of your previous year's tax bill on the 8th of each month from January to October. If your income is less in the current year than the previous year, the tax office will stop payments when it has received the full amount. On the other hand, if you earned more in the previous year than the year before, the tax office will automatically deduct further payments in November and December. Monthly payments are a good budgeting aid, particularly if you're a spendthrift and are likely to rush out and spend your salary as soon as you receive it. However, most Frenchmen prefer to pay in three instalments, with the advantage that you can invest the amount set aside for tax until each payment is due.

If you believe you have paid too much tax (who doesn't?), you must make a claim by the end of the third year after the year in question, e.g. by 31st December 1999 for the 1996 tax year. Claims must be made in writing with a special form. If possible, you should file a claim before a payment is made for the current year, in order to claim a deferment of payment.

RESIDENTIAL & REAL ESTATE TAXES

There are two kinds of local property taxes (*impôts locaux*) in France: residential tax (*taxe d'habitation*) and real estate tax (*taxe foncière*). Residential tax is payable by anyone who lives in a property in France, whether as an owner, tenant or rent free. Real estate tax is paid only by owners of property in France. Both taxes are payable whether the property is a main or a second home, or the owner is a French or foreign resident. Taxes pay for local services including rubbish collection, street lighting and cleaning, local schools and other community services, and include a contribution to departmental and regional expenses. You may be billed separately for rubbish collection (*ordures*). If your property is a second home (*résidence secondaire*) this should be stated on your bill, which should be reduced accordingly.

Real Estate Tax: Real estate tax (*taxe foncière*) is paid by owners of property in France and is similar to the property tax (or rates) levied in most countries. It's payable even if a property isn't inhabited, providing it's furnished and habitable. Real estate tax is levied on buildings and shelters for persons or goods that are considered to be buildings, warehouses, house boats (fixed mooring) and on certain land. The tax is split into two amounts: one for the building (*taxe foncière bâtie*) and a smaller one for the land (*taxe foncière non bâtie*). Tax is payable on land whether or not it's built on. Real estate tax isn't applicable to buildings and land used exclusively for agricultural or religious purposes, or to government and public buildings.

New and restored buildings used as main or second homes are exempt from real estate tax for two years from the 1st January following the completion date (certain new houses and apartments are exempt for 10 or 15 years). An application for a temporary exemption from real estate tax must be made to your local tax office (*centre des impôts fonciers* or *bureau du cadastre*) before 31st December for exemption the following year. Applications must be made within 90 days of the completion of a new or restored building.

Residential Tax: Residential tax (*taxe d'habitation*) is payable by anyone who resides in a property in France on 1st January, whether as an owner, tenant or rent-free. It's payable on residential properties (used as main or second homes), outbuildings (e.g. accommodation for servants, garages) located less than one kilometre from a residential property, and on business premises that are an indistinguishable part of a residential property. Residential tax is levied by the town where the property is located. Premises used exclusively for business, farming, student lodging and classes, and official government offices are exempt from residential tax. Tax is usually payable on assessment in autumn of the same year.

If a property is your family's main home, there are obligatory deductions for dependants including children, parents, grandparents (depending on their age) and handicapped dependants of any age. Deductions are calculated as a percentage of the rental value and are 10 per cent for each of the first two dependants and 15 per cent for each additional dependant. If you aren't liable for income tax or paid little income tax for the previous year, or your main home has a rental value of less than 130 per cent of the average local rental value, you may be entitled to a reduction. Residential tax isn't paid by residents aged over 60 and others living in their principal home who were exempt from income and wealth tax the previous year. In 1999 new lower income levels were introduced whereby if your 1998 revenue was less than 43,900F (with additional income of 11,740F for each half-part quotient) you're exempt from Residential Tax. In an effort to stimulate the letting market, residential tax was doubled in recent years (in certain areas only, on an experimental basis) when a property has been left empty for over two years.

Valuation: Residential tax is based on the average (notional) rental value of property in the previous year, adjusted for inflation, as calculated by the land registry (*Service du Cadastre*). It's calculated on the living area of a property, including outbuildings, garages and amenities, and takes into account factors such as the quality of construction, location, renovations, services (e.g. mains water, electricity and gas) and amenities such as central heating, swimming pool, the number of bathrooms, covered terrace, garage, etc. Properties are placed in eight categories ranging from 'very poor' to 'luxurious'. Changes made to a building, such as improvements or enlargements, must be notified to the land registry within 90 days. In principle, the notional rental value is the same for both residential tax and real estate tax. If you think a valuation is too high, you can contest it. The amount of tax due is calculated by multiplying the base figure (50 per cent of the rental value) by the tax rate for the tax year. A nationwide reassessment of property taxes has taken place in recent years and they have been increased considerably.

Payment: Forms for the assessment of both residential and real estate tax are sent out by local councils and must be completed and returned to the regional tax office (*Centre des Impôts*) by a specified date. They will calculate the tax due and send you a bill. You may be given up to two months to pay and a 10 per cent penalty is levied for late payment. It's possible to pay residential tax monthly (in ten equal instalments from January to October) by direct debit from a French bank account, which helps soften the blow.

Residential tax is payable by anyone who occupies a property in France on 1st January and if you vacate or sell a property on January 2nd, you must pay residential tax for the whole year. However, real estate tax is apportioned by the notary between the seller and buyer from the date of the sale. Taxes vary from area to area and are higher in cities and towns than in rural areas and small villages, where few community services are provided. In rural areas, the total residential and real estate tax is around 4,000F a year for an average dwelling, although they range from 750F for a basic small cottage to 10,000F or more for a luxury villa. In some areas a regional or sundry tax (*taxe assimilée*) is also levied, particularly if a property is in a popular tourist area. This is because the local authorities must spend more than usual on amenities and the upkeep of towns (gardens, etc).

WEALTH TAX

A wealth tax (*impôt sur la fortune/ISF*) was introduced on 1st January 1989 (since when billions of francs have disappeared into foreign banks!) and is payable on an individual's net estate when it exceeds 4.7 million francs. If you're domiciled in France, the value of your estate is based on your worldwide assets. If you're resident in France but not domiciled there, the value of your estate is based on your assets in France only. Wealth tax is assessed on the net value of your assets on 1st January each year and is payable by the following 15th June on filing the return (15th July for other European residents and 15th August for all others). On 1st January 1999 the rates were:

Assets (F)	Rate (%)	Liability (F)
up to 4.70m	zero	0
from 4.70m to 7.64m	0.55	16,170
from 7.64m to 15.16m	0.75	54,400
from 15.16m to 23.54m	1.0	83,800
from 23.54m to 45.58m	1.3	286,520
from 45.58m to 100.00m	1.65	897,930
Above 100.00m	1.8	

The amount payable is reduced by 1,000F for each dependant. The taxable estate doesn't include 'professional assets' (*biens professionnels*), which may include shares in a company in which you play an active role, providing they total at least 25 per cent of the equity. It excludes companies with property investment as their main activity.

CAPITAL GAINS TAX

Capital gains tax (*impôt sur les plus values*) is payable on the profit from sales of certain property in France including antiques, art and jewellery, securities and real estate. After paying capital gains tax (CGT), gains are added to other income and are liable to income tax.

Principal Residence: CGT isn't payable on a profit made on the sale of your principal residence in France, providing that you have occupied it since its purchase or for a minimum of five years. You're also exempt from CGT if you're forced to sell for family or professional reasons, e.g. you're transferred abroad by your employer. Income tax treaties usually provide that capital gains on property are taxable in the country where the property is located. Note that if you move to France permanently and retain a home abroad, this may affect your position regarding capital gains. If you sell your foreign home before moving to France, you will be exempt from CGT as it's your principal residence. However, if you establish your principal residence in France the foreign property becomes a second home and is thus liable to CGT when it's sold. **Note that EU tax authorities co-operate in tracking down capital gains tax dodgers.**

Second Homes: Capital gains on second homes in France are payable by both residents and non-residents. Long and short-term gains are treated differently. Short-term gains are classified as profits on the sale of a property owned for less than two years and are taxed at 33.3 per cent for non-residents and as ordinary income for residents. Long-term gains are categorised as gains on a property owned for more than two years and less than 22 years. The taxable gain is the difference between the purchase and sales price reduced by 5 per cent for the third and each subsequent year up to 22 years, and multiplied by an index linked multiplier (*coefficient*) of the sale price. After a property has been owned for 22 years it's exempt from CGT.

Residents are exempt from CGT on a second home in France if they don't own their main residence, i.e. you're a tenant or lease holder. You or your spouse mustn't be the owner of your permanent residence and the sale of the second home must take place more than five years after its acquisition or completion, and more than two years after that of a principle residence. The exemption applies only to the first sale of a second home in France.

Where applicable, CGT is withheld by the *notaire* handling the sale. The tax calculation is made by the *notaire*, although the local tax office can claim further tax if the assessment proves to be incorrect. On the other hand, if the amount withheld is too high, you should (eventually) receive a refund. You may be able to agree with the *notaire* what the CGT should be. Before a sale the *notaire* prepares a form calculating the tax due and appoints an agent (*agent fiscal accredité*) or guarantor to act on your behalf concerning tax. If the transaction is straightforward, the local tax office may grant a dispensation (*dispense*) of the need to appoint a guarantor, providing that you apply *before* completion of the sale. If you obtain a dispensation, the proceeds of the sale can be released to you in full after CGT has been paid. The *notaire* handling the sale must apply for the dispensation.

Everyone is given an allowance of 6,000F to set against a short or long-term capital gain. You should keep all bills for the fees associated with buying a property (the *notaire*, agent, surveyor, etc.), plus any bills for renovation, restoration, modernisation and improvements of a second home, as these can be offset against CGT and are index-linked. If you work on a house yourself, you should keep a copy of bills for materials and tools, as these can be multiplied by three and the total offset against CGT. Painting and decorating costs (*embellissement*) cannot be claimed against CGT. Costs relating to the sale can also be offset against any gain, as can part of the interest paid on a loan taken out to purchase or restore a property.

INHERITANCE & GIFT TAX

As in most other western countries, dying doesn't free your assets from the clutches of French tax inspectors. France imposes both inheritance (*droits de succession*) and gift (*droits de donation*) taxes on its inhabitants.

Inheritance Tax: Inheritance tax, called estate tax or death duty in some countries, is levied on the estate of a deceased person. Both residents and non-residents are subject to inheritance tax if they own property in France. The country where you pay inheritance tax is decided by your domicile (see **Liability** on page 92). If you're living permanently in France at the time of your death, you will be deemed to be domiciled there by the French tax authorities. If you're domiciled in France inheritance tax applies to your worldwide estate (excluding property), otherwise it applies only to assets located in France. It's important to make your domicile clear, so that there's no misunderstanding on your death.

When a person dies in France, an estate tax return (*déclaration de succession*) must be filed within six months of the date of death and within 12 months if the death occurred outside France. The return is generally prepared in France by a *notaire*. If the estate doesn't have any property or if the sole beneficiary is the spouse and the gross value is less than 10,000F, no return is necessary.

Inheritance tax in France is paid by individual beneficiaries, irrespective of where they are domiciled, and not by the estate. Tax may be paid in instalments over five or, in certain cases, ten years or may be deferred. The rate of tax and allowances vary depending on the relationship between the beneficiary and the deceased. French succession laws are quite restrictive compared with the law in many other countries. The surviving spouse has an allowance of 400,000F (500,000F from 1st January 2000) and the children and parents of the deceased an allowance of 300,000F. After the allowance has been deducted there's a sliding scale up to a maximum of 40 per cent on assets over 11.2 million francs, as shown in the table below:

	Amount (F)	
Tax Rate (%)	Spouse	Children/Parents
5	up to 50,000	up to 50,000
10	50,000 to 100,000	50,000 to 75,000
15	100,000 to 200,000	75,000 to 100,000
20	200,000 to 3.4m	100,000 to 3.4m
30	3.4m to 5.6m	3.4m to 5.6m
35	5.6m to 11.2m	5.6m to 11.2m
40	over 11.2m	over 11.2m

As you can see from the above table, it's best to leave property in France to your spouse, children or parents, in order to take advantage of the relatively low tax rates.

There's an allowance of 100,000F for each brother and sister if the deceased was single, widowed, divorced or separated, over 50 years old, was incapable of working due to a medical condition, *and* the brother or sister had lived continuously with the deceased for at least five years before his death. If the 100,000F allowance isn't applicable, the allowance for brothers and sisters is just 10,000F. After the 100,000F or 10,000F allowance, the tax rate for brothers and sisters is 35 per cent up to 150,000F and 45 per cent above this amount. Mentally or physically handicapped beneficiaries who are unable to earn a living receive a special allowance of 300,000F, in addition to the 100,000F for brothers and sisters (if applicable). Any beneficiary who doesn't benefit from any other allowance has an allowance of 10,000F. Between relations up to the fourth degree, i.e. uncles/aunts, nephews/nieces, great uncles/aunts, great nephews/nieces and first cousins, there's a flat rate tax of 55 per cent. For relationships beyond the fourth degree or between unrelated persons, the tax rate is 60 per cent.

Exemptions from inheritance tax include certain woodlands and rural properties, and legacies to charities and government bodies. Many people take out a life insurance policy to reduce the impact of inheritance tax, as the beneficiaries of life insurance policies aren't liable to inheritance tax. Note that if you're a resident in France and receive inheritance from abroad, you're subject to French inheritance tax. However, if you've been resident for less than six years in France you're exempt or if you paid the bill in another country the amount is deducted from your French tax bill.

Gift Tax: Gift tax is calculated in the same way as inheritance tax, according to the relationship between the donor and the recipient and the size of the gift. A reduction of gift tax is granted depending on the age of the donor (the younger the donor the larger the reduction). If the donor is under 65 years of age the tax is reduced by 50 per cent and for those aged 65 to 75 there's a 35 per cent reduction. Over 75 there's no reduction. Any gifts made before the death of the donor (*inter vivos*) must be included in the estate duty return. Note that gift tax is payable on gifts made between spouses in France and therefore assets should be equally shared before you're domiciled there.

It's important for both residents and non-residents with property in France to decide in advance how they wish to dispose of their French property. This should be decided <u>before</u> buying a house or other property in France. There are a number of ways of limiting or delaying the impact of French inheritance laws including inserting a clause (such as a *clause tontine*) in a property purchase contract (*acte de vente*), officially changing your marital regime in France (e.g. to joint ownership or *communauté universelle*), and by buying property through a civil real estate company (*Société Civile Immobilière*), possibly with a clause *tontine*. The clause *tontine* allows a property to be left in its entirety to a surviving spouse, without it being shared among the children (see **Wills** below). A surviving spouse can also be given a life interest (*usufruit*) in an estate in priority to children or parents through a gift between spouses (*donation entre époux*), although this may not apply to non-residents. Note that French law doesn't recognise the rights to inheritance of a non-married partner, although there are a number of solutions to this problem, e.g. a life insurance policy.

French inheritance law is an extremely complicated subject and professional advice should be sought from an experienced lawyer who understands both French law and that of any other country involved. Your will (see below) is also a vital component in reducing French inheritance and gift tax to the minimum or delaying its payment.

WILLS

It's an unfortunate fact of life that you're unable to take your hard-earned assets with you when you take your final bow (or come back and reclaim them in a later life!). All adults should make a will (*testament*) regardless of how large or small their assets. The disposal of your estate depends on your country of domicile (see **Inheritance & Gift Tax** above). As a general rule, French law permits a foreigner who *isn't* domiciled in France to make a will in any language and under the law of any country, providing it's valid under the law of that country.

Note, however, that 'immovable' property (or immovables) in France, i.e. land and buildings, *must* be disposed of (on death) in accordance with French law. All other property in France or elsewhere (defined as 'movables') may be disposed of in accordance with the law of your country of domicile. Therefore, it's extremely important to establish where you're domiciled under French law. One of the best solutions for a non-resident who wishes to avoid French inheritance laws regarding immovable property located in France may be to buy it through a French holding company, in which case the shares of the company are 'movable' assets and are therefore governed by the succession laws of the owner's country of domicile.

French law is restrictive regarding the distribution of property and the identity of heirs and gives priority to children, including illegitimate and adopted children, and the living parents of a deceased person. Under French law (*code Napoléon*) you cannot disinherit your children, who have absolute priority over your estate, even before a surviving spouse. There are, however, many legal ways to safeguard the rights of a surviving spouse, some of which are mentioned above under **Inheritance & Gift Tax.** The part of a property that must be inherited by certain heirs (*héritiers réservataires*) is called the legal reserve (*réserve legale*). Once the reserved portion of your estate has been determined, the remaining portion is freely disposable (*quotité disponible*). Only when there are no descendants or ascendants is the whole estate freely disposable.

If you die leaving one child, he must inherit one half of your French estate and two children must inherit at least two-thirds. If you have three or more children, they must inherit three-quarters of your estate. If a couple has no surviving children, their parents inherit their estate. The reserve for parents is 25 per cent per parent and if there's only one surviving parent it remains 25 per cent. Brothers and sisters are next in line after children and parents, and can only be disinherited if specified in a will.

There are three kinds of will in France: holographic (*testament olographe*), authentic (*testament authentique*) and secret (*testament mystique*), described below.

A **holographic will** is the most common form of will used in France. It must be written by hand by the person making the will (i.e. it cannot be typewritten or printed) and be signed and dated by him. No witnesses or other formalities are required. In fact it shouldn't be witnessed at all, as this may complicate matters. It can be written in English or another language, although it's preferable if it's written in French (you can ask a *notaire* to prepare a draft and copy it in your own handwriting). It can be registered in the central wills registry (*fichier de dernières volontés*).

An **authentic or notarial will** is used by some 5 per cent of French people. It must be drawn up by a *notaire* in the form of a notarial document and can be handwritten or typed. It's dictated by the person making the will and must be witnessed by two *notaires* or a *notaire* and two other witnesses. Unlike a holographic will, an authentic will is automatically registered in the central wills registry.

A **secret will** is rarely used and is a will written by or for the person making it and signed by him. It's inserted and sealed in an envelope in the presence of two witnesses. It's then given to a *notaire* who records on the envelope a note confirming that the envelope has been handed to him and that the testator has affirmed that the envelope contains his will.

A gift between spouses (*donation entre époux*) can be used to leave property to a spouse and delay the inheritance of an estate by any surviving children. It must be prepared by a *notaire* and signed in the presence of the donor and the donee. For anyone with a modest French estate, for example a small property in France, a holographic will is sufficient. Note that where applicable, the rules relating to witnesses are strict and if they aren't followed precisely they may render a will null and void. In France, marriage doesn't automatically revoke a will, as in some other countries, e.g. Britain. A holographic or secret will must be handed to a *notaire* for filing. He sends a copy to the local district court where the estate is administered. Wills aren't made public in France and aren't available for inspection.

Under French law, the role of the executor is different from many other countries and his duties are supervisory only and last for a year and a day. He's responsible for paying debts and death duties and distributing the balance in accordance with the will. On your death, the executor who's dealing with your affairs in France must file a *déclaration de succession* within one year of your death. At death your property passes directly to your heirs and it's their responsibility to pay any outstanding debts and their own inheritance tax. Note that winding-up an estate takes much longer than in many other countries and is usually given a low priority by *notaires*.

It's possible to make two wills, one relating to French property and the other to foreign property. Opinion differs on whether you should have separate wills for French and foreign property, or a foreign will with a codicil (appendix) dealing with your French property (or vice versa). However, most experts believe it's better to have a French will from the point of view of winding up your French estate (and a will for any country where you own immovable property). If you have French and foreign wills, make sure that they don't contradict one another (or worse still, cancel each other out, e.g. when a will contains a clause revoking all other wills). Note that a foreign will written in a foreign language must be translated into French (a certified translation is required) and proven in France in order to be valid there.

Keep a copy of your will(s) in a safe place and another copy with your lawyer or the executor of your estate. Don't leave them in a bank safe deposit box, which in the event of your death is sealed for a period under French law. You should keep information regarding bank accounts and insurance policies with your will(s), but don't forget to tell someone where they are!

Note that French inheritance law is a complicated subject and it's important to obtain professional legal advice when writing or altering your will(s).

COST OF LIVING

No doubt you would like to try to estimate how far your French francs will stretch and how much money (if any) you will have left after paying your bills. Inflation in France in 1998 was around 1 per cent and the French have enjoyed a stable and strong economy in recent years, reflected in the strong French franc. Salaries are generally high and the French enjoy a high standard of living, although some 5.5. million people live below the poverty threshold (those with a monthly net income of less than half the average national income). Social security costs are very high, particularly for the self-employed, and the combined burden of social security, income tax and indirect taxes make French taxes among the highest in the EU.

Anyone planning to live in France, particularly retirees, should take care not to underestimate the cost of living, which has increased considerably in the last decade. France is a relatively expensive country by American standards, particularly if your income is earned in $US. You should be wary of cost of living comparisons with other countries, which are often wildly inaccurate (and often include irrelevant items which distort the results). It isn't just residents who need to watch the *centimes*, as in recent years many visitors have found it difficult or impossible to remain within their budgets. The cost of living in France is similar to that of Germany and some 25 per cent lower than in Britain and around 25 per cent higher than the USA.

It's difficult to calculate an average cost of living in France as it depends on each individual's particular circumstances and life-style. With the exception of Paris and other major cities, where the higher cost of living is offset by higher salaries, the cost of living in France is around average for western European countries. The actual difference in your food bill will depend on what you eat and where you lived before arriving in France. Food in France costs around 50 per cent more than in the USA, but is similar overall to most other western European countries, although you may need to modify your diet. From 2,000F to 2,500F should feed two adults for a month, excluding fillet steak, caviar and alcohol (other than a moderate amount of inexpensive beer or wine). Shopping for selected 'luxury' and 'big-ticket' items such as stereo equipment, household apparatus, electrical and electronic goods, computers and photographic equipment abroad can result in significant savings.

A list of the approximate **MINIMUM** monthly major expenses for an average single person, couple or family with two children are shown in the table below (most people will no doubt agree that the figures are either too HIGH or too LOW). When calculating your cost of living, deduct *at least* 15 per cent for social security contributions and the appropriate percentage for income tax (see page 92) from your gross salary. The numbers (in brackets) refer to the notes following the table.

MONTHLY COSTS (F)			
	Single	**Couple**	**Couple with 2 children**
Housing (1)	2,500	3,500	4,500
Food (2)	1,300	2,250	2,800
Utilities (3)	300	500	700
Leisure (4)	600	1,000	1,200
Transport (5)	600	600	800
Insurance (6)	400	700	800
Clothing	300	600	1,200
TOTAL	6,000	9,150	12,000

(1) Rent or mortgage payments for a modern or modernised apartment or house in an average suburb, excluding Paris and other high-cost areas. The properties envisaged are a studio or one-bedroom apartment for a single person, a two-bedroom property for a couple and a three-bedroom property for a couple with two children.

(2) Doesn't include luxuries or liquid food (alcohol).

(3) Includes electricity, gas, water, telephone, cable TV and heating costs.

(4) Includes entertainment, restaurant meals, sports and vacation expenses, plus newspapers and magazines.

(5) Includes running costs for an average family car plus third party insurance, annual taxes, petrol, servicing and repairs, **but excludes depreciation or credit purchase costs.**

(6) Includes 'voluntary' insurance such as supplementary health insurance, disability, home contents, third party liability, legal, travel, automobile breakdown and life insurance.

4.

FINDING YOUR DREAM HOME

After having decided to buy a home in France, your first task will be to choose the region and what sort of home to buy. **If you're unsure where and what to buy, the best decision is to rent for a period.** The secret of successfully buying a home in France (or anywhere else for that matter) is research, research and more research, preferably before you even set foot there. You may be fortunate and buy the first property you see without doing any homework and live happily ever after. However, a successful purchase is much more likely if you thoroughly investigate the towns and communities in your chosen area; compare the range and prices of properties and their relative values; and study the procedure for buying property. It's a wise or lucky person who gets his choice absolutely right first time, but there's a much higher likelihood if you do your homework thoroughly.

One of the things that attracts many buyers to France is the relatively low cost of property compared with many other European countries. However, the French don't generally buy domestic property as an investment, but as a home for life, and you shouldn't expect to make a quick profit when buying property in France. Property values generally increase at an average of around 5 per cent a year (or in line with inflation), meaning you must own a house for around three years simply to recover the high fees associated with buying. Property prices rise faster than average in some fashionable areas, although this is generally reflected in higher purchase prices. The stable property market in most areas acts as a discouragement to speculators wishing to make a quick profit, particularly as many properties require a substantial investment in restoration or modernisation before they can be sold at a profit. Note that capital gains tax (see page 103) can wipe out a third of any profit made on the sale of a second home.

A slice of *la bonne vie* needn't cost the earth, with habitable cottages and terraced village homes available from around 200,000F, modern apartments from around 300,000F and large detached homes from as little as 400,000F. However, if you're seeking a home with a large plot of land and a swimming pool you will need to spend at least 600,000F (depending on the area) and for those with the financial resources the sky's the limit, with luxury apartments in Paris and villas in the south of France costing many millions of francs.

This chapter is designed to help you decide what sort of home to buy and, most importantly, its location. It will also help you avoid problems and contains information about regions, research, location, renting, cost, auctions, business properties, fees, buying new and old, community properties, timeshare (and other part-ownership schemes), estate agents, inspections and surveys, garages and parking, conveyancing, purchase contracts, completion, renovation and restoration, moving house, moving in, security, utilities, heating and air-conditioning, property income and selling a home.

REGIONS

France is divided into 21 geographical regions, although not everyone agrees on their names and the departments they comprise. The regions described below are roughly the most common division and are depicted on the map in **Appendix C**.

Alsace: Alsace is one of France's smallest regions containing the departments of Bas-Rhin and Haut-Rhin. It's located in the extreme east of France bordering Germany, to which it has belonged at various times in its colourful history. Not surprisingly it has a Germanic feel, which is reflected in its architecture, cuisine, dress, dialects (German is still widely spoken), names and people (called Alsatians). Sandwiched between the Vosges mountains and the Rhine, Alsace is gloriously scenic and largely unspoiled, with delightful hills (cross-country skiing is a popular winter sport), dense forests, rich farmland and pretty vineyards. It's noted for its many picturesque villages, particularly on the Wine Road (*Route du Vin*) stretching from Marlenheim west of Strasbourg down to Thann beyond Mulhouse.

The region's capital is Strasbourg, home of the European Parliament, the European Court and the European Commission on Human Rights. Other notable towns include Colmar, an attractive town with multi-coloured houses and an important artistic and cultural centre, and Mulhouse, a prominent industrial city. The region has excellent road connections with Paris, the south of France, Germany and Switzerland. Alsace is famous for its beer (such as Kronenbourg) and wines, particularly its white wines which many consider to be the best in France. Somewhat surprisingly, Alsace has more Michelin restaurant stars than any other region of

France, which no doubt contributes to its acclaimed quality of life. Property prices in Alsace are higher than the average in France and there are few bargains to be found. Rundown or derelict rural properties for sale are rare in Alsace, where (unlike many other regions) there hasn't been a mass exodus from the farms and countryside.

Aquitaine: Aquitaine contains the departments of Dordogne, Gironde, Landes, Lot-et-Garonne and Pyrénées-Atlantiques. It's a largely agricultural region noted for its temperate climate, unspoiled and sparsely populated countryside, and its tranquility. The region has a long Atlantic coastline with a number of popular coastal resorts including Arcachon (with the largest beach in Europe), Biarritz (with its faded 19th century grandeur), Capbreton, Cap Ferrat, Hendaye, Hossegor and Saint-Jean-de-Luz, a charming fishing village.

The Gironde department in the north is home to the celebrated Bordeaux vineyards, the most famous wine-producing region in the world, which has made it the richest area in France. It embraces some 3,000 wine *châteaux* and is a haven for touring tipplers (Saint-Émilion is the most attractive of the Bordeaux wine villages). Bordeaux, the capital of the region, is a wealthy new 'techno' centre and a popular convention and exhibition venue with excellent *autoroute*, air and rail connections (it's just three hours from Paris by TGV). It isn't, however, one of France's most attractive or interesting cities. Other important towns in the region include Agen, Bayonne, Bergerac, Biarritz, Hendaye, Perigueux and Pau (birthplace of Henry IV and site of the first golf course in mainland Europe in 1856, when it was 'colonised' by the British).

South of Gironde is the Landes department, renowned for the largest pine forests in southern Europe (planted in the mid-19th century to secure the shifting sand dunes), which reach almost to the Atlantic coast. It's also noted for its sleepy farming villages with traditional half-timbered houses, beautiful white sandy beaches and excellent country fare. The department of the Pyrénées-Atlantiques (*Pays Basque*) in the extreme south (bordering Spain) is known for its Basque chalet-style and *Béarn* houses, charming villages and fine cuisine (Basque food is renowned for its excellence). Some 80,000 Basques live in France, while the remaining 600,000 reside over the border in Spain.

The departments of the Dordogne (the third largest in France) and Lot-et-Garonne are celebrated for their lush woodland, rolling green countryside and fertile valleys, and offer some of the best landscape scenery in France. Dordogne, named after one of France's longest and most beautiful rivers (at its most picturesque between Bort-les-Orgues and Beaulieu-sur-Dordogne), is one of the most scenic departments in France. The region also contains some of France's prettiest and most dramatic towns and villages including Brantôme, Domme, Les Eyzies-de-Tayac, Monpazier, La Roque-Gaseac, Sarlat-la-Canéda and Trémolat. The area is noted for its *bastides*, fortified towns surrounded by ramparts often built on cliff tops, of which Monpazier is a fine example. Sarlat-la-Canéda and Domme are the jewels of the Dordogne and are so popular that they are in danger of being ruined by tourism (they are best avoided in high summer). The local cuisine includes truffles and *foie gras* and is noted for its rich goose and duck dishes. Winters are usually very wet and cold, and summers hot and humid; the most pleasant seasons are spring and autumn, when the Dordogne is at its most beautiful. The Dordogne is often referred to as Périgord, which was the old name for the area before it was renamed in the 18th century (Périgord is further divided into Périgord Vert in the north, Périgord Blanc in the centre and Périgord Noir in the south).

Dordogne has long been popular with the British (the French call it 'little England'), Dutch and latterly the Germans, particularly for second homes. Its popularity created a boom in the late '80s when it was the number one area in France with the British and property prices went through the roof. Demand has died down somewhat in recent years and prices fell sharply after many foreign buyers (mainly British) who over-extended themselves were forced to sell. Property is now more reasonably priced with some bargains still around, although it doesn't offer the best value for money. However, properties tend to be cheaper the further you travel from the Dordogne river, with those priced at 1 to 1½ million francs usually offering the best value. Apart from the Dordogne, Lot-et-Garonne (which is cheaper than the Dordogne and offers many of its attractions) and the Atlantic coastal resorts, the region isn't particularly popular with foreign property buyers.

Auvergne: The Auvergne region is at the very heart of France and contains the departments of Allier, Cantal, Haute-Loire and Puy-de-Dôme. It's one of the least known and most remote regions of France and entirely unspoiled. The Auvergne is famous for its rugged scenery which includes extinct volcanoes, spectacular gorges, lakes, geysers, mountain streams, rivers and vast forests. Although often depicted as bleak and isolated, the region is home to two of France's most spectacular national parks, the *Parc Naturel Régional des Volcans d'Auvergne* and the *Parc Naturel Régional du Livradois-Forez*. They contain a profusion of magnificent mountains, rivers (the Dordogne has its source here), lush pastures and dense woodland, and together comprise France's largest protected area, quite unlike the rest of the region. The Auvergne is largely agricultural and is noted for its peaceful, slow pace of life, and is renowned for its hot springs and mineral cold springs (sold as bottled water), of which there are some two hundred in Vichy alone.

The region's main towns include Ambert, Aurillac, Clermont-Ferrand (the capital city of the region), Le-Puy-en-Velay, Moulins and Vichy, a famous spa town. Auvergne has good road, rail and air connections via Clermont-Ferrand, which is connected to Paris and the south of France by the A71 and A72 *autoroutes* respectively. The region is bitterly cold in winter, when there's good skiing in the Massif Central range, and very hot in summer. Auvergne is the most sparsely populated region in France and the local people, known as *Auvergnats*, are slow to accept outsiders. Property is excellent value for money and the least expensive in France, although due to its anonymity and remoteness, it isn't popular with foreign buyers.

Brittany (Bretagne): Brittany is the western-most region of France (and Europe) and comprises the departments of Côtes d'Armor, Finistère, Ille-et-Vilaine and Morbihan. Although not as spectacular as some other regions, Brittany has over 1,200km (750mi) of Atlantic coastline noted for its attractive coves, wide estuaries, sandy beaches, rugged cliffs and picturesque harbours (the area is popular with sailors). The inland region is largely agricultural, unspoiled and scenic, with delightful wooded valleys. The major towns include Brest, Dinard, Lorient, Quimper, Rennes (the historic capital of Brittany), Saint-Brieuc and Saint-Malo. Although its summers are warm and pleasant, the weather can be stormy in winter (Brest is reputedly the wettest city in France), although the northwest coast is milder as it's influenced by the Gulf Stream. The local people (Bretons) are of Celtic origin with a rich maritime tradition and a unique culture. Proud and independent (they claim that Bretagne is a country apart), they even have their own language which has been revived in recent years. The local Breton costume is still worn on special occasions, one of the most colourful of which is the *Fêtes des Filets Bleus* held in the fishing village of Concarneau in August.

Brittany is popular with both holidaymakers and second homebuyers, particularly the British, due to its excellent connections via the ports of Roscoff and Saint-Malo, and the Normandy ports. Among the most popular homes are the characteristic Breton cottage, built mainly of granite with slate roofs. Property is expensive on the west coast, particularly around Quimper and Bénodet. The area around Dinan, Dinard and Saint-Malo is also popular, which is reflected in relatively high prices. Less expensive properties can be purchased in the Roscoff area and the west coast between Quimper and Vannes is also good value. The interior, known as the *Argoat* (land of woods), is quieter and cheaper. As in all regions, there's a huge difference between the price of properties with a sea-view and those situated further inland.

Burgundy (Bourgogne): Burgundy contains the departments of Côte-d'Or, Nièvre, Saône-et-Loire and Yonne. The region is of little economic importance and has few industries, which means it's almost totally unspoiled and one of France's most beautiful and fertile areas (it has been dubbed the rural soul of France). Burgundy has a rich and colourful history (it was an independent kingdom for some 600 years) and a wealth of historic towns. It's a timeless land where little has changed over the centuries and a haven of peace and serenity (particularly the Parc du Morvan at its heart). The region's most important towns include Autun, Auxerre, Beaune, Chalon-sur-Saône, Dijon (of mustard fame and capital of the region), Fontenay, Mâcon, Nevers, Paray-le-Monial and Vézelay.

The name Burgundy is synonymous with magnificent wines such as Nuits-Saint-Georges, Meursault, Beaune, Puligny-Montrachet, Gevrey-Chambertin and Pouilly-Fuissé, grown on the 60km (37mi) Côte d'Or hillside, fine cuisine (noted for its rich sauces) and the good life. The region is also noted for its many canals and canal boats, and has some 1,200km (750mi) of navigable waterways including the Burgundy Canal and the rivers Saône and Yonne. Burgundy is located just 100km (around 65mi) south of Paris and 80km (50mi) north of Lyon, and has excellent connections with both the north and south of France via the A6 and A31 *autoroutes* and TGV trains.

Somewhat surprisingly Burgundy isn't popular with foreign property buyers, perhaps due to its relative isolation, and there are few holiday and retirement homes there. It rarely features in international property magazines and although the region has a wealth of beautiful *châteaux*, manor houses and watermills, these (and vineyards) are rarely on the market. Prices tend to be higher than average for France, but inexpensive, habitable village houses and farmhouses in need of restoration can be found in most areas.

Champagne: The Champagne region (also called Champagne-Ardennes) contains the departments of Ardennes, Aube, Haute-Marne and Marne. Celebrated for the bubbly stuff after which it's named, the production of Champagne dominates most aspects of life in the region. Its main towns include Charleville-Mézières, Épernay, Reims (the region's capital) and Troyes. Reims is home to the *Grandes Marques* of Champagne such as Veuve Cliquot and Charles Heidsieck, although Épernay is the centre of Champagne production. Reims cathedral is one of the most beautiful and historically important in France, where the country's kings were crowned.

The region is highly cultivated and although not one of France's most attractive areas, it's noted for its rolling landscape, immense forests (Verzy forest contains beech trees that are over 1,000 years old), deep gorges and vast rivers. Champagne also contains the largest artificial lake in Europe, Lac du Der-Chantecoq, located at Saint-Dizier. The Ardennes (which shares a border with Belgium) is the region's most picturesque department and its rolling, wooded landscape is dotted with ramparts, fortified castles and farmhouses. The Champagne region isn't popular with foreign homebuyers, despite property being relatively inexpensive, particularly in the Ardennes. However, it gets more expensive the nearer you get to Brussels in the north and Paris in the west (the western Aube is the most expensive area). The area has good road connections and is served by the A4 and A26 *autoroutes.*

Corsica (Corse): Containing the departments of Corse du Sud and Haute Corse, Corsica is situated 160km (99mi) from France and 80km (50mi) from Italy, covering an area of 8,721km² (3,367mi²) with a coastline of around 1,000km (620mi). It's further from France than Italy, with which it has strong historical ties, having been an Italian possession until 1768 when France purchased it from Genoa. There's a strong local identity (and independence movement) and Corsica enjoys a larger degree of autonomy than the mainland regions. The main towns include Ajaccio (the capital town and birthplace of Napoléon), Bastia, Bonifacio, Calvi and Porto-Vecchio, all situated on the coast.

Corsica is quite different from the mainland regions, not only its geography but its people, culture, customs, language and way of life. It has a stark, primitive beauty and is sparsely populated with huge areas devoid of human life. Corsica is one of the most beautiful Mediterranean islands and is a popular holiday destination (particularly the western coast), with superb beaches and picturesque hillside villages. Mountains cover most of its surface, including some 200 peaks over 2,000 metres (6,500ft) with the highest reaching to over 2,700m/9,000ft (skiing is possible in the winter). Around half the island is covered in vegetation including beech, chestnut and pine forests, and the ubiquitous *maquis*, a dense growth of aromatic shrubs (heather and myrtle) and dark holm oak.

Tourism is the island's main industry and it remains completely unspoiled and a haven for outdoor lovers (hikers and bikers) and those seeking peace and serenity. Not surprisingly, Corsica has a slow pace of life, which is epitomised by its ancient and spectacular mountain railway. The island has a Mediterranean climate with hot summers and mild (but windy) winters. It's popular with holiday home owners, particularly the Italians, and prices have risen in recent years following increased interest. It has, however, avoided the devastation wrought in many other Mediterranean islands by high-rise developments and buildings are restricted to a maximum of two storeys and construction is forbidden close to beaches.

Franche-Comté: Franche-Comté (literally 'free country') dates back to the 12th century and contains the departments of Doubs, Haute-Saône, Jura and the Territoire-de-Belfort. It's a little known region situated in eastern France bordering Switzerland, with which it shares much of its architecture, cuisine and culture. Franche-Comté is acclaimed for its beautiful, unspoiled scenery (more Swiss in appearance than French) and recalls a fairy-tale land where time has almost stood still. Its main towns include Belfort and Besançon, the region's capital on the river Doubs and the first official green town in France. Besançon is served by the A36 *autoroute* and has good connections with the centre and south of France, Germany and Switzerland.

Sandwiched between the Vosges range to the north and the Jura mountains to the south, the landscape consists of rolling cultivated fields, dense pine forests and rampart-like mountains. Although not as majestic as the Alps, the Jura mountains are more accessible and are a mecca for nature lovers and winter sports fans. The Doubs and Loue Valleys (noted for their timbered houses perched on stilts in the river) and the high valley of Ain are popular areas. The Franche-Comté is largely ignored by foreign tourists and homebuyers. Property prices are higher than the French average, although some bargains can be found, particularly if you're seeking a winter holiday home.

Languedoc-Roussillon: Languedoc-Roussillon, often referred to simply as the Languedoc or Midi, is situated in southern central France and contains the departments of Aude, Gard, Hérault, Lozère and Pyrénées-Orientales. It's bordered by the Pyrénées, Andorra and Spain in the south and extends north as far as the Massif Central (where Lozère is France's most sparsely populated department). Languedoc has a long Mediterranean coastline of virtually uninterrupted sandy beaches, stretching some 180km (110mi) from the Carmargue to the Spanish border. The region's main towns include Béziers, Carcassonne (with the largest fortress in Europe), Montpellier, Narbonne, Nîmes (the best example of a Roman town outside Italy) and Perpignan. Montpellier is the region's capital and one of the most progressive towns in France (it also has a famous university).

Few French regions are more steeped in history than Languedoc, home of the heretical Cathars, offering an abundance of sun, sea, mountains and excellent (but under-rated) wines such as Corbières, Minervois and Côtes du Roussillon. It's one of the great wine growing regions of France (Béziers is the wine capital of France) and encompasses the largest wine production area in Europe. The region has a vast range of scenery and landscape including the beautiful Cévennes national park, the Tarn valley, the tranquil Canal du Midi, the gentle rolling foothills of the Pyrénées and the dramatic beauty of the high Pyrénées peaks. It's a popular region with sports fans (e.g. skiing, camping, hiking, aerial and water sports), with a wealth of facilities on the doorstep, and is the stronghold of French rugby. Languedoc is noted for its relaxed pace of life and is a popular hideaway for those seeking peace and tranquility. It has its own ancient language (Occitan) and many towns close to the Spanish border have a Catalan feel (Catalan is also spoken here).

A number of purpose-built resorts have been created on the Côte Vermeille (vermillion coast) in the last few decades including Argelès-sur-Mer, Gruissan, Saint-Cyprien-Plage, Port Bacarès, Port Leucate, Cap d'Agde (site of one of Europe's largest naturist resorts) and La Grande Motte. Most are unattractive and to be avoided if you're looking for a home of character. Collioure is the best known and most picturesque port in Roussillon (and also the most expensive), which also has a number of attractive fishing villages such as Palavas and Sète. The Mediterranean coast is noted for its hot summers and mild winters, in stark contrast to the region's northern areas which can be bitterly cold in winter.

The Languedoc is popular with holidaymakers and second homeowners, and property is much cheaper here than in Provence/Côte d'Azur and it also has a lower cost of living. Apart from the popular coastal resorts, where expensive tiny apartments and studios are commonplace, property is reasonably priced. In recent years Languedoc has attracted an increasing number of northern Europeans, many seeking a combined winter and summer holiday home or a retirement home, and the recently opened Pas de l'Escalette tunnel (Hérault) has opened up the area to more potential buyers. Languedoc has good access from the A9 and A61 *autoroutes* and is connected to Paris by the TGV. There are also good air connections via Toulouse and inexpensive charter flights to Gerona and Barcelona (just over the border in Spain) from many countries.

Limousin: Limousin contains the departments of Corrèze, Creuse and Haute-Vienne. Sparsely populated and the least populous of the mainland regions, it's popular with those seeking the mythical *France profonde* (the French heartland). The region's main towns include Brive, Guéret and Limoges, famous for its pottery since the 12th century and the region's capital. It's one of the most remote and rural regions of France, scenic, unspoiled and peaceful, and a haven for country lovers. The Limousin (particularly the Haute-Vienne) is noted for its deep gorges, numerous rivers, '1,000' lakes (a mecca for watersports enthusiasts) and excellent fishing. A farming region with few towns of any size, Limousin is a pastoral delight depicting a bygone age that has largely disappeared from Western Europe. Property prices and the cost of living are among the lowest in France. Largely undiscovered by foreign buyers, Limousin is much cheaper than its more famous neighbours (such as the Dordogne) and a wide range of property is available.

Loire Valley (Val de Loire): The Loire Valley (sometimes called the Central Loire and the heart of France) contains the departments of Cher, Eure-et-Loir, Indre, Indre-et-Loire, Loir-et-Cher and Loiret. It's named after the Loire river, which gives its name to many departments. The Loire is France's longest river (1,020km/628mi), with its source in the Vivarais mountains (south of Saint-Etienne) and its outlet at Saint-Nazaire in the Western Loire. Its basin covers 115,120km² (44,450mi²) or one-fifth of France's landmass and it has a number of important tributaries, notably the Indre and Cher rivers. The Loire is considered to be the dividing line between the colder regions of northern France and the warmer south, although the change is gradual.

The Loire Valley, which traditionally refers to the stretch from Orléans to Nantes, is one of the most alluring areas of France. It's renowned for its magnificent historic *châteaux* (a legacy of sumptuous living) and cathedrals, and architecturally is France's most impressive region (dubbed the 'soul of France'). The Loire is noted for its natural beauty and fertility, consisting of pleasant undulating woodland, lakes, rivers, orchards, and fields of maize and sunflowers (it's the market garden of France). The region's chief towns include Blois, Bourges, Chartres (with its magnificent Gothic cathedral, widely considered to be the most beautiful in Europe), Orléans and Tours. One of its most attractive areas is the old province of Berry, comprising the departments of Cher and Indre, and the majestic medieval city of Bourges, its ancient capital.

The Loire valley is unspoiled by industry, mass tourism or a surfeit of holiday homes, although it's popular with retirees and second home owners. Property prices vary considerably depending on the proximity to major towns, although they are generally well above the French average and bargains are rare. The region has excellent road connections via the A10, A11 and A71 *autoroutes*.

Lorraine: Lorraine (or Lorraine-Vosges as it's also called) is situated in the northeastern corner of France bordering Germany, Belgium and Luxembourg, and contains the departments of Meuse, Meurthe-et-Moselle, Moselle and Vosges. Like the Alsace, Lorraine has been fought over for centuries by France and Germany, between whom it has frequently swapped ownership (the region retains a strong Germanic influence). Although mainly an industrial area, Lorraine is largely unspoiled and is popular with nature lovers and hikers. It's noted for its meandering rivers, rolling hills, wooded valleys, and delightful medieval towns and villages.

Lorraine is famous for its celebrated Moselle wines and *quiche*. The main towns include Nancy, the region's capital city, and Metz, plus a wealth of picturesque villages including Bussang, Ferrette, Le Hohwald, Saint-Amerin and Schirmeck, and resort towns such as Masevaux and Plimbières-les-Bains. Lorraine has few foreign residents and is largely ignored by tourists and second homebuyers, despite the relatively low cost of living and reasonable property prices. The region has good road access via the A4 and A31 *autoroutes*.

Midi-Pyrénées: The Midi-Pyrénées region is one of the largest in France and contains the departments of Aveyron, Ariège, Gers, Haute-Garonne, Hautes-Pyrénées, Lot, Tarn and Tarn-et-Garonne. The region encompasses the old province of Gascony (dubbed France's answer to Tuscany), which takes in the department of Gers and parts of the Landes, Haut-Garonne and the Hautes-Pyrénées. The Midi-Pyrénées borders Spain in the south and embraces the French Pyrénées and the towns of Albi, Auch, Cahors, Lourdes, Montauban, Tarbes and Toulouse (the region's capital). Although considered by many to be a grey industrial city, Toulouse is actually an attractive, historic city full of character. Lourdes receives some six million pilgrims a year in search of a miracle cure and is second only to Rome as a centre of pilgrimage.

The region is largely unspoiled and has a wide variety of terrain, ranging from the wild beauty of the Lot Valley in the north to the rugged majesty of the Pyrénées in the south. The Lot river is one of the prettiest in France and wends its way through limestone cliffs dotted with the occasional *château* or village nestling precariously on an overhanging crag, amid a strikingly beautiful landscape. The northern area is noted for its medieval towns and villages (with Gothic half-timbered houses) such as Cadenac-le-Haut and Saint-Cirq-Lapopie. The French Pyrénées are a popular hiking, cycling and skiing area, and home to some 35 ski resorts including Barèges and Cauterets. Although catering more for beginners and intermediates rather than expert skiers, the Pyrénées' resorts are generally much cheaper than those in the Alps. The region is also noted for its numerous spa towns (of which Bagnères-de-Luchon is the most celebrated), whose thermal springs can allegedly cure a multitude of ailments including sterility in women!

The region is popular for holiday and retirement homes, particularly Gascony and the Lot (also known as Quercy), where a surprising around 50 per cent of all properties are purportedly second homes. Although becoming more expensive, the region offers good value for money and substantial homes can still be purchased for reasonable prices. The Midi-Pyrénées is served by the A61 and A62 *autoroutes*, which link it with both the Atlantic and Mediterranean coasts, and Paris is five hours away by TGV.

Nord/Pas-de-Calais: The Nord/Pas-de-Calais region in the far north of France contains the departments of Nord and Pas-de Calais. It's one of France's smallest regions and shares a border with Belgium, from where it gets its Flemish influence and beer-producing traditions. The region was (along with Picardy) the birthplace of 19th century manufacturing in France and is the country's only major conurbation outside Paris, although it has historically been neglected. Although derided as industrialised, over-populated and one of France's least attractive regions, it has many attractive areas and is noted for its clean beaches, undulating countryside, secluded woods, beautiful river valleys (particularly the Canche and Authie), market gardens, fine golf courses and many pretty, peaceful villages.

The region's main towns include Amiens, Arras, Calais, Cambrai, Dunkerque, Lille, Montreuil, Roubaix, Saint-Omer, Tourcoing and Valenciennes. Lille is the capital of the region and is a stylish, prosperous and vibrant city, with a unique cultural identity and five universities. It has a flamboyant old town and a revitalised city centre with its new TGV station and other major developments. Paris and Brussels are just a few hours away by TGV. The region's coastline (the Opale coast) has a number of pleasant resorts including Berck, Boulogne, Etaples, Hardelot, Le Touquet (the most fashionable resort) and Wimereux. The region is popular with the British due to its accessibility, although there wasn't been the expected surge in property prices after the opening of the Channel Tunnel. Homes in the region remain relatively inexpensive, although coastal areas are naturally more expensive than inland areas, although not outrageously so. The area has excellent road connections with Paris and the rest of France via the A26 and A25 *autoroutes*, and with Belgium and northern Europe, and is linked with Britain, Paris and the rest of France via TGV and Eurostar trains.

Normandy (Normandie): Normandy contains the departments of Calvados, Eure, Manche, Orne and Seine-Maritime, and is officially sub-divided into two areas: High Normandy (*Haute-Normandie*), along the Seine Valley and with similar scenery to the Ile-de-France, and Low Normandy (*Basse-Normandie*), more rugged and similar to Brittany. Normandy is noted for its lovely countryside (called the *bocage*) and wide variety of scenery including lush meadowland, ubiquitous orchards, numerous rivers and babbling brooks, quiet country lanes, and over 600km (370mi) of coastline (famous for the Normandy D-Day landings in June 1944). The area to the south of Caen is known as La Suisse Normande (Swiss Normandy) for its similarity to the Swiss landscape, with its deep gorges and rocky peaks. Normandy is famous for its cider, calvados (apple brandy) and superb cuisine (including exquisite shellfish).

The region contains many chic and fashionable resorts, particularly on the *Côte Fleurie*, including Cabourg, Deauville, Honfleur, Houlgate and Trouville. Other historic towns include Barfleur (the port that launched the Norman conquest of England), Bayeux (and its famous tapestry), Falaise (birthplace of William the Conqueror) and the fishing port of Fécamp, home to the Bénédictine liquor distillery housed in a glorious 'Disney' fantasy of a building. Mont Saint-Michel (on the region's southern coast) is one of France's premier tourist attractions, despite being

overcrowded, exploited and expensive (it's packed with over-priced cafés, restaurants and tourist junk shops). It's best seen outside the peak summer season, preferably in the early morning before the tourist hordes arrive. Normandy's other main towns include Alençon, Caen (completely destroyed during the second-world war), Dieppe (France's oldest seaside resort with one of its longest bathing beaches), Rouen (the region's capital on the River Seine) and Saint-Lô.

Normandy has long been popular with the British for holidays and second homes, particularly in and around the Channel ports and resorts. With the exception of Nord/Pas-de-Calais and Picardy regions, it's the most accessible region from Britain via the ports of Caen, Cherbourg and Le Havre. Most cheaper properties close to the coast have long been snapped up, although there are still bargains to be found further inland, particularly in the Contentin (Cherbourg) peninsular. Coastal property is relatively expensive and prices increase the closer you get to Paris (Parisians weekend on the Normandy coast). Honfleur has a surfeit of British residents and Deuville is packed with chic Parisians, and both are very expensive. Normandy is famous for its half-timbered *colombage* houses, which are much in demand. Although served by the A13 and A15 *autoroutes* to Paris and beyond, the region isn't one of France's most accessible.

Paris/Ile-de-France: The region of Paris/Ile-de-France contains the departments of Essone, Hauts-de-Seine, Seine-et-Marne, Seine-Saint-Denis, Val-de-Marne, Val-d'Oise, Ville de Paris and Yvelines. Paris needs no introduction and is one of the world's great cities, famous for its beauty, chic, romance, fine restaurants and vibrant nightlife. However, despite its excellent public transport system, which is one of the best in the world, it increasingly suffers from air pollution caused by vehicle exhaust fumes. The departments that make up the Ile-de-France are largely unspoiled with a marked absence of urban sprawl, and have mostly retained their historic character (the eastern department of Seine-et-Marne is surprisingly rural). The main towns around Paris include Bobigny, Créteil, Fontainbleau, Mantes, Marne-la-Vallée, Meaux, Melun, Nanterre, Pontoise, Provins, Rambouillet, Saint-Germain-en-Laye, Saint-Denis and Versailles.

Few people choose to live in Paris unless it's absolutely necessary, particularly as the price of property (50,000F or more per square metre in fashionable areas) and the cost of living is the highest in France. However, property here is usually a good long-term investment, particularly if you plan to let it, although values have fallen in the last decade. Paris is popular among the rich and famous for 'second' homes and is an excellent spot for a 'little' *pied-à-terre*. Most Parisians rent in central Paris and buy a home in the country or live in one of the commuter areas surrounding Paris, particularly the Seine Valley (which consequently is relatively expensive). Not surprisingly Paris has excellent road, rail and air connections, both nationally and internationally.

Picardy (Picardie): The region of Picardy (north of Paris) contains the departments of Aisne, Oise and Somme, and is one of the least known regions of France. It's mainly famous for its battlegrounds from the first and second world wars, particularly the Somme, although the region is rich in history and architecture. Picardy has a generally flat and uninteresting agricultural landscape, with just a small coastal strip around Boulogne and Le Touquet, although it has a number of attractive areas, particularly the valleys of the Somme, Aisne and Oise rivers. The region's main towns include Amiens (the capital city), Beauvais, Compiègne, Chantilly, Saint-Omer and Saint-Quentin. Picardy has some of the lowest property prices in

France (the Somme Valley is the most attractive area), although it isn't popular with foreign buyers. The Oise department is the most expensive due to its proximity to Paris.

Poitou-Charentes: The Poitou-Charentes region is situated in the west of France and contains the departments of Charente, Charente-Maritime, Deux-Sèvres and Vienne. The région is completely unspoiled with virtually no industry and is one of the most tranquil in France. Its long Atlantic coastline is noted for its sandy beaches, marinas, golf courses and islands, and contrasts sharply with the relatively flat and uninteresting landscape in inland areas, particularly the Charente, a land of mixed farming and livestock breeding. Among the most popular resorts are Brouage, La Rochelle, Royan and the islands of Ile d'Oléron and Ile de Ré, with their pine-shaded beaches and superb shellfish. The fishing port of La Rochelle is a beautiful and charming town, popular with holidaymakers and noted for its excellent seafood. One of the most interesting areas is the marshlands of Le Marais Poitevin bordering the Vendée, an area reclaimed from the sea and criss-crossed by dykes. It's one of the most remarkable landscapes in France and has been described as a green Venice. The region's main towns include Angoulême, Cognac (producers of the world's finest brandy), Niort, La Rochelle, Poitiers (the region's capital), Roquefort and Saintes. The Futuroscope 'park of the moving image' just north of Poitiers is a major attraction.

Poitou-Charentes is a popular region with tourists, holiday homeowners and retirees, particularly British property buyers, many of whom favour the area around Cognac and Saintes. There's a huge difference between the relatively high cost of property on the coast and inland areas, where homes are good value for money. A large number and variety of properties are available in rural areas, particularly farmhouses and village homes in need of restoration. The Atlantic coast of Charente-Maritime has an excellent micro-climate and is noted for its long hot summers and mild winters, although it can be very cold inland. Most of Charente-Maritime has good access from the A10 *autoroute*, although the inland department of Charente is relatively isolated.

Provence/Côte d'Azur: The region of Provence/Côte d'Azur in the southeast of France contains the departments of Alpes-de-Haute-Provence, Alpes Maritimes (often classified as the separate region of Côte d'Azur), Bouches-du-Rhône, Hautes-Alpes, Var and Vaucluse. Provence is a fascinating land of romance, history and great beauty, and is celebrated for its excellent climate, attractive scenery, fine beaches, cuisine and fashionable resorts. It's a region of stark contrasts with a huge variety of landscape and scenery encompassing rugged mountains, rolling hills, spectacular gorges, dramatic rock formations, lush and fertile valleys carpeted with lavender, extensive vineyards (which stretch to the foot of the rugged Alpilles mountains), and a ravishing coastline dotted with quaint fishing villages and fine beaches.

A journey through Provence is an indulgence of the senses and its diverse vegetation includes cypresses, gnarled olive trees, almond groves, umbrella pines, lavender, wild rosemary, thyme and savory, all of which add to the unique and seductive sights and smells of Provence. The region contains many beautiful areas, notably the Lubéron National Park, the heart of the provençal countryside and a fashionable area for holiday homes. The Carmargue, between Arles and the sea (from which it was reclaimed), is one of the most spectacular nature reserves in France and famous for its lagoons, white horses, pink flamingoes and black fighting bulls.

Provence produces a number of excellent wines and includes the prestigious vineyards of Châteauneuf-du-Pape, Gigondas and Lirac, plus the popular provençal *rosés*.

Provence contains a wealth of beautiful historic Roman towns and dramatically sited medieval villages such as Les Baux-de-Provence and Sainte-Agnès. The region's main towns include Aix-en-Provence, Antibes, Arles, Avignon (City of the Popes), Cagnes-sur-Mer, Cannes, Digne-les-Bains, Fréjus, Grasse (France's perfume capital), Hyères, Marseille, Menton, Nice, Orange, Saint-Raphaël, Saint-Tropez and Toulon (France's largest naval base). Marseille, capital of the south and one of France's great cities, is also its oldest (founded by the Greeks). It's one of the country's most important ports and the gateway to Corsica and North Africa. It isn't, however, a popular tourist destination and is infamous for its crime underworld of 'French Connection' fame.

The Côte d'Azur (Azure Coast) was 'discovered' by the British in the 19th century, who dubbed it the French Riviera. It stretches from Menton close to the Italian border to beyond Cannes (the actual area is disputed) and takes in the independent principality of Monaco, centred on Monte Carlo (and its famous casino). Monaco is very, very expensive due to its small size and the influx of the many 'tax-dodging' millionaires who live there (only 6,000 of its 30,000 inhabitants are native Monégasques). It's the ultimate playground of the rich and famous, with property costing around five times that of a fashionable French Riviera town.

The Côte d'Azur was the world's first coastal playground for the rich and famous, and is one of the most exclusive areas of France. Almost nowhere in France compares with its ambience and allure, beautiful sea and landscapes, fine weather, glamorous resorts, sandy beaches and beautiful people. Popular resorts include Antibes (Cap d'Antibes), Cannes, Cogolin, Juan-les-Pins, Menton, Nice, Port Grimaud, Ramateulle and Saint-Jean-Cap-Ferrat. Nice, affectionately dubbed the Big Olive, is the capital of the French Riviera and a glamourous and sophisticated city. One of the best ways to appreciate the beauty of the coast is to take the train from Menton to Marseille (there's also a spectacular narrow-gauge line between Digne-les-Bains and Nice). On the negative side, the Côte d'Azur has one of the highest costs of living in France and is overdeveloped, overcrowded and vulgar, with an unsavoury reputation for crime and corruption.

Provence/Côte d'Azur is the most popular region in France for holiday and retirement homes, and has a large foreign community with the Italians and British among the largest buyers of second homes. Although prices dropped during the recession, they have since recovered and the region has the most expensive real estate in France outside Paris, with large luxury properties routinely costing over 100 million francs! When money is no object this is usually the region of France that wealthy buyers choose. The price of a small studio apartment on the coast will buy you a large detached property almost anywhere else in France. On the plus side, property has excellent, almost year-round letting potential and is generally a good investment.

Provence has a superb climate with hot summers and mild winters (apart from the Mistral), although it gets quite cold in some inland areas. The area has good *autoroute* connections with other regions of France and with Italy and Switzerland, plus good rail and air connections. Some of the world's best skiing is available just a few hours away in the French and Italian Alps.

Rhône-Alpes: The Rhône-Alpes region in the southeast of France contains the departments of Ain, Ardèche, Drôme, Haute-Savoie, Isère, Loire, Rhône and Savoie. It has borders with Switzerland and Italy and is noted for its majestic mountain scenery, which is unrivalled at almost any time of year. Although largely unspoiled by development, the Rhône Valley is one of France's major industrial regions. Lyon (the capital of the region) has a beautiful old medieval quarter and is France's second city and its gastronomic capital. The Rhône-Alpes is one of France's most scenic and beautiful regions with dense forests, lush pasture land, fast-flowing rivers, huge lakes, deep gorges and spectacular mountains. The Rhône river (which has its source high in the Swiss Alps) is a vital artery for river, road and rail traffic between the north and south.

It's a land made for sports fans and those with a love of the outdoors, with superb summer (e.g. climbing, hiking, biking, canoeing and white-water rafting) and winter sports facilities, including some of the best skiing in the world. Top ski resorts include Chamonix (also France's mountaineering capital), Courchevel, Megève, Meribel, Val d'Isère and Val Thorens. The region's major towns include Aix-les-Bains, Albertville, Annecy (the cleanest lake of its size in Europe), Bourg-en-Bresse, Chambéry, Chamonix, Grenoble, Lyon, Montélimar, St. Etienne and Vienne. Grenoble, a centre for high-tech industries and the most important city in the Alps, is one of France's fastest-growing cities.

The price of property in the Rhône-Alpes region is well above the average, particularly in the Alps, although there are some inexpensive areas in the east. The Ardèche with its spectacular gorge is increasingly popular with foreign buyers and consequently is becoming more expensive. It's also worth taking a look at the Drôme department, particularly around Nyons (famous for its olive oil), which although not as dramatic as the Ardèche is quieter and just as beautiful. Village houses are rarely for sale in or near ski resorts, where prices held up well in the recession in the early '90s. Properties in French ski resorts are usually an excellent investment and also make fine summer holiday homes, particularly if you're a keen biker, climber or hiker. Like Franche-Comté, Rhône-Alpes is popular with the Swiss, many of whom live in the region and commute to their workplaces in Geneva and other Swiss cities. Note that buying in a ski resort is best done in summer as snow can hide a multitude of sins. The region is noted for its great extremes of temperature and is usually freezing in winter and hot in summer, and most pleasant in spring and autumn. The Rhône-Alpes has excellent road, rail and air connections and Lyon is just two hours from Paris by TGV.

Western Loire (Pays de la Loire): The Western Loire (the Pays de la Loire literally means 'lands of the Loire river') contains the departments of Loire-Atlantique (formerly part of Brittany), Maine-et-Loire, Mayenne, Sarthe and Vendée. It includes the lower reaches of the Loire river, after which it's named, which has its outlet on the Atlantic at Saint-Nazaire. The region has an Atlantic coastline of over 160km (100mi) of sandy beaches stretching from Beauvoir-sur-Mer almost to La Rochelle (La Baule has one of the finest white sand beaches in Europe). The region is picturesque rather than dramatic, with gentle rolling hills, woodland, valleys and meandering rivers, and some of France's loveliest coastal scenery. It's particularly popular with hikers, cyclists and golfers, most of whom wisely don't care for an excess of hills. The area between Angers and Tours is known as the 'garden of France' for its orchards, market gardens and vineyards, and is also famous for its seafood. The Western Loire is noted for its tranquility and gentle pace of life and is one of the great 'undiscovered' areas of France.

The region's main towns include Angers, Cholet, Laval, Le Mans (home of the world's most famous road race), Nantes, Saumur and Saint-Nazaire, where the new Pont de Saint-Nazaire is the longest road bridge in France. Nantes (formerly the capital of Brittany) is the region's beautiful capital and commercial centre of the region. The Western Loire has a rich and fascinating history and a wealth of interesting historic towns, striking abbeys, magnificent cathedrals and beautiful *châteaux*. It's popular with second home owners and retirees, and property is reasonably priced away from the main resorts and towns. The A11 *autoroute* provides good connections to Paris and the south and the region is also served by the TGV.

RESEARCH

There's an overwhelming choice of property for sale in France, which is a buyers market in most areas and likely to remain that way for many years. As when buying property anywhere, it's never advisable to be in too much of a hurry. Have a good look around in your chosen region and obtain an accurate picture of the types of properties available, their relative values and what you can expect to get for your money. However, before doing this you should make a comprehensive list of what you want (and don't want) from a home, so that you can narrow the field and save time on wild goose chases.

Note that it's often difficult to compare homes in different regions as they usually vary considerably and few houses are exactly comparable. In most areas properties range from derelict farmhouses, water mills and barns to modern townhouses and apartments with all modern conveniences; from crumbling *châteaux* and manor houses requiring complete restoration to luxury chalets and villas. You can also buy a plot of land and have an individual, architect-designed house built to your own specifications. If, however, after discussing the decision with your partner, one of you insists on a brand new luxury apartment in Cannes and the other on a 17th century *château* in the Loire Valley, the easiest solution may be to get a divorce!

Although property in France is relatively inexpensive compared with many other European countries, the fees associated with the purchase of properties older than five years are the highest in Europe and add 10 to 15 per cent to the cost. To reduce the chances of making an expensive error when buying in an unfamiliar region, it's often prudent to rent a house for a period (see **Renting** on page 135), taking in the worst part of the year (weather-wise). This allows you to become familiar with the region and the weather, and gives you plenty of time to look around for a home at your leisure. Wait until you find something you fall head over heels in love with and then think about it for another week or two before rushing headlong to the altar! One of the advantages of buying property in France is that there's usually another 'dream' home around the next corner – and the second or third dream home is often even better than the first. It's better to miss the 'opportunity of a lifetime' than end up with an expensive pile of stones around your neck. **However, don't dally too long as good properties at the right price don't remain on the market for ever.**

One of the most common mistakes people make when buying a rural property in France is to buy a house that's much larger than they need with acres of land, simply because it seems to offer such good value. Don't, on the other hand, buy a property that's too small. Bear in mind that extra space can easily be swallowed up, and when you have a home in France you will inevitably discover that you have many more relatives and friends than you ever thought possible! For many foreign buyers, France provides the opportunity to buy a size or style of home that they could never afford in their home countries.

Buying a huge house with a few acres may seem like a good investment, but bear in mind that should you wish to sell buyers may be thin on the ground, particularly when the price has doubled or trebled after the cost of renovation. In most areas there's a narrow market for renovated rural property. There are usually many buyers in the lower 300,000F to 500,000F price range, but they become much scarcer at around one million francs unless a property is exceptional, i.e. outstandingly attractive, in a popular area and with a superb situation. In some areas even desirable properties remain on the market for a number of years. Although it's tempting to buy a property with a lot of land, you should think about what you're going to do with it. After you've installed a swimming pool, tennis court and croquet lawn, you still have a lot of change left out of even a few acres. Do you like gardening or are you prepared to live in a jungle? Can you afford to pay a gardener? A large garden needs a lot of upkeep (i.e. work). Of course you can always plant an orchard or vineyard, create a lake or take up farming!

If you're looking for a holiday home (*résidence secondaire*), you may wish to investigate mobile homes or a scheme that restricts your occupancy of a property to a number of weeks each year. These include shared ownership, leaseback (*nouvelle propriété*), time-sharing (*multipropriété*) and a holiday property bond (see page 157). Don't rush into any of these schemes without fully researching the market, and before you're absolutely clear about what you want and what you can realistically expect to get for your money.

Bear in mind that foreign buyers aren't welcome everywhere, particularly when they 'colonise' a town or area. There has been some resistance to foreigners buying property in certain areas and a few towns have even blocked sales to foreigners to deter speculators. Understandably, the French don't want property prices driven up by foreigners (particularly second home owners) to levels they can no longer afford. However, foreigners are generally welcomed by the local populace (and are infinitely preferable to most country folk than Parisians!), not least because they boost the local economy and in rural areas often buy derelict properties that the French won't touch. Permanent residents in rural areas who take the time and trouble to integrate with the local community are invariably warmly welcomed.

The more research you do before buying a property in France the better, which should (if possible) include advice from people who already own a house there, from whom you can usually obtain invaluable information (often based on their own mistakes). In the last decade or so a number of specialist English-language French property magazines and newspapers have been established in Britain including *Focus on France*, *French Property News* and *Living France*, an excellent monthly 'lifestyle' magazine for francophiles noted for its beautiful photography (see **Appendix A** for addresses). In France, property is advertised for sale (under *vente maisons/appartements*) in all major Parisian and provincial newspapers, plus many free newspapers. Weekly property newspapers such as *De Particulier à Particulier*, *Le Journal des Particuliers*, *La Centrale des Particuliers* and *La Semaine Immobilière* are all good sources of information. Information about properties for sale is also available via Minitel and the Internet (see page 27).

AVOIDING PROBLEMS

The problems associated with buying property abroad have been highlighted in the last decade or so, during which the property market in many countries has gone from boom to bust and back again. From a legal viewpoint, France is one of the safest places in the world in which to buy a home and buyers have a high degree of protection under French law, which applies to all buyers irrespective of whether they are French citizens or foreign non-residents. However, you should take the usual precautions regarding contracts, deposits and obtaining proper title.

Many people have had their fingers burnt by rushing into property deals without proper care and consideration. It's all too easy to fall in love with the beauty and ambience of France and to sign a contract without giving it sufficient thought. If you're uncertain, don't allow yourself to be rushed into making a hasty decision, e.g. by fears of an imminent price rise or because someone else is interested in a property. Although many people dream of buying a holiday or retirement home in France, it's vital to do your homework thoroughly and avoid the 'dream sellers' (often fellow countrymen) who will happily prey on your ignorance and tell you anything in order to sell you a property.

The vast majority of people who buy homes in France don't obtain independent legal advice and most of those who experience problems take no precautions whatsoever. Of those that do take legal advice, many do so only *after* having paid a deposit and signed a contract or, more commonly, after they have run into problems. The most important point to bear in mind when buying property in France is to obtain expert legal advice from someone who's familiar with French law. As when buying property in any country, you should never pay any money or sign anything without first taking legal advice. You will find that the relatively small cost (in comparison to the cost of a home) of obtaining legal advice is excellent value for money, if only for the peace of mind it affords. Trying to cut corners to save a few francs on legal costs is foolhardy in the extreme when a large sum of money is at stake. You may be able to obtain a list of lawyers who speak your national language and are experienced in handling French property sales, either in France or in your home country, e.g. British buyers can obtain a list from the Law Society in Britain.

There are professionals speaking English and other languages in all areas of France, and many expatriate professionals (e.g. architects and surveyors) also practise there. However, don't assume that because you're dealing with a fellow countryman that he'll offer you a better deal or do a better job than a Frenchman (the contrary may be true). It's wise to check the credentials of all professionals you employ, whether French or foreign. Note that it's *never* advisable to rely solely on advice proffered by those with a financial interest in selling you a property, such as a builder or estate agent, although their advice may be excellent and totally unbiased.

Declared Value: Don't be tempted by the 'quaint' French 'custom' of tax evasion, where the 'official' (*prix déclaré*) sale price declared to the tax authorities is reduced by an 'under the table' (*dessous-de-table*) cash payment. It's possible when buying a property direct from the vendor that he may suggest this, particularly if he's selling a second home and must pay capital gains tax on the profit. Obviously if the vendor can show a smaller profit, he pays less tax. You will also save money on taxes and fees, but will have a higher capital gains tax bill when you sell if it's a second home. **You should steer well clear of this practice, which is naturally strictly illegal (although widespread).** If you under-declare the price, the authorities can revalue the property and demand that you pay the shortfall in tax plus interest and fines. They can even prosecute you for fraud, in which case you can receive a prison sentence! The authorities can also decide to buy a property at the under-declared price plus 10 per cent within three months of the date of purchase. If you're selling a property, you should bear in mind that if the buyer refuses to make the under-the-table payment after the contract has been signed, there's nothing you can do about it!

Among the most common problems experienced by buyers in France are buying in the wrong area (**rent first!**); buying a home that's unsaleable; buying too large a property and grossly underestimating restoration and modernisation costs; not having a survey done on an old property; not taking legal advice; not including the necessary conditional clauses in the contract; buying a property for business, e.g. to convert to *gîtes*, and being too optimistic about the income; paying too much; taking on too large a mortgage; and property management companies doing a moonlight flit with the owners' rental receipts.

It's advisable to have your finance in place before you start looking for a property in France and if you need a mortgage, to obtain a mortgage guarantee certificate from a lender that guarantees you a mortgage at a certain rate, which is usually subject to a valuation (see **Mortgages** on page 88). Note, however, that there's a mandatory conditional clause in French contracts that allows buyers to withdraw from a contract and have their deposit returned (under certain conditions) if they're unable to obtain a mortgage. You will also need a 10 per cent deposit when buying a property older than five years plus the fees and taxes associated with buying, which are 10 to 15 per cent of the purchase price (see **Fees** on page 146).

Finally, if there's any chance that you will need to sell (and recoup your investment) in the short to medium term, it's important to buy a home that will be saleable. A property with broad appeal in a popular area (particularly a waterside property) usually fits the bill, although it will need to be very special to sell quickly in some areas. A modest, reasonably priced property is usually likely to be much more saleable than a large expensive home, particularly one needing restoration or modernisation.

CHOOSING THE LOCATION

The most important consideration when buying a home anywhere is usually its location – or as the old adage goes, the *three* most important points are location, location and location! A property in a reasonable condition in a popular area is likely to be a better investment than an exceptional property in a less attractive location. There's no point in buying a dream property in a terrible location. France offers almost anything that anyone could want, but you must choose the right property in the right spot. **The wrong decision regarding location is one of the main causes of disenchantment among foreigners who have purchased property in France.**

Where you buy a property will depend on a range of factors including your personal preferences, your financial resources and, not least, whether you plan to work in France. If you already have a job there, the location of a home will probably be determined by the proximity to your place of employment. However, if you intend to look for employment or start a business, you must live in an area that allows you the maximum scope. Unless you have reason to believe otherwise, you would be foolish to rely on finding employment in a particular area. If, on the other hand, you're seeking a holiday or retirement home, you will have a huge choice of areas. When choosing a permanent home, don't be too influenced by where you have spent an enjoyable holiday or two. A town or area that was acceptable for a few weeks holiday may be far from suitable, for example, for a retirement home, particularly regarding the proximity to shops, medical facilities and other amenities.

If you have little idea about where you wish to live, read as much as you can about the different regions of France (see page 113) and spend some time looking around your areas of interest. Note that the climate, lifestyle and cost of living can vary considerably from region to region (and even within a particular region). Before looking at properties it's important to have a good idea of the kind of home that you're looking for and the price you wish to pay, and to draw up a shortlist of the areas or towns of interest. If you don't do this, you're likely to be overwhelmed by the number of properties to be viewed. Real estate agents usually expect serious buyers to know where they want to buy within a 30 to 40km (20 to 25mi) radius and some even expect clients to narrow it down to specific towns and villages.

The 'best' area in which to live depends on a range of considerations including the proximity to your place of work, schools, bar, country or town, shops, public transport, sports facilities, beach, etc. There are beautiful areas to choose from throughout France, most within easy travelling distance of a town or city. Don't, however, believe the times and distances stated in adverts and by estate agents. According to some agents' magical mystery maps everywhere in the north is handy for Paris or a Channel port and all homes in the south are a stone's throw from Lyon or Nice. If you buy a remote country property, the distance to local amenities and services could become a problem, particularly if you plan to retire to France. If you live in a remote rural area you will need to be much more self-sufficient than if you live in a town. Don't forget that France is a <u>BIG</u> country and those living in remote areas need to use the car for everything. It has been calculated that it costs some 40,000F a year (including depreciation costs) to run a new small car doing 15,000km (9,300mi) a year (which is less than average). **The cost of motoring is high in France and is an important consideration when buying a home there.**

If possible you should visit an area a number of times over a period of a few weeks, both on weekdays and at weekends, in order to get a feel for the neighbourhood (don't just drive around, but walk!). A property seen on a balmy summer's day after a delicious lunch and a few glasses of *vin rouge* may not be nearly so attractive on a subsequent visit *sans* sunshine and the warm inner glow. You should also try to visit an area at different times of the year, e.g. in both summer and winter, as somewhere that's wonderful in summer can be forbidding and inhospitable in winter. If you're planning to buy a winter holiday home, you should also view it in the summer, as snow can hide a multitude of sins! In any case, you should view a property a number of times before making up your mind to buy it. If you're unfamiliar with an area, most experts recommend that you rent for a period before deciding to buy (see **Renting** on page 136). This is particularly important if you're planning to buy a permanent or retirement home in an unfamiliar area. Many people change their minds after a period and it isn't unusual for families to move once or twice before settling down permanently.

If you will be working in France, obtain a map of the area and decide the maximum distance you will consider travelling to work, e.g. by drawing a circle with your workplace in the middle. Obtain large scale maps of the area where you're looking. The best maps are the *Institut Géographique National (IGN)* blue series, with a scale of 1:25,000, i.e. 1cm to 250m (or 2.5in to a mile). These often show individual buildings, so it's easy to mark off the places that you've seen. You could do this using a grading system to denote your impressions. If you use an estate agent, he will usually drive you around and you can return later to those that you like most at your leisure (providing that you have marked them on your map!).

There are many points to consider regarding the location of a home. These can roughly be divided into the local vicinity, i.e. the immediate surroundings and neighbourhood, and the general area or region. Take into account the present and future needs of all members of your family, including the following:

- For most people the climate (see page 48) is one of the most important factors when buying a home in France, particularly a holiday or retirement home. Bear in mind both the winter and summer climate, the position of the sun, the average daily sunshine, plus the rainfall and wind conditions. The orientation or aspect of a building is vital and if you want morning or afternoon sun (or both) you must ensure that balconies, terraces and gardens face the right direction. If you're seeking guaranteed sunshine you need to head south. Generally south of the Loire river is considered to be the point where the colder northern European climate starts to get warmer, although the change is gradual.

Note, however, that even southern France hasn't abolished winter and it can be extremely cold, wet and windy in some areas.

- Check whether an area is particularly prone to natural disasters such as floods, storms or forest fires. If a property is located near a waterway, it may be expensive to insure against floods, which are a constant threat in some areas.

- Noise can be a problem in some cities, resorts and developments. Although you cannot choose your neighbours, you can at least ensure that a property isn't located next to a busy road, industrial plant, commercial area, discotheque, night club, bar or restaurant (where revelries may continue into the early hours). Look out for objectionable neighbouring properties which may be too close to the one you're considering and check whether nearby vacant land has been 'zoned' for commercial activities. In community developments (e.g. apartment blocks) many properties are second homes and are let short-term, which means you may need to tolerate boisterous holidaymakers as neighbours throughout the year (or at least during the summer months).

- Bear in mind that if you live in a popular tourist area, e.g. almost anywhere in the south of France, you will be inundated with tourists in summer. They won't only jam the roads and pack the public transport, but may even occupy your favourite table at your local café or restaurant (heaven forbid!). Although a 'front-line' property on the beach or in a marina development may sound attractive and be ideal for short holidays, it isn't usually the best choice for permanent residents. Many beaches are hopelessly crowded in the high season, streets may be smelly from restaurants and fast food outlets, parking impossible, services stretched to breaking point, and the incessant noise may drive you crazy. You may also have to tolerate water restrictions in some areas.

- Do you wish to live in an area with many of your fellow countrymen and other expatriates or as far away from them as possible? If you wish to integrate with the local community, avoid foreign 'ghettos' and choose an area or development with mainly local inhabitants. However, unless you speak French fluently or intend to learn it, you should think twice before buying a property in a village. Note that the locals in some villages resent 'outsiders' moving in, particularly holiday home owners, although those who take the time and trouble to integrate into the local community are usually warmly welcomed. If you're buying a permanent home, it's important to check your prospective neighbours, particularly when buying an apartment. For example, are they noisy, sociable or absent for long periods? Do you think you will get on with them? **Good neighbours are invaluable, particularly when buying a second home in France.**

- Do you wish to be in a town or do you prefer the country? Inland or on the coast? How about living on an island? Bear in mind that if you buy a property in the country, you will also probably have to put up with poor public transport (or none at all), long travelling distances to a town of any size, solitude and remoteness. You won't be able to pop along to the local *boulangerie* for a *baguette* and *croissants*, drop into the local bar for a glass of your favourite tipple with the locals, or have a choice of restaurants on your doorstep. In a town or large village, the weekly market will be just around the corner, the doctor and pharmacy close at hand, and if you need help or run into any problems, your neighbours will be close by.

In the country you will be closer to nature, will have more freedom (e.g. to make as much noise as you wish) and possibly complete privacy, e.g. to sunbathe or swim *au* naturel. Living in a remote area in the country will suit nature lovers looking for solitude who don't want to involve themselves in the 'hustle and bustle' of town life (not that there's much of this in French rural towns). If you're after peace and quiet, make sure that there isn't a busy road or railway line nearby or a local church within 'DONGING!' distance. Note, however, that many people who buy a remote country home find that the peace of the countryside palls after a time and they yearn for the more exciting city or coastal night-life. If you have never lived in the country, it's advisable to rent first before buying. Note also that while it's cheaper to buy in a remote or unpopular location, it's usually much more difficult to find a buyer when you want to sell.

- If you're planning to buy a large country property with a sizeable garden or plot of land, bear in mind the high cost and amount of work involved in its upkeep. If it's to be a second home, who will look after the house and garden when you're away? Do you want to spend your holidays mowing the lawn and cutting back the undergrowth? Do you want a home with a lot of outbuildings? What are you going to do with them? Can you afford to convert them into extra rooms, guest accommodation or *gîtes*?

- How secure is your job or business and are you likely to move to another area in the near future? Can you find other work in the same area, if necessary? If there's a possibility that you may need to move in some years time, you should rent or at least buy a property that will be relatively easy to sell and recoup the cost.

- What about your partner's and children's jobs, or your children's present and future schooling? What is the quality of local schools? Note that even if your family has no need or plans to use local schools, the value of a home may be influenced by the quality and location of schools.

- What local health and social services are provided? How far is the nearest hospital with an emergency department?

- What shopping facilities are provided in the neighbourhood? How far is it to the nearest town with good shopping facilities, e.g. a super/hypermarket? How would you get there if your car was out of commission? Note that many rural villages are dying and have few shops or facilities, and aren't usually a good choice for a retirement home.

- What is the range and quality of local leisure, sports, community and cultural facilities? What is the proximity to sports facilities such as a beach, golf course, ski resort or waterway? Bear in mind that properties in or close to ski and coastal resorts are considerably more expensive, although they also have the best letting potential. If you're interested in a winter holiday home, which area should you choose? The Alps are one of the few areas in France where property prices held up well during the recession in the early '90s.

- Is the proximity to public transport, e.g. an international airport, port or railway station, or access to an *autoroute* important? Note that the *autoroute* network is continually being expanded and will eventually cover the whole country. The expansion of the TGV rail network also means that many remote areas are now linked to Paris and other major cities in just a few hours. Don't, however, believe all you're told about the distance or travelling times to the nearest *autoroute*, airport, railway station, port, beach or town, but check it for yourself.

• If you're planning to buy in a town or city, is there adequate private or free on-street parking for your family and visitors? Is it safe to park in the street? In some areas it's important to have secure off-street parking if you value your car. Parking is a problem in many towns and most cities, where private garages or parking spaces can be very expensive. Bear in mind that an apartment or townhouse in a town or community development may be some distance from the nearest road or car park. How do you feel about carrying heavy shopping hundreds of metres to your home and possibly up several flights of stairs? Traffic congestion is also a problem in many towns and tourist resorts, particularly during the high season.

• What is the local crime rate? In some areas the incidence of housebreaking and burglary is extremely high. Due to the higher than average crime rate, home insurance is higher in Paris and on the Côte d'Azur and some other popular areas. Check the crime rate in the local area, e.g. burglaries, housebreaking, stolen cars and crimes of violence. Is crime increasing or decreasing? Note that professional crooks like isolated houses, particularly those full of expensive furniture and other belongings, which they can strip bare at their leisure. You're much less likely to be a victim of theft if you live in a village, where crime is usually virtually unknown (strangers stand out like sore thumbs in villages, where their every move is monitored by the local populace).

• Do houses sell well in the area, e.g. in less than six months? Generally you should avoid neighbourhoods where desirable houses routinely remain on the market for six months or longer (unless the property market is in a severe slump and nothing is selling).

FRENCH HOMES

French homes are usually built to high structural standards and whether you buy a new or an old home, it will usually be extremely sturdy. Older homes often have metre-thick walls and contain numerous rooms. Most have a wealth of interesting period features including vast fireplaces, wooden staircases, attics, cellars (*caves*), and a profusion of alcoves and annexes. Many houses have a basement (*sous-sol* or *cave*), used as a garage and cellar. In most old houses, open fireplaces remain a principal feature even when central heating is installed. In warmer regions, floors are often tiled and walls are painted rather than papered, while in cooler northern regions, floors are carpeted or bare wood, and walls are more likely to be papered. When wallpaper is used, it's often garish and may cover everything including walls, doors and ceilings! Properties throughout France are usually built in a distinct local (often unique) style using local materials. There are stringent regulations in most areas concerning the style and design of new homes and the restoration of old buildings.

In older rural properties, the kitchen (*cuisine*) is the most important room in the house. It's usually huge with a large wood-burning stove for cooking, hot water and heating, a huge solid wood dining table and possibly a bread oven. French country kitchens are worlds apart from modern fitted kitchens (called American kitchens in France) and are devoid of shiny formica, plastic laminates and pristine order. They are often stark in comparison with modern kitchens, with stone or tiled floors and a predominance of wood, tiles and marble. In contrast with modern kitchens in most countries, kitchens in apartments in Paris and other cities may be very basic.

Refrigerators (*frigo*) and stoves (*cuisinière*) are usually quite small in French homes. Stoves in rural homes are usually run on bottled gas or a combination of bottled gas and electricity. Many homes have a gas water heater (*chaudière*) that heats the water for the bathroom and kitchen. Most French homes don't have a separate utility room and the washing machine and drier are usually kept in the kitchen. Homes often have a separate toilet (*toilette* or *WC/water*) and the bathroom (*salle de bains*) often has a toilet, a *bidet*, a bath (*baignoire*) and/or a shower (*douche*). Baths are more common than showers in older homes, although showers are found in most modern homes. Note that many old, unmodernised homes don't have a bath, shower room or an inside toilet.

Many rural properties have shutters fitted (with catches to secure them to a wall), both for security and as a means of insulation. External shutters are often supplemented by internal shutters that are fixed directly to the window frames. French casement windows open inwards rather than outwards, as in most other countries. In the south and southwest many rural homes have outdoor swimming pools and homes throughout France have a paved patio or terrace, which is often covered. Old farmhouses invariably have a number of outbuildings such as barns that can usually be converted into additional accommodation.

Although new properties are often lacking in character, they are usually spacious and well endowed with modern conveniences and services, which certainly cannot be taken for granted in older rural properties. Standard fixtures and fittings in modern houses are more comprehensive and of better quality than those found in old houses. The French generally prefer modern homes to older houses with 'charm and character', which to the locals means it's expensive to maintain and in danger of falling down. You do, however, often find pseudo period features such as beams and open fireplaces in new homes. Central heating, double glazing and good insulation are common in new houses, particularly in northern France, where they are essential. Central heating may be electric, gas or oil-fired. However, on the French Riviera, where winter temperatures are higher, expensive insulation and heating may be considered unnecessary (don't you believe it!). Air-conditioning is rare, even in the south of France.

Note that most French families live in apartments or detached homes, and semi-detached and terraced properties are relatively rare in France. Some 45 per cent of the population lives in apartments (although less than 10 per cent in tower blocks), which are more common in France than in most other European countries. In cities and suburbs, most people have little choice as houses are in short supply and prohibitively expensive. In the major cities there are many *bourgeois* apartments built in the 19th or early 20th century, with large rooms, high ceilings and huge windows. Unless modernised they have old fashioned bathrooms, kitchens and non 'public' rooms (the rooms visitors don't see), and are expensive to decorate, furnish and maintain. Many apartments don't have their own source of hot water and heating, which is shared with other apartments in the same building.

RENTING

If you're uncertain about exactly what sort of home you want and where you wish to live, it's advisable to rent a property for a period in order to reduce the chances of making a costly error. **Renting long-term before buying is particularly prudent for anyone planning to live in France permanently!** If possible, you should rent a similar property to that which you're planning to buy, during the time of year when you plan to occupy it. Renting allows you to become familiar with the weather, the amenities and the local people; to meet other foreigners who have made their homes in France and share their experiences; and not least, to discover the cost of living for yourself. Providing you still find France alluring, renting 'buys' you time to find your dream home at your leisure. You may even wish to consider renting a home in France long-term (or 'permanently'), as it saves tying up your capital and can be surprisingly inexpensive in many regions. Some people let out their family homes abroad and rent one in France for a period (you may even make a profit!).

If you're looking for a rental property for a few months, e.g. three to six months, it's best not to rent unseen, but to rent a holiday apartment for a week or two to allow yourself time to look around for a longer term rental. Properties for rent are advertised in local newspapers and magazines, particularly expatriate publications, and can also be found through property publications in many countries (see **Appendix A** for a list) and the Internet. Many real estate agents offer short-term rentals and builders and developers may also rent properties to potential buyers.

Long-Term Unfurnished Rentals: France has a strong rental market and it's possible to rent every kind of property, from a tiny studio apartment (bedsitter) to a huge rambling *château*. Most rental properties in France are let unfurnished (*non-meublé*), particularly for lets longer than one year, and long-term furnished (*meublé*) properties are difficult to find. If you're looking for a home for less than a year, you're usually better off looking for a furnished apartment or house. A rental contract or lease (*bail*) for an unfurnished property is usually a standard document in France and must be for a minimum period of three years if it's for a named individual (*Bail un Nom Propre/personne physique*) and cannot be for an unspecified period.

Rental costs vary considerably depending on the size (number of bedrooms) and quality of a property, its age and the facilities provided. However, the most significant factor affecting rents is the region of France, the city and the particular neighbourhood. In Paris, a tiny studio apartment of around 20 square metres in a good area costs around 3,000F a month, while a two or three-bedroom apartment in a fashionable area can cost from 15,000F to 30,000F a month. In the provinces you can rent a two-bedroom apartment or cottage for 3,000F or less per month.

Short-Term Furnished Rentals: France has an abundance of self-catering accommodation and the widest possible choice. You can choose from literally thousands of cottages (*gîtes*), apartments, villas, bungalows, mobile homes, chalets, and even *châteaux* and manor houses. However, most property is available for short holiday lets only, particularly during the peak summer season, and little furnished property is let long-term (although it's increasing due to tax incentives). However, a growing number of foreign owners who are unable to sell their French homes are letting them long-term, particularly outside the peak summer period. Note that when the rental period includes the peak letting months of July and August, the rent can be prohibitive.

Standards vary considerably, from dilapidated ill-equipped cottages to luxury villas with every modern convenience. Many short-term lets are *gîtes*, which simply means a home or shelter, but is nowadays widely used to refer to most furnished, self-catering holiday accommodation. A typical *gîte* is a small cottage or self-contained apartment with one or two bedrooms (sleeping four to eight and usually including a sofa bed in the living room), a large living room/kitchen with an open fire or stove, and a toilet and shower room. In certain parts of France, notably the overcrowded French Riviera, *gîtes* may be no more than purpose-built concrete rabbit hutches, built to a basic standard and strictly regulated. Check whether a property is fully equipped (which should mean whatever you want it to mean!) and whether it has central heating if you're planning to rent in winter.

For short-term lets the cost is calculated on a weekly basis (Saturday to Saturday) and depends on the standard, location, number of beds and the facilities provided. The rent for a *gîte* sleeping six is typically from 1,500F to 2,000F per week in June and September, and 2,000F to 2,500F in July and August. The rent is higher for a *gîte* with a pool. However, when renting long-term outside the high season, you can rent a two-bedroom property for around 3,000F a month in most regions. Rentals can be booked via travel agents, French Government Tourist Offices (who are agents for *Gîtes de France*) and via the Internet (e.g. www.villa-rentals.com/france). You can also contact owners directly via the publications listed in **Appendix A** and those mentioned under **Property Income** on page 191.

Note that rental laws and protection for tenants doesn't extend to holiday lettings, furnished lettings or sub-lettings. For holiday letting, the parties are free to agree such terms as they see fit concerning the period, rent, deposit and the number of occupants permitted, and there's no legal obligation on the landlord to provide a written agreement. However, you should never rent a furnished property without a written contract, which should be drawn up or checked by a notary for long-term rentals. This is important if you wish to get a deposit returned. A long-term rental contract for a furnished property is called a *contrat de location de locaux meublés*, while a seasonal contract is an *engagement de location meublée saisonnière*. All rental contracts, whether for unfurnished or furnished properties, must be signed by all parties involved, including the agent handling the contract, if applicable. Next to their signature each party must also write the words *lu et approuvé* (read and approved).

Hotels & Motels: Hotel rates in France vary depending on the time of year, the exact location and the individual establishment, although you may be able to haggle over rates outside the high season and for long stays. In most towns, a single room costs from 150F to 200F and a double from 150F to 300F. They aren't a cost-effective solution for home hunters, although there's little other choice if you need accommodation for a short period only. Bed and breakfast accommodation is also available in France, although it isn't usually considered budget accommodation (see the books listed in **Appendix B**). For real budget accommodation you need to choose a hostel.

Many hotels have rooms for three or four guests at reduced rates or provide extra beds for children in a double room free or for a small charge. A double room may contain one or two 'double' beds, although they may not be full-size double beds; often a room will have a double bed and one or two single beds. The backbone of the French hotel network is the *Logis et Auberges de France*, the world's largest hotel consortium representing over 5,000 privately run hotels in the French countryside. Most are one or two-star hotels in popular locations, with prices ranging from 150F to 400F per night for a double room. The *Logis* guide is available from French Government Tourist Offices and a *Logis de France* handbook is also available from bookshops. There are a number of budget hotel/motel chains in France with hotels close to *autoroutes* and major towns and cities. These include Formule 1 (☎ 01.36.68.56.85), Mister Bed (☎ 01.46.14.38.00), Première Classe (☎ 01.64.62.46.46) and Village Hotels (☎ 01.80.71.50.60). Rooms cost around 150F per night for up to three people sharing a room with a double and single bed and a colour TV.

Home Exchange: One alternative to renting is to exchange your home abroad for a period with one in France. This way you can experience home living in France for a relatively small cost and may save yourself the expense of a long-term rental. Although there's an element of risk involved in exchanging your home with another family (depending on whether your swap is made in heaven or hell!), most agencies thoroughly vet clients and many have a track record of successful swaps. There are home exchange agencies in most countries, many of which are members of the International Home Exchange Association (IHEA). There are many home exchange companies in the USA including HomeLink International (16,500 members in around 50 countries), Box 650, Key West, FL 33041, USA (☎ 305-294 7766 or 800-638 3841). Two long-established home exchange companies in Britain are HomeLink International, Linfield House, Gorse Hill Road, Virginia Water, Surrey GU25 4AS, UK (☎ 01344-842642, Internet: www.homelink.org), who publish a Directory of homes and holiday homes for exchange, and Home Base Holidays, 7 Park Avenue, London N13 5PG, UK (☎ 0181-886 8752, Internet: www.homebase-hols.com). Other agencies include Green Theme International (☎ UK 01208-873123, Internet: www.green-theme.zb.net), Intervac Home Exchange (☎ UK 01225-892208, Internet: www.intervac.com) and the Worldwide Home Exchange Club (☎ UK 01892-619300, Internet: www.wwhec.com).

COST

Property prices in France rose considerably in the '80s in most areas, fuelled by the high demand for holiday homes, particularly from foreigners. However, as the world recession deepened in the early '90s, property prices plummeted as buyers disappeared and although prices have stabilised in the last few years the market remains stagnant in most areas. There have been many unprecedented bargains in the last five years as foreign buyers who over-extended themselves or found the cost of living too high sold up and went home. France remains a buyers' market in most regions and there are still good buys to be had in most regions. The best bargains are often to be had at auction (see page 143), where properties repossessed by banks are sold. Property in France remains excellent value for money compared with most other countries, particularly rural properties with a plot of land.

Property prices in France generally rise slowly and steadily and are fairly stable, without the unpredictable swings experienced in some other countries. In rural areas where there's no strong local demand, prices are unlikely to rise or fall dramatically. As in most countries, property is cheapest in rural areas where the exodus in the last 30 years has left the countryside with a surfeit of empty properties (and where employment prospects are poor or non-existent). The French tend to live close to their work and the idea of commuting long distances doesn't appeal to them. With the exception of major commuter areas such as the Seine Valley and a few popular holiday areas such as Provence, the Alps and most coastal areas, the price of rural property in France is relatively low. Prices have been driven up by foreign buyers in some regions, particularly in border regions such as the Rhine departments, Savoy and the Lyon-Grenoble-Annecy triangle, and some areas in the southwest, e.g. the Dordogne. However, prices are highest in areas where the French demand for holiday homes is strongest, which generally includes anywhere along the Atlantic and Mediterranean coasts. Note that you usually pay a premium for a property with a sea view, although it's also more saleable.

Coastal and city properties are at a premium and cost up to double the price of similar rural properties. Property on the French Riviera is among the most expensive in the world, despite prices having fallen in the last decade. Property prices have also fallen in Paris and although it isn't cheap, it's much more affordable than it was a decade ago. New properties are widely available and include coastal and city apartments, sports (e.g. ski or golf) developments, and a wide range of individually designed houses and chalets. Many new properties are part of huge purpose-built developments, often located along the coast or in the mountains, encompassing a golf course, swimming pool, tennis and squash courts, a gym or fitness club, and a restaurant.

Although there has been evidence of dual pricing in the past, the practice of quoting higher prices to foreigners is rare. The prices advertised abroad are invariably identical to those advertised in France. What is certainly true is that the French drive a much harder bargain than most foreigners when buying a property, particularly an old one. French owners are sometimes astonished at the prices foreign buyers are prepared to pay for nondescript homes in uninspiring areas, although they *never* complain about foreigners pushing up prices when they are on the receiving end! The French think that the British are particularly insane for buying up their tumbled down farmhouses and crumbling *châteaux*. Few Frenchmen (although it's becoming more common) share the British passion for spending their holidays and weekends up to their elbows in bricks and mortar! They do, however, have a grudging admiration for the British for their painstaking and sensitive restorations.

Apart from obvious points such as size, quality and land area, the most important factor influencing the price of a house is its location. A restored or modernised two-bedroom house costing 300,000F in the northwest (e.g. Normandy), sells for double or treble that price in the southeast (e.g. Provence). Similarly, the closer you are to the coast (or Paris), the more expensive a property will be, with properties on the French Riviera the most expensive of all. A Charente farmhouse with a barn and land costs around the same as a tiny studio apartment in Paris or on the Côte d'Azur. Note that when people talk about inexpensive (cheap) homes, they invariably mean something that needs restoring, which usually necessitates spending as much as the purchase price (or much more) to make it habitable.

In most rural areas it's still possible to buy an old property for as little as 100,000F to 200,000F, although you usually need to carry out major restoration work. Modern studio and one-bedroom apartments cost from around 250,000F and two-bedroom apartments from 400,000F. A rural two-bedroom renovated cottage costs from around 300,000F and a modern two-bedroom bungalow from 400,000F. Property in ski resorts varies considerably in price depending on the particular resort and the location of the property. A tiny studio in a purpose-built resort costs from around 200,000F, while a one-bedroom apartment close to the ski lifts in a resort such as Courcheval, Méribel or Tignes costs between 500,000F to 600,000F, rising to around 800,000F in Chamonix or Val d'Isère. Small chalets start at around one million francs, although you need to spend over two million francs to buy a family-sized chalet in an average resort.

When property is advertised in France, the total living area in square metres (*mètres carrés*) is usually stated (written as m²) and the number of rooms (*pièces*), including bedrooms and reception rooms (such as a lounge or living room). A two-room (*deux pièces*) apartment has one-bedroom and a three-room (*trois pièces*) house has two bedrooms. Prices in Paris are similar to other international cities such as London and New York. In central Paris, 800,000F barely buys a one-bedroom apartment in some areas and it isn't unusual to pay ten million francs for a luxury apartment in a fashionable area. Prices are calculated per m², ranging from around 10,000F in the cheaper areas to 100,000F or more for a luxury property in the chic 8th and 16th districts (*arrondissement*). The average price in most other French cities is between 8,000F and 12,000F per m².

The total fees payable when buying a house in France are higher than in most other countries. The *notaire's* fees and taxes usually amount to between 10 and 15 per cent of the selling price for a small to medium sized property over five years old; fees for properties less than five years old are around 3 to 4 per cent. Note that prices may be quoted inclusive or exclusive of agency fees. Make sure you know whether *all* agents' fees are included in the price quoted and **who must pay them**. If you negotiate a reduction, check that the agent or vendor hasn't just excluded some fees from the price (to be added later). Additional *notaire's* fees are payable if you have a French mortgage, plus lender's fees.

To get an idea of property prices in different regions of France, check the prices of properties advertised in English-language property magazines and French newspapers, magazines and property journals (see **Appendix A**). Property price indexes for different areas are published by some French property magazines, although these should be taken as a rough guide only. **Before deciding on the price, make sure you know <u>exactly</u> what's included, as it isn't unusual for French sellers to strip a house bare and take everything including internal doors and the kitchen sink (it's true!).** If applicable, have fixtures and fittings listed in the contract.

The table below is designed to give you a *rough* idea of what you can expect to receive for your money in France. Cheaper properties, say under 500,000F, requiring restoration are rare in the more expensive areas such as Paris/Ile-de-France, Provence/Côte d'Azur, major cities, and popular coastal and mountain resort areas. Inexpensive properties (e.g. for restoration) are also difficult to find in the regions of

Alsace, Franche-Comté and Rhône-Alpes. Unless otherwise stated, the prices listed below refer to property in all regions of northern, western, central and southern France, with the exception of the eastern regions from Alsace in the north to the Côte d'Azur in the south. Note that rural properties such as farmhouses invariably come with a large plot of land (one or two acres is common).

Price (FF)	Will Buy?
100,000 to 200,000	A rural cottage or farmhouse requiring extensive restoration and modernisation; a large stone barn for conversion.
200,000 to 300,000	A small habitable restored or partly restored village or rural property (possibly with some land); a large rural property in need of restoration; a tiny studio apartment (e.g. 30 square metres) on the Côte d'Azur.
300,000 to 400,000	A restored or partly restored two or three-bedroom rural property with some land; a farmhouse requiring renovation in the Dordogne; a one-bedroom apartment in a popular resort (excluding the Côte d'Azur); a village house for restoration in some western parts of Provence.
400,000 to 500,000	A restored farmhouse or village house in good condition; a three or four-bedroom rural detached house in good condition; a small two-bedroom modern house; a one-bedroom apartment in a popular coastal resort on the Côte d'Azur.
500,000 to 750,000	A large three or four-bedroom rural property in good condition with a large garden or a small plot of land (possibly with a pool); a one or two-bedroom apartment in a popular resort; a rural village house or farmhouse for restoration in Provence.
750,000 to 1 million	A restored four-bedroom rural property with a swimming pool and a substantial plot of land; a modern four-bedroom rural property; a two or three-bedroom apartment in most resorts; a studio or one-bedroom apartment in a good area of Paris; a modest village or rural home in an unfashionable area of Provence or the Alps.
1m to 1.5 million	A small chalet in the Alps off the beaten track; a restored or partly restored manor house or small run-down *château*; a large restored rural property with a pool and a large plot of land; a large modern rural house or villa; a three-bedroom apartment in a fashionable resort on the Côte d'Azur; a small restored village house in a fashionable part of Provence; a one or two-bedroom apartment in central Paris.
1.5m to 3 million	A family-sized chalet in the Alps (excluding the most popular resorts); a large manor house in good condition; a

small habitable *château* or a large *château* requiring restoration; a restored farmhouse (*mas*) or modern villa (with pool) in rural Provence; a large luxury apartment in a fashionable resort on the Côte d'Azur; a good-sized apartment in a fashionable Paris suburb.

3 million plus   A habitable or restored *château* or large manor house; a large restored farmhouse in Provence; a large villa on the Côte d'Azur; a large chalet in a fashionable Alpine resort; a luxury Parisian three or four-bedroom apartment; a small vineyard.

Negotiating the Price

When buying a property it usually pays to haggle over the price, even if you think it's a bargain. Prices in the south of France are usually more negotiable than in the north, but they are also higher. Don't be put off by a high asking price, as most sellers are willing to negotiate. In recent years many properties have sold for much less than their original asking prices, particularly properties priced at over one million francs. Sellers generally presume buyers will bargain and rarely expect to receive the asking price for a property (although some vendors ask an unrealistic price and won't budge a *centime*!). In popular areas (e.g. Paris and Provence), asking prices may be unrealistically high (up to double the real market price), particularly to snare the unsuspecting and ignorant foreign buyer. It's usually worthwhile obtaining an independent valuation (appraisal) to determine a property's market value.

If you're using an agent you should ask him what to offer, although he may not tell you (and indeed, shouldn't, if he's also acting for the seller). Note that if you make an offer that's too low you can always raise it, but it's impossible to lower an offer once it has been accepted (if your first offer is accepted without haggling, you will never know how low you could have gone). If an offer is rejected it may be worth waiting a week or two before making a higher offer, depending on the market and how keen you are to buy a particular property. If you make a low offer, it's advisable to indicate to the owner a few negative points (without being too critical) that merit a reduction in price. Note that if you make a very low offer, an owner may feel insulted and refuse to do business with you! If a property has been realistically priced, you shouldn't expect to obtain more than a 5 or 10 per cent reduction. Cash buyers in some areas may be able to negotiate a considerable price reduction for a quick sale, depending on the state of the local property market and how urgent the sale. An offer should be made in writing, as it's likely to be taken more seriously than a verbal offer. **Be prepared to walk away from a deal rather than pay too high a price.**

If you simply want to buy a property at the best possible price as an investment, then shopping around and buying a 'distress sale' from an owner who simply must sell is likely to result in the best deal. Obviously you will be in a better position if you're a cash buyer and able to close quickly. Note, however, that if you're seeking an investment property it's advisable to buy in an area that's in high demand, preferably with both buyers and renters. For the best resale prospects, it's usually best to buy in an area or community (and style) that's attractive to French buyers. You should find out as much as possible about a property before making an offer, such as when it was built; how long the owners have lived there; whether it's a permanent or holiday home; why they are selling (they may not tell you outright, but may offer clues); how keen they are to sell; how long it has been on the market; the condition of the property; the neighbours and neighbourhood; local property taxes and insurance rates; and not least, whether the asking price is realistic.

Timing is of the essence in the bargaining process and it's essential to find out how long a property has been on the market (generally the longer it has been for sale, the more likely a lower offer will be accepted) and how desperate the vendor is to sell. Some people will tell you outright that they must sell by a certain date and that they will accept any reasonable offer. You may be able to find out from neighbours why someone is selling, which may help you decide whether an offer would be accepted. If a property has been on the market for a long time, e.g. longer than six months in a popular area, it may be overpriced (unless it has obvious defects). If there are many desirable properties for sale in a particular area or development that have been on the market a long time, you should find out why. For your part, you must ensure that you keep any sensitive information from a seller and give the impression that you have all the time in the world (even if you must buy immediately). All this 'cloak and dagger' stuff may seem unethical, but you can be assured that if you were selling and a prospective buyer knew you were desperate and would accept a low (lower) offer, he certainly wouldn't be in a hurry to pay you any more!

Buying at Auction

The best property bargains are generally to be found at auctions (*ventes aux enchères*), where properties that have been repossessed by mortgage lenders are commonly sold (called *ventes judiciares*). Other frequent reasons for selling at auction are family disputes over inheritance and when the previous owner died without leaving any heirs. Properties usually have a reserve price, which is often as little as half the real market price. When a property is sold by a bank, the reserve price is usually the amount owed to them, above which they aren't interested. Somewhat surprisingly, there often isn't a lot of competition for properties sold at auction, particularly as many are old properties in rural areas which aren't of much interest to French buyers.

Properties due to be sold at auction are advertised in local papers by the *Tribunal de Grande Instance* (local county court) responsible for the auction and details are published around six weeks in advance by the person (e.g. the notary or lawyer) responsible for the sale. The form (*fiche*) contains the date and place of the sale; a description of the property; land details with *cadastre* references; the name and address of the lawyer handling the sale; details regarding property inspections; and the reserve price. **Before making a bid it's imperative to accurately assess the market value of a property and (if applicable) what it will cost to bring it to habitable condition.**

To make a bid you need to appoint a lawyer (*avocat*) or notary (*notaire*) who's registered with the *Tribunal de Grande Instance*, as they are the only people permitted to make bids. Instructions regarding the maximum price that you're prepared to pay must be provided in writing and bids are delivered in sealed envelopes. You must deposit a (returnable) bidding entry fee of from 1,000F to 20,000F via a cheque (drawn on a French bank) or banker's draft (certified cheque) in French francs, the amount of which is decided by the auctioneer. If you're successful you will be required to pay a deposit equal to 10 per cent of the purchase price immediately after the bid (which may be requested prior to bidding). It isn't necessary to attend an auction in person as you can appoint a lawyer to act on your behalf.

Note that higher fees must be paid for properties purchased at auction, usually amounting to between 15 and 20 per cent of the purchase price. In addition to normal fees (see page 146), you must pay for the publication of the judgement (*hypothèque*), court expenses and the lawyer's fees. You can calculate the fees to be paid, based on your offer price. The fees must be paid within one month and the purchase price usually within two months. It's possible to arrange a mortgage after a successful bid, although if you fail to raise a loan you will lose your deposit.

A judge presides over the auction proceedings and bids, which start at the reserve price and increase in increments of 1,000F. The sale usually takes place *à la chandelle* (by candle) or more commonly *aux trois feux* (by three lights). As the lot is knocked down, the court usher lights the first candle (or first light), which burns for 20 seconds and is followed by the second and third candles until the third candle or light (*feu d'adjudication*) has been extinguished, indicating that the sale is concluded. Note, however, that the candle or light sequence must be restarted each time a new bid is made. The system is similar to the 'going once, going twice, gone' system employed at auctions in Britain, although it's much more dramatic.

The successful bidder must wait ten days, during which time someone can make a higher bid providing it's at least 10 per cent above the auction price. If a higher bid is made the property must be re-auctioned, usually within two months. Such interventions are rare and are permitted once only. You can, of course, also decide not to bid on a property and wait until a successful bid has been made. Then, if you decide that it's worth more you can make a higher bid. Some British agents such as Consultancy in France (☎ UK 01935-850274) provide details of properties to be sold at auction in a given area in return for a registration fee and a flat fee as commission on a successful sale.

Buying a Business Property

A large variety of residential properties are purchased with a business which usually include farms, vineyards, hotels, restaurants and bars. For the purpose of this section a business property doesn't include a secondary or 'part-time' business such as *gîtes* or bed and breakfast, which are discussed under **Property Income** on page 191.

Before buying any property-based business you must do your homework thoroughly, particularly regarding the history and viability of the business. You must also be certain that you have or can acquire the skills necessary to run the business successfully. When taking over an existing and operating company, French labour law requires new owners to respect existing employment contracts, which isn't a bad thing if you require help as experienced staff are priceless. However, you aren't compelled to employ staff if you cannot afford them.

As when buying any property, many people wear (thick) rose-tinted spectacles when seeking a business property in France and only really investigate the pros and cons after they have committed themselves. **Buying a business in France is a complicated undertaking that should be concluded only after taking expert legal and professional advice.** A number of companies are only too willing to help you through the jungle, but you should bear in mind that they are usually trying to sell you a business and aren't necessarily interested in whether you get a good deal or can make a success of it.

Goodwill & Premises: When buying certain businesses in France there are usually separate prices for the 'goodwill' and stock-in-trade (*fonds* or *fonds de commerce*) and the building or 'walls' (literally *murs*), e.g. the building housing a hotel or restaurant. If you don't buy the building, a separate rental contract (lease) must be negotiated. If possible, it's advisable to purchase a business with the building, particularly if you need to raise a loan. You can obtain a mortgage of up to 80 per cent on the bricks and mortar, but you must fund the goodwill yourself. Note that the protection afforded domestic tenants doesn't extend to business rentals. Therefore if you rent business premises it's essential to take legal advice regarding a lease, which *must* contain a right to rent clause to ensure the future value of the business.

Duty, Fees & Taxes: It's important to check the duty, fees and taxes payable when buying a business. Taking over the assets of a company such as the stock, the client list, business name, premises, (etc.) can be expensive with regard to taxes. Registration duty of around 18 per cent is payable on the transfer of most of the elements of a business (*fonds de commerce*) such as the immovable property, leasehold rights, furniture, fittings and equipment, business name, client list and licences. Stock is subject to 20.6 per cent VAT. Note that the authorities can reassess the value of a business if they consider that it's been undervalued and impose fines. The notary's (*notaire's*) fees when buying a business property are usually around 20 per cent of the purchase price.

Farms: In recent years an increasing number of foreigners have purchased farms in France, including many British, Dutch, German and Swiss buyers. The price of farming land varies considerably and is prohibitively expensive in some areas, while in others it's practically given away with farmhouses. In general, farmland is cheaper in France than in any other western European country. However, it isn't easy for foreigners to raise loans from French banks to buy farms and it's common to buy the farm buildings and rent the land. Note that if you're seriously under-capitalised, as many farmers are, your chances of success are remote. Young farmers under 35 years with recognised farming qualifications can obtain financial incentives to buy farms in France including government grants and low interest loans. Information and advice on any aspect of farming can be obtained from the *Fédération Nationale des Sociétés d'Aménagement Foncier et d'Etablissement Rural (FNSAFER)*, 3, rue de Turin, 75008 Paris (☎ 01.42.93.66.06), which advises and controls all transactions of agricultural land in France and has regional offices throughout the country. Information about grants can be obtained from the *Centre Nationale pour l'Aménagement des Structures des Expositions*, 7, rue Ernest Renan, BP 1, 92136 Issy les Moulineaux Cedex (☎ 01.46.48.40.00).

More foreigners have had their fingers burnt buying farms or farming land than any other property-based business venture in France. As in all countries, farming in France is fraught with problems, particularly the vagaries of the weather (e.g.

droughts, floods, frosts, etc.), declining food prices and under-capitalisation. Many foreign farmers have fled with their tails between their legs within a few years, having learnt the reality of French farming the hard way (it isn't for nothing that the French are deserting their farms in droves). **Although rare, you should be aware that there's open hostility to foreign farmers in some regions and there have been a number of reports of foreigners being sold substandard stock (cull cattle) and land, and some have even had their crops sabotaged!** Problems are more likely in remote regions where the locals are unused to foreigners and are often insular or even xenophobic.

Vineyards: There are usually vineyards for sale in most wine-producing regions and there have been a number of bargains around in recent years, although you're unlikely to find a *premier grand cru* Bordeaux or Burgundy property for sale (and if you did you would need a King's ransom to buy it). Buying and operating a vineyard isn't something to be taken lightly as it requires a lot of hard work and resources. It's essential to hire experienced staff if you're inexperienced, as it take years to become a viticulture expert. Nevertheless, if you're successful the financial rewards can be enormous as a number of Australian, British and Swiss owners can testify.

There are restrictions or prohibitions on planting new vines in many areas due to over-production and therefore if you wish to expand production it's essential to buy a vineyard which already has the necessary permits. As with all farming, the weather is the biggest threat to your livelihood and a frost in late spring can destroy the entire grape crop overnight. Vineyard prices vary enormously, e.g. from around 70,000F a hectare for an *appellation* red wine vineyard in an average area, e.g. Bergerac in the Dordogne, to over 250,000F a hectare for a top quality vineyard in a good area. White wine vineyards are generally cheaper than red wine vineyards. Note that the sale price of a vineyard doesn't usually include current wine stocks, which must usually be purchased separately. A commercial property is likely to be owned by a company, which is cheaper to buy in terms of transaction costs. FNSAFER (see above) also assists foreigners seeking to buy a vineyard in France. See also **Self-Employment** on page 20 and **Starting a Business** on page 21.

FEES

A variety of fees (also called closing or completion costs) are payable when you buy a property in France, which vary considerably depending on the price, whether you're buying via an agent or a *notaire* (or direct from the vendor), and whether you have employed a lawyer or other professionals. Most property fees are based on the 'declared' value of the property, which may be less than the purchase price or its 'market' value. You should never be tempted to under-declare the price in order to pay lower fees as it can have serious consequences if it's discovered (see **Avoiding Problems** on page 128).

The mandatory fees associated with buying a property in France that's over five years old are among the highest in Europe and include stamp duty (*droits d'enregistrement*), land registry fees and the *notaire's* fees. All are payable on the completion of a sale (or before) and most are subject to VAT at 20.6 per cent. They are usually around 10 per cent for an old property and from 3 to 4 per cent for a new property, although total fees for an old property can 15 per cent or higher if you have a French mortgage and buy through an agent. In recent years the taxes payable on both new and old properties have been reduced to boost sales, although it has had only limited impact. Before signing a preliminary contract, check exactly what fees are payable and how much they are, and have them confirmed in writing.

Stamp Duty: Stamp duty (*droits d'enregistrement*) varies depending on whether you're buying a new or an 'old' property. On a 'old' property over five years old (on which TVA has previously been paid) stamp duty is around 6 per cent, which comprises 4.2 to 5 per cent departmental tax (*taxe départmentale*) and 1.2 per cent communal tax (*taxe communale/locale*). Regional tax (*taxe régionale*) was abolished on residential property in 1999. The stamp duty on property less than five years old (on which TVA applies) is 0.6 per cent. Duty on building plots (and commercial property) purchased by individuals is 3.6 per cent plus 1.2 per cent communal tax (total 4.8 per cent), but VAT is no longer payable.

Notaire's Fees: The *notaire's* conveyance fees are levied on a sliding scale as shown below:

Portion of Purchase Price	Fee
up to 20,000F	5%
20,001F to 40,000F	3.3%
40,001F to 110,000F	1.65%
over 110,000F	0.825%

Based on the above rates the *notaire's* fees for a property costing 400,000F would be 5,207.5F (or around 1.3 per cent).

Land Registry Fee: There's a fee of around 1 per cent of the sale price for registration of a property older than five years at the land registry (*bureau des hypothèques*) and 0.6 per cent (of the price exclusive of VAT) for new properties built within the last five years.

Value Added Tax (VAT): VAT (TVA) at 20.6 per cent is included in the purchase price of properties less than five years old when they are sold for the first time. If you sell a new property within five years, you must pay TVA on any profit (plus capital gains tax). Since 1998 there has been no VAT on building plots purchased by individuals.

Selling Agent's Commission: An estate agent's fees (see page 158) in France may be paid by the vendor, the buyer or they may be shared, although it's usual for the vendor to pay. However, when the selling 'agent' is a *notaire,* his commission is always paid by the buyer. Before signing a contract, check who must pay the selling agent's fees and what they will be.

Mortgage Fees: Mortgage fees may include a commitment fee, an arrangement fee (*frais de dossier*), which is usually 1 per cent of the loan amount, an administration fee (e.g. 1 per cent), and an appraisal or valuation fee. There's also a fee payable to the *notaire* for registration of the mortgage at the *bureau des hypothèques*, which amounts to around two-thirds of the conveyance fees listed above.

Miscellaneous Fees: Other fees may include legal fees, surveyor's or inspection fees, architect's fees, and utility connection and registration fees.

Running Costs: In addition to the fees associated with buying a property you must also take into account the running costs. These include local property taxes (rates); building and contents insurance (see page 57); standing charges for utilities (electricity, gas, telephone, water); community fees for a community property (see page 152); garden and pool maintenance; plus a caretaker's or management fees if you leave a home empty or let it. Annual running costs usually average around 2 to 3 per cent of the cost of a property.

BUYING A NEW HOME

France's bold and innovative architecture, as portrayed in its many striking public buildings, doesn't often extend to private dwellings, many of which seem to have been designed by the same architect. However, although new properties may lack the charm and character of older buildings, they offer attractive financial and other advantages. These include a lower deposit (5 per cent rather than 10 per cent), cheaper conveyancing fees (3 to 4 per cent rather than 10 to 15 per cent), lower property taxes, a 10-year warranty, and no costs or problems associated with renovation or modernisation. It's often cheaper to buy a new home than restore a derelict property, as the price is fixed, unlike the cost of renovation which can soar way beyond original estimates (as many people have discovered to their cost!). If required, a new property can usually be let immediately and modern homes have good resale potential and are considered a good investment by French buyers. On the other hand, new homes are usually smaller than old properties, have smaller gardens and rarely come with a large plot of land.

The standard of new buildings in France is strictly regulated and houses are built to official quality standards. They are built to higher specifications than old houses and usually include double-glazing; roof, cavity and under-floor insulation; central heating; and ventilation and dehumidifying systems. Most new buildings use low maintenance materials and must (by law) have good insulation and ventilation, providing lower heating bills and keeping homes cooler in summer. New properties are also covered by a 10-year warranty (*garantie décennale*) against structural defects and it's against the law to sell a new house without a warranty. Other systems and equipment are covered by a minimum two-year warranty. The French government encourages the building of new energy-efficient homes and France builds more new homes than most other European countries (some 60 per cent of French homes have been built since 1945). Security is a top priority for most new developments (which usually have security gates) and homes often have security blinds and other security features.

A new house is generally defined as one built in the last five years. Value added tax (TVA) at 20.6 per cent is included in the price of properties less than five years old when they are sold for the first time. The buyer also pays conveyancing and other fees of around 3 to 4 per cent of the price. In recent years the taxes payable on new (and old) properties have been reduced for a limited period to boost sales, although it has had only limited impact. If you sell a new property within five years, the buyer will also pay reduced *notaire's* fees, although you must pay TVA on any profit plus capital gains tax. New buildings have two years exemption from property tax (*taxe foncière*).

A huge variety of new properties are available in France including homes in coastal and city apartments and rural sports developments (e.g. skiing or golf), and a wide range of individually-designed, detached houses. Many new properties are part of purpose-built developments, often located near the coast or in the mountains, and encompassing a range of sports facilities that may include a golf course, swimming pool, tennis and squash courts, a gymnasium or fitness club and a restaurant. Some even have their own village and shops. Note, however, that many of these developments are planned as holiday homes and they may not be attractive as permanent homes (they are also generally expensive). If you're buying an apartment or house that's part of a development, check whether your neighbours will be mainly French or other foreigners. Some people don't wish to live in a *commune* of their fellow countrymen and this will also deter French buyers when you want to sell. Prices of new properties vary considerably depending on their location and quality, from around 300,000F for a studio or one-bedroom apartment in a resort, 400,000F to 500,000F for a two-bedroom cottage or townhouse, and from around 600,000F for a four-bedroom house. The cost of land is usually extra when buying a detached, one family home on its own plot.

Most new properties are sold by developers (*promoteurs*) and builders, although they are also marketed by estate agents. All new developments and builders must be underwritten by a bank (*garantie extrinsèque*) or the developer himself (*garantie intrinsèque*) providing he meets certain liquidity and other requirements. These guarantees are known as *garantie d'achèvement* and protect buyers from defaulting builders and developers. Where applicable, the deposit is made out to the underwriting bank and cannot be used by the developer. It's possible to check a developer's financial status, although your best insurance when buying a new property is the reputation of the developer or builder. Most new developments have a sales office (*bureaux de vente*) and a show house or apartment (*maison/appartement témoin*).

When buying a new property in a development, you're usually obliged to buy it off-plan (*vente en état futur d'achèvement*), also confusingly called 'on plan', i.e. before it's built. In fact, if a development is built and largely unsold, particularly a quality development in a popular area, it usually means that there's something wrong with it! The contract (*contrat de réservation* or more correctly *contrat préliminaire*) is subject to a cooling-off period of seven days from the date of receipt of a registered letter of notification, which usually accompanies a copy of the signed contract. The contract contains the timetable for the property's completion; payment dates; the completion date and penalties for non-completion; guarantees for building work; and a copy of the plans and drawings. The floor plan and technical specifications are signed by both parties to ensure that the standard and size of construction is adhered to. The vendor is referred to as the *réservant* (reserving party) and the buyer as the *réservataire*.

Payments are spread over 12 to 18 months, with a typical payment schedule shown below (although they can vary considerably):

Payment	Stage
5%	initial deposit
30%	completion of foundations
30%	completion of roof (waterproofing)
5%	connection of water and services
10%	completion of internal walls
10%	tiling and completion of wall surfaces
5%	final completion
5%	delivery of keys

If completion isn't planned for at least two years the deposit (*dépôt de garantie*) is 2.5 per cent. The final 5 per cent may be retained by the buyer if there are any defects still to be rectified or there's a dispute over performance of the contract. The *notaire's* fees are usually paid on completion of the foundations.

If you're buying a property off-plan, you can usually choose your bathroom suite, kitchen, fireplace, wallpaper, paint, wall and floor tiles, and carpet in bedrooms, all of which may be included in the price. You may also be able to alter the interior room layout, although this will increase the price. New homes usually contain a high level of 'luxury' features which may include tiled kitchens, deluxe bathroom suites, fitted cupboards, fitted kitchens (with dishwashers, cookers and refrigerators), smoke and security alarms, and optional coordinated interior colour schemes. New homes are usually, but not always, sold *décorée*, which means that they are decorated, have a fitted kitchen and are ready for occupation. Most developers will negotiate over the price or include 'free' extras (such as a fitted kitchen when it isn't included in the price), particularly if a development isn't selling well. Note that it's advisable to make any changes or additions to a property during the design stage, such as including an American kitchen, chimney or additional shower room, which will cost much more to install later.

If you want to be far from the madding crowd, you can buy a plot of land and have a house built to your own design or to a standard design provided by a French builder such as Ferinel, Maison Bouygues, Maison Individuelle or a small local builder (*pavilloner*). Builders usually also have a selection of building plots for sale. Although French builders have a range of standard designs, they will accommodate almost any interior or exterior variations (for a price), providing they are permitted under the local building codes. Shop around and compare prices, which can vary considerably (small family builders often provide the best value). If you want a wooden house, Troy Europe (☎ UK 01494-520883) build everything from 'sheds' to family-sized chalets, and Topsiders (☎ UK 0181-892 4503), an American company with a wealth of experience of building prefabricated timber homes, has a range of interesting designs. If you decide to build your own home, you must ensure that the proposed size and style of house is legal by checking the local commune's *Plan d'Occupation des Sols (POS)*. Don't rely on the builder or developer to do it for you, but check yourself or have your lawyer do it for you. If a mistake is made a building may need to be demolished!

Resale Homes: Buying new doesn't necessarily mean buying a brand new home where you're the first occupant. There are many advantages in buying a modern resale home which may include better value for money; an established development with a range of local services and facilities in place; more individual design and style; the eradication of 'teething troubles'; furniture and other extras included in the price; a mature garden and trees; and a larger plot of land. With a resale property you can see exactly what you will get for your money (unlike when buying off-plan), most problems will have been resolved, and the previous owners may have made improvements or added extras such as a swimming pool that may not be fully reflected in the asking price. The disadvantages of buying a resale home depend on its age and how well it has been maintained. They may include a poor state of repair and the need for refurbishment; few benefits of a new home unless it has been modernised; the need for redecorating and new carpets; poorer build quality and inferior design; no warranty, i.e. with a home that's over ten years old; termite or other infestations; and the possibility of incurring high assessments for repairs in community properties.

BUYING AN OLD HOME

In France, the term 'old home' usually refers to a building that's pre-war and possibly hundreds of years old, and which is either in need of restoration and modernisation or which has already been restored. It also refers, at least as far as the fees associated with buying a property are concerned, to any property over five years old that has already had at least one owner. If you want a property with abundant charm and character, a building for renovation or conversion, outbuildings, or a large plot of land, you must usually buy an old property. In many rural areas it's still possible to buy old properties for as little as 100,000F to 200,000F, although you will need to carry out major renovation work, which may double or treble the price. Because the purchase price is often low, many foreign buyers are lulled into a false sense of security and believe they are getting a wonderful bargain, without fully investigating the renovation costs. **Bear in mind that renovation or modernisation costs will invariably be higher than you imagined or planned!**

Old properties are often better value than new homes and there are some good bargains around, although you must carefully check their quality and condition. As with most things in life, you generally get what you pay for, so you shouldn't expect a fully restored property for 200,000F. At the other end of the scale, for those who can afford them there's a wealth of beautiful *châteaux*, manor houses and water mills, many costing no more than an average four-bedroom house in many other countries. However, if you aspire to live the life of the landed gentry in your own *château*, bear in mind that the reason there are so many on the market (and the seemingly low prices) is that the cost of restoration and upkeep is *astronomical*.

Although property is cheaper in France than in many other western European countries, most of the cheaper rural homes require complete renovation and modernisation. Some even lack basic services such as electricity, a reliable water supply and sanitation. If you're planning to buy a property that needs restoration or renovation, obtain an *accurate* estimate of the costs *before* signing a contract. As a rough guide, a property in need of total restoration is likely to cost as much to restore as it does to buy, e.g. a 200,000F house will eventually cost 400,000F and may cost you much more.

Don't buy a derelict property unless you have the courage, determination and money to overcome the many problems you will certainly face. **Taking on too large a task in terms of restoration is a common mistake among foreign buyers in all price ranges.** Unless you're prepared to wait until you can occupy it or are willing to live in a caravan for a long time while you work on it, it's best to spend a bit more and buy something habitable but untidy, rather than a property that needs completely gutting before you can live in it. Note that although many old rural properties are described as *habitable*, this word should immediately set the alarm bells ringing as it has an infinite number of interpretations in French. The *Concise Oxford Dictionary* ventures: 'that can be inhabited', which doesn't help much (a field can be inhabited if you have a tent). In French *habitable* can mean anything from derelict and unfit for pigs to something that just needs redecorating. When a property is described as *habitable* you should be prepared to ask a lot of questions and should ensure that it means exactly what you need it to mean.

Bear in mind that if you buy and restore a property with the intention of selling it for a profit, you must take into account not only the initial price and the restoration costs, but also the fees and taxes included in the purchase, plus capital gains tax if it's a second home. It's difficult to sell an old renovated property at a higher than average market price, irrespective of its added value. The French have little interest in old restored properties, which is an important point if you need to sell an old home in a hurry in an area that isn't popular with foreign buyers. If you want to make a profit you're better off buying a new home.

If you aren't into do-it-yourself in a big way, you're usually better off buying a property that has already been partly or wholly restored. This often works out cheaper in the long run, as the cost of restoration (to say nothing of the sweat) is rarely fully reflected in the sale price. If you need to pay for the whole cost of restoration it can be prohibitively expensive (see **Renovation & Restoration** on page 170). If you want a restored home, you're usually better off buying one from a foreigner, such as a Briton, who has lovingly and sensitively restored it, rather than from someone who has transformed it out of all recognition.

COMMUNITY PROPERTIES

In France, properties with common elements (whether a building, amenities or land) shared with other properties are owned outright through a system called co-ownership (*copropriété*), similar to owning a condominium in the USA. Community properties include apartments, townhouses, and detached (single-family) homes on a private estate with communal areas and facilities. Almost all French properties that are part of a development are owned *en copropriété*. In general, the only properties that don't belong to a community are detached houses on individual plots in public streets or on rural land. Under the system of *copropriété*, owners of community properties not only own their homes (*parties privatives*), but also a share (*quote-part*) of the common elements (*parties communes*) of a building or development including foyers, hallways, lifts, patios, gardens, roads, and leisure and sports facilities.

Some 45 per cent of the French population live in apartments, which are common in cities and resorts (or anywhere building land is limited). Many community developments are located near coastal or mountain resorts and they may offer a wide range of communal facilities including a golf course, swimming pools, tennis and squash courts, a gymnasium or fitness club, and a restaurant. Most also have landscaped gardens, high security and a full-time caretaker (*gardien/gardienne*), and some even have their own 'village' and shops. At the other extreme, some developments consist of numerous cramped, tiny studio apartments. Note that community developments planned as holiday homes may not be attractive as permanent homes.

Advantages: The advantages of owning a community property include increased security; lower property taxes than detached homes; a range of community sports and leisure facilities; community living with lots of social contacts and the companionship of close neighbours; no garden, lawn or pool maintenance; fewer of the responsibilities of home ownership; ease of maintenance; and they are often situated in locations where owning a single-family home would be prohibitively expensive, e.g. a beach-front or town centre.

Disadvantages: The disadvantages of community properties may include excessively high community fees (owners may have no control over increases); restrictive rules and regulations; a confining living and social environment and possible lack of privacy; noisy neighbours (particularly if neighbouring apartments are rented to holidaymakers); limited living and storage space; expensive covered or secure parking; and acrimonious owners' meetings, where management and factions may try to push through unpopular proposals (sometimes using proxy votes).

Before buying a *copropriété* property it's advisable to ask current owners about the community. For example do they like living there, what are the fees and restrictions, how noisy are other residents, are the recreational facilities easy to access, would they buy there again (why or why not), and, most importantly, is the community well managed. You may also wish to check on your prospective neighbours. If you're planning to buy an apartment above the ground floor, you may wish to ensure that the building has a lift. Note that upper floor apartments are both colder in winter and warmer in summer and incur extra charges for the use of lifts. They do, however, offer more security than ground floor apartments. Note that an apartment that has apartments above and below it will generally be more noisy than a ground or top floor apartment.

Cost: Prices vary considerably depending on the location, for example from around 300,000F for a studio or one-bedroom apartment in an average location to millions of francs for a luxury apartment or townhouse in a prime location. Garages and parking spaces must often be purchased separately in developments, with a lock-up garage usually costing between 60,000F and 90,000F and a parking space from 20,000F to 30,000F. If you're buying a resale property, check the price paid for similar properties in the same area or development in recent months, but bear in mind that the price you pay may have more to do with the seller's circumstances than the price fetched by other properties. Find out how many properties are for sale in a particular development; if there are many on offer you should investigate why, as there could be management or structural problems. If you're still keen to buy you can use any negative aspects to drive a hard bargain. Under a recent law (Carrez), the exact surface area (excluding cellars, garages, parking areas or anything less than 8m²) must be stated in the preliminary contract.

Management: The management and co-ownership of a *copropriété* building is regulated by French law and the rules and regulations are contained in a document called the *règlement de copropriété*. If you don't understand it you should have it explained or get it translated. All decisions relating to the management and upkeep of a community development are decided by a general committee (*syndicat des copropriétaires*) presided over by a manager (*gérant/syndic*). He's responsible for the management, efficient daily running and the apportioning of charges relating to the building, e.g. insurance, repairs and maintenance. The *syndic* bills individual owners for service charges and management fees. A syndicat must hold a meeting at least once a year to approve the budget, discuss other matters of importance such as capital expenditure and, if necessary, appoint a new *syndic*. Owners must be given 15 days notice by registered letter of the annual meeting or a special meeting and the opportunity to place items on the agenda no later than six days before the meeting. All decisions are made by a majority vote. Owners who are unable to attend may vote by proxy.

Community Fees: Owners must pay service charges for the upkeep of communal areas and for communal services. Charges are calculated according to each owner's share of the development and not whether they are temporary or permanent residents. For example, 20 apartments of equal size in an apartment block would each pay 5 per cent of the community fees. General charges include such services as caretaking, upkeep of the garden and surrounds, swimming pool maintenance and refuse collection. In addition to general charges, there may also be special charges for collective services and common equipment such as lifts, central heating and hot water, which may be divided according to the share of the utility allocated to each apartment. Fees vary considerably and can be relatively high for luxury developments with a range of amenities such as a swimming pool and tennis courts, e.g. 6,000F a year for a two-room apartment and double this for a four-room property. However, high fees aren't necessarily a negative point (assuming you can afford them), providing you receive value for money and the community is well managed and maintained. The value of a community property depends to a large extent on how well the development is maintained and managed.

Check the level of general and special charges before buying an apartment. Service charges are usually billed each quarter (although this varies) and the amount is adjusted at the end of the year when the annual accounts have been approved by the committee. If you're buying a resale apartment, ask to see a copy of the service charges for previous years and the minutes of the last annual general meeting, as owners may be 'economical with the truth' when stating service charges, particularly if they are high. When buying a *copropriété* property the managing agent should send the *notaire* handling the sale a statement of the seller's account regarding the payment of community fees and any work in progress, but not yet completed (for which owners are liable). The vendor should obtain a *certificat de l'article 20* stating that he doesn't owe any money to the *copropriété*, otherwise the *notaire* must withhold payment to cover any fees due.

Maintenance & Repairs: If necessary owners can be assessed an additional amount to make up any shortfall of funds for maintenance or repairs. You should check the condition of the common areas (including all amenities) in an old development and whether any major maintenance or capital expense is planned for which you could be assessed. Beware of bargain apartments in buildings requiring a lot of maintenance work or refurbishment (note that properties in ski resorts usually require more maintenance than those is coastal areas). However, under French law, disclosure of impending expenditure must be made to prospective buyers before they sign a contract. Owners' meetings can become rather heated when finances are discussed, particularly when assessments are being made to finance capital expenditure.

Restrictions: The rules and regulations (*règlement de copropriété*) governing a *copropriété* development allow owners to run their community in accordance with the wishes of the majority, while at the same time safeguarding the rights of the minority. Rules usually include such things as noise levels; the keeping of pets (usually permitted); renting; exterior decoration and plants (e.g. the placement of shrubs); rubbish disposal; the use of swimming pools and other recreational facilities; parking; business or professional use; and the hanging of laundry. Permanent residents should avoid buying in a development with a high percentage of rental units, i.e. units that aren't owner-occupied. Check the regulations and discuss any restrictions with residents.

Holiday Apartments: If you're buying a holiday apartment that will be vacant for long periods (particularly in winter), don't buy in an apartment block where heating and/or hot water charges are shared, otherwise you will be paying towards your co-owners' heating and hot water bills. You should also check whether there are any rules regarding short or long-term rentals or leaving a property unoccupied for any length of time. Note that when buying in a large development, communal facilities may be inundated during peak periods, e.g. a large swimming pool won't look so big when 100 people are using it and getting a game of tennis or using a fitness room may be difficult.

TIMESHARE & PART-OWNERSHIP SCHEMES

If you're looking for a holiday home abroad, you may wish to investigate a scheme that provides sole occupancy of a property for a number of weeks each year. These include co-ownership, leaseback, timesharing and a holiday property bond. **Don't rush into any of these schemes without fully researching the market and before you're absolutely clear what you want and what you can realistically expect to get for your money.**

Co-Ownership: Co-Ownership (*bi-propriété*) includes schemes such as a consortium of buyers owning shares in a property-owning company and co-ownership between family, friends or even strangers. Some developers offer a turn-key deal whereby a home is sold fully furnished and equipped. Co-ownership allows you to recoup your investment in savings on holiday costs and still retain your equity in the property. A common deal is a 'four-owner' scheme (which many consider to be the optimum number of co-owners), where you buy a quarter of a property and can occupy it for up to three months a year. However, there's no reason why there cannot be as many as 12 co-owners, with a month's occupancy each per year (usually shared between high, medium and low seasons).

Co-ownership provides access to a size and quality of property that would otherwise be unimaginable, and it's even possible to have a share in a substantial *château*, where a number of families could live together simultaneously and hardly ever see each other if they didn't want to. Co-ownership can be a good choice for a family seeking a holiday home for a few weeks or months a year and has the added advantage that (because of the lower cost) a mortgage may be unnecessary. Note that it's cheaper to buy a property privately with friends than through a developer, when you may pay well above the market price for a share of a property (check the market value of a property to establish whether it's good value). **Co-ownership is _much_**

better value than a timeshare and needn't cost much more. Note, however, that a water-tight contract must be drawn up by an experienced lawyer to protect the co-owners' interests.

One of the best ways to get into co-ownership, if you can afford it, is to buy a house yourself and offer shares to others. This overcomes the problem of getting together a consortium of would-be owners and trying to agree on a purchase in advance, which is difficult unless it's just a few friends or family members. You can form a French company (*Société Civile Immobilière*) to buy and manage the property that can in turn be owned by a company in the co-owners' home country, thus allowing for any disputes to be dealt with under local law. Each co-owner is given a number of shares according to how much he has paid, entitling him to so many weeks occupancy a year. Owners don't need to have equal shares and can all be made direct title holders. If a co-owner wishes to sell his shares, he must give first refusal to other co-owners. However, if they don't wish to buy them and a new co-owner cannot be found (which is unlikely), the property must be sold.

Sale & Leaseback: Sale and leaseback (*nouvelle propriété/propriété allégée*) schemes are designed for those seeking a holiday home for a limited number of weeks each year. Properties sold under a leaseback scheme are always located in popular resort areas, e.g. golf, ski or coastal resorts, where self-catering accommodation is in high demand. Buying a property through a leaseback scheme allows you to buy a new property at less than its true cost, e.g. 30 per cent less than the list price. In return for the discount the property must be leased back to the developer, usually for 9 to 11 years, so that he can let it as self-catering holiday accommodation. The buyer (in effect) becomes the landlord and qualifies for a refund of the VAT (20.6 per cent) that was included in the purchase price. The developer pays the buyer all the holiday rental in advance by adding a further percentage to the VAT refund, therefore instead of paying the full price the buyer is given a discount (e.g. 25 or 30 per cent) off the purchase price. The buyer owns the freehold of the property and the full price is shown in the title deed.

The buyer is also given the right to occupy the property for a period each year, usually six or eight weeks, spread over high, medium and low seasons. These weeks can usually be let to provide income or possibly even exchanged with accommodation in another resort (as with a timeshare scheme). The developer furnishes and manages the property and pays all the maintenance and bills (e.g. for utilities) during the term of the lease (even when the owner is in occupation). **Note that it's important to have a contract checked by your legal adviser to ensure that you receive vacant possession at the end of the leaseback period, <u>without</u> having to pay an indemnity charge, otherwise you could end up paying more than a property is worth.**

Timesharing: Timesharing (*multipropriété*, but also called *interpropriété, polypropriété, pluripropriété, multijouissance* and *multivacances*) isn't as popular in France as in some other countries, notably Spain and the USA (particularly Florida). In France timeshare owners purchase a right to occupy a property (*jouissance*) at designated times. Since 1986, timeshare properties have been owned by a limited company such as a *Société Civile Immobilière (SCI)*, in which owners hold voting shares intended to give them a say in how a property is managed. However, this is impractical when owners are spread around France or further afield and management is generally performed completely arbitrarily by a developer or agent.

Timesharing (also called 'holiday ownership', 'vacation ownership' and 'holidays for life') has earned a poor reputation in the last few decades, although things are slowly improving. In recent years the Organisation for Timeshare in Europe (OTE) has been trying to restore respectability to timesharing and its members (which include France) are bound by a code of conduct. This includes a requirement that buyers have secure occupancy rights and that their money is properly protected prior to the completion of a new property. Since April 1997, an EU Directive has required timeshare companies to disclose information about the vendor and the property, and allow prospective buyers a 'cooling off period' during which they may cancel any sales agreement they have signed without penalty. However, although the directive technically binds timeshare companies, if they flout it you'll need to seek redress in a court of law, which may not be something you want (or can afford) to do!

The best timeshare developments are on a par with luxury hotels and offer a wide range of facilities including bars, restaurants, entertainment, shops, swimming pools, tennis courts, health clubs, and other leisure and sports facilities. If you don't wish to take a holiday in the same place each year, choose a timeshare development that's a member of an international organisation such as Resort Condominium International (RCI) or Interval International (II), which allow you (usually for a fee) to exchange your timeshare with one in another area or country. The highest rated RCI timeshares are classified as Gold Crown Resorts and allow you to exchange with any timeshare anywhere in the world (RCI has over 2,000 member resorts in some 70 countries).

France isn't plagued by the timeshare touts common in some other countries (such as Spain). However, you may be 'invited' to a presentation in a popular resort and should know what to expect. If you're tempted to attend a sales pitch (usually lasting at least two hours), you should be aware that you may be subjected to some of the most persuasive, high-pressure sales methods employed anywhere on earth and many people are simply unable to resist (the sales staff are experts). If you do attend, don't take any cash, credit cards or cheque books with you so that you won't be pressured into paying a deposit without thinking it over. Although it's illegal for a timeshare company to accept a deposit during the 10-day cooling-off period, many companies will try to get you to pay one. Don't rely on being able to get your money back if you pay by credit card. If you pay a deposit your chances of getting it back are slim and if it's repaid, it's likely to take a long time. Bear in mind that of those who agree to buy a timeshare, around half cancel within the cooling-off period.

A personal guarantee must be provided by a timeshare company that the property is as advertised and, where applicable, the contract must be in the language of the EU country where the buyer is resident or the language of the buyer's choice (you cannot sign away any of your rights irrespective of what's written in the contract). If you're an EU citizen and get into a dispute, you can take legal action in your home country for a sale made in France. There are so many scams associated with timeshares that it would take a dedicated book to recount them all (and you would need to update it every few months!). **Suffice to say that many people bitterly regret the day they signed up for a timeshare!**

It isn't difficult to understand why there are so many timeshare companies and why salespersons often employ such intimidating, hard-sell methods. A week's timeshare in an apartment worth around 500,000F can be sold for up to 80,000F, making a total income of some 4,000,000F for the timeshare company if they sell 50 weeks (eight times the market value of the property!), plus management and other fees. **Most experts believe that there's little or no advantage in a timeshare over** a normal holiday rental and that it's simply an expensive way to pay for your holidays in advance. It doesn't make any sense to tie up your money for what amounts to a long-term reservation on an annual holiday.

Top-quality timeshares usually cost up to 80,000F for one week in a one or two-bedroom apartment in a top-rated resort at a peak period, to which must be added annual management fees, e.g. 1,500F to 2,000F a week, plus other miscellaneous charges. Most financial advisers believe that you're better off putting your money into a long-term investment, where you retain your capital and may even earn sufficient interest to pay for a few weeks holiday each year. If you wish to buy a timeshare, it's best to buy a resale privately from an existing owner or from a timeshare resale broker, which sell for a fraction of their original cost. When buying privately you can usually drive a hard bargain and may even get a timeshare 'free' simply by assuming the current owner's maintenance contract.

Often timeshares are difficult or impossible to sell at any price and 'pledges' from timeshare companies to sell them for you or buy them back at the market price are usually just a sales ploy, as timeshare companies aren't interested once they have made a sale. **Note that there's no real resale market for timeshares and if you need to sell you're highly unlikely to get your money back.** Further information about timesharing can be obtained from the Timeshare Council (☎ UK 0171-821 8845) and the Timeshare Helpline (☎ UK 0181-296 0900) in Britain. The Timeshare Consumers Association (Hodsock, Worksop, Notts, S81 0TF, UK, ☎ 01909-591100, e-mail: tca@netcomuk.co.uk) publish a useful booklet entitled *Timeshare: Guide to Buying, Owning and Selling*.

A **Holiday Property Bond** is a good alternative to timesharing for those with a minimum of around GB£2,000 to invest. Holiday Property Bond (operated by Villa Owners Club Ltd., HPB House, Newmarket, Suffolk CB8 8EH, UK, ☎ 01638-660066) owns over 600 properties in some ten countries, including France. Each GB£1 invested is equal to one point and each week's stay in each property is assigned a points rating depending on its size, location and the time of year. There are no extra fees apart from a 'user' charge when occupying a property to cover cleaning and utility costs. Furthermore, there's a buy-back guarantee after two years, when an investment can be sold at the market value.

ESTATE AGENTS

Unlike many other countries, only some 50 per cent of property sales in France are handled by (real) estate agents (*agent immobilier*). The other 50 per cent are directly between vendors and buyers or are handled by *notaires*. However, where foreign buyers are concerned the vast majority of sales are made through agents. It's common for foreigners in many countries, particularly Britain, to use an agent in their own country who works with one or more French agents. A number of French agents also advertise abroad, particularly in the publications listed in **Appendix A**, and many have English-speaking staff (so don't be discouraged if you don't speak fluent French). If you want to find an agent in a particular town or area, look under estate agents (*immobilier*) in the local French Yellow Pages (available at main libraries in many countries).

Qualifications: French estate agents are regulated by law and must be professionally qualified and licensed and hold indemnity insurance. To work in his own right in France, an agent must possess a *carte professionnelle*, which is granted only to those with certain professional qualifications or considerable experience. You shouldn't view properties with anyone who cannot produce a *carte professionnelle* (or who isn't employed by someone with one), as if you have an accident while visiting a property you won't be able to claim unless an agent is legal and registered. Very few foreign agents in France possess the coveted *carte professionnelle*. There are a number of unlicensed illegal agents operating in France, who should be avoided. Note that a *marchand de biens* is a property developer and speculator who's only permitted to sell property that he has owned for at least three months (some licensed real estate agents are also *marchand de biens*). Most French estate agents are members of a professional body such as the *Fédération Nationale des Agents Immobiliers et Mandataires (FNAIM)*, the leading French association of estate agents, or the *Syndicat National des Professionnels Immobiliers (SNPI)*.

Deposits: Never pay any money to an agent who isn't a holder of a *carte professionnelle*. Agents must be bonded in respect of the money they can hold on behalf of their clients and must display the sum of their financial guarantee (*pièce de garantie*). If it's less than 500,000F an agent isn't entitled to receive buyers' deposits, which must then be paid to a *notaire* (all of whom can hold deposits). **Ensure that you're dealing with an agent who fulfils these requirements and if in doubt ask to see his qualifications.**

Fees: There are no government controls on agents' fees, although they are obliged to post a list (*barème*) in their offices. The agent's commission is usually paid by the vendor and included in the purchase price. It's usually paid on a sliding scale between 5 and 10 per cent, e.g. 10 per cent on properties priced at 100,000F reducing to 5 per cent on properties costing one million francs or more (the cheaper the property, the higher the fee as a percentage of the sale). On the more expensive properties an agent's fee may be negotiable. An agent's fees may be paid by the vendor, the buyer or be shared, although it's normal for the vendor to pay. The term *net vendeur* is the amount the seller will receive, to which must be added fees such as the selling agent's or *notaire's* fees. Commission included (*commission comprise*, written as C/C) is the amount the seller receives including the agent's commission. Make sure when discussing the price that it's C/C and not *net vendeur*. Many foreign agents work with French agents and share the standard commission, so buyers usually pay no more by using a foreign agent. The agent's fee is usually payable on completion, but may be payable sooner. **When buying, check in advance whether you need to pay commission or any extras on top of the sale price (apart from the normal fees and taxes associated with buying a property in France).**

Notaries: Around 15 per cent of property sales in France are negotiated by notaries (*notaires*), who also have a monopoly on conveyancing (see page 163) for all property sales in France. *Notaires* have a strict code of practise and aren't, for example, permitted to display property details in their offices, and therefore most have a working relationship with a number of real estate agents. When a notaire is the selling agent his seller's commission *isn't* included in the asking price and is paid by the buyer. However, this doesn't cost the buyer any more as an estate agent's commission is usually included in the asking price and paid by the buyer, and the fees charged by a *notaire* are usually lower than those levied by estate agents (see above). For example 5 per cent up to 175,000F and 2.5 per cent above this figure. Although there may appear to be a conflict of interest when a *notaire* is instructed by the seller but receives his fee from the buyer, in practice there are usually no problems. VAT at 20.6 per cent must be added to all fees.

Viewing: If possible, you should decide where you want to live, what sort of property you want and your budget *before* visiting France. Obtain details of as many properties as possible in your chosen area and make a shortlist of those you wish to view (it's also advisable to mark them on a map). Usually the details provided by French estate agents are sparse and few agents provide detailed descriptions of properties. Often there's no photograph and even when there is, it usually doesn't do a property justice. Obviously with regard to many old properties in need of renovation, there isn't a lot that can be said apart from stating the land area and the number and size of all buildings. Note that there are no national property listings in France, where agents jealously guard their list of properties, although many work with overseas agents in areas popular with foreign buyers. French agents who advertise in foreign journals or who work closely with overseas agents usually supply coloured photographs and a full description, particularly for the more expensive properties. The best agents provide an abundance of information. Agents vary enormously in their efficiency, enthusiasm and professionalism. If an agent shows little interest in finding out exactly what you want, you should go elsewhere.

If you have made an appointment to see certain properties, make a note of their reference numbers in case the French agent hasn't been informed (or has lost them). Note, however, that it isn't unusual for a French agent's reference numbers not to match those you're given abroad! Some agents, particularly outside France, don't update their records frequently and their lists may be way out of date. If you're using a foreign agent, confirm (and reconfirm) that a particular property is still for sale and the price before travelling to France to view it.

Note that a French agent may ask you to sign a document (*bon de visite*) before showing you any properties, which is simply to protect his commission should you obtain details from another source or try to do a deal with the owner behind his back. Most French agents expect customers to know where they want to buy within a 30 to 40km (20 to 25mi) radius and some even expect them to narrow their choice down to certain towns or villages. If you cannot define where and what you're looking for, at least tell the agent so that he will know that you're undecided. If you're 'just looking' (window shopping), say so. Many agents will still be pleased to show you properties, as they are well aware that many people fall in love with (and buy) a property on the spot.

In France you're usually shown properties personally by agents and won't be given the keys (especially to furnished properties) or be expected to deal with tenants or vendors directly. One reason is that many properties are almost impossible to find if you don't know the area and it isn't unknown for agents to get hopelessly lost when looking for properties! Many rural properties have no numbers and street names are virtually non-existent (if someone invites you to dinner in rural France, make sure you have their telephone number for when you get lost).

You should make an appointment to see properties, as agents don't like people just turning up. **If you make an appointment, you should keep it or call and cancel it.** If you happen to be on holiday it's okay to drop in unannounced to have a look at what's on offer, but don't expect an agent to show you properties without an appointment. If you view properties during a holiday, it's advisable to do so at the beginning so that you can return later to inspect any you particularly like a second or third time. Note that French agents and *notaires* don't usually work during lunch hours and most close on Saturday afternoons, Sundays and possibly also on Mondays.

You should try to view as many properties as possible during the time available, but allow sufficient time to view each property thoroughly, to travel and get lost between houses, and for breaks for sustenance (it's *mandatory* to have a good lunch in France). Although it's important to see enough properties to form an accurate opinion of price and quality, don't see too many in one day (between six and eight is usually a manageable number), as it's easy to become confused as to the merits of each property. If you're shown properties that don't meet your specifications, tell the agent immediately. You can also help the agent narrow the field by telling him exactly what's wrong with the properties you reject.

It's advisable to make notes of both the good *and* bad features and take lots of photographs of the properties you like, so that you're able to compare them later at your leisure (but keep a record of which photos are of which house!). It's also shrewd to mark each property on a map so that should you wish to return, you can find them without getting lost (too often). The more a property appeals to you, the more you should look for faults and negative points; if you still like it after stressing all the negative points it must have special appeal.

INSPECTIONS & SURVEYS

When you have found a property that you like, you should make a close inspection of its condition. Obviously this will depend on whether it's a ruin in need of complete restoration, a property that has been partly or totally modernised, or a modern home. One of the problems with a property that has been restored is that you don't know how well the job has been done, particularly if the current owner did it himself. If work has been carried out by registered local builders, you should ask to see the bills, as all building work in France is guaranteed for ten years (*garantie décennale*).

Some simple checks you can do yourself include testing the electrical system, plumbing, mains water, hot water boiler and central heating. Don't take someone's word that these are functional, but check them for yourself. If a property doesn't have electricity or mains water, check the nearest connection point and the cost of extending the service to the property, as it can be *very* expensive in remote rural areas. If a property has a well or septic tank, you should have them tested. An old property may show visible signs of damage and decay, such as bulging or cracked walls, rising damp, missing roof slates (check it using binoculars) and rotten woodwork. Some areas are prone to flooding, storms and subsidence, and it's advisable to check an old property after a heavy rainfall, when any leaks should come to light. You may also wish to have a property checked for termites, which are found in over 50 departments.

You should ensure that a property over ten years old is structurally sound as it will no longer be covered by a warranty (warranties are transferable if a property is sold during the warranty period). Although France is noted for its high building standards, you should never assume that a building is sound, as even relatively new buildings can have serious faults (although rare). The cost of an inspection is a small price to pay for the peace of mind it affords. Some lenders insist on a 'survey' before approving a loan, although this usually consists of a perfunctory valuation to confirm that a property is worth the purchase price.

Although a vendor must certify that a property is free from 'hidden defects', this provides little assurance as he can usually just plead ignorance and it's usually difficult or expensive to prove otherwise. A Frenchman wouldn't make an offer on a property before at least having it checked by a builder. A master builder (*maître d'oeuvres*) will also be able to tell you whether the price is too high, given any work that needs to be done. If a property is pre-1945 a builder could be employed to check it for soundness, although an architect (*architecte*) is usually better qualified to check a modern house (unless he designed it himself!). Alternatively you can employ a professional valuer or surveyor (*expert immobilier*) who usually specialises in a particular segment of the property market, such as residential housing, commercial property or farmland. You can find a valuer through local real estate agents, architects or Yellow Pages, or failing that you can contact the *Chambres des Experts Immobiliers*, c/o FNAIM, 129, rue du Fauberg St-Honoré, 75008 Paris (☎ 01.42.25.24.26). You can also have a full structural survey (*le bilan de santé immobilier*) carried out, although this is rare in France. However, if you would have a survey carried out if you were buying the same property in your home country, then you should have one done in France. You will usually need to pay around 1,000F for a 'rough' appraisal (*expertise*) and from around 3,000F for a 'full' survey.

You may be able to make a 'satisfactory' survey a condition (*clause suspensive*) of the preliminary contract, although this isn't usual in France and a vendor may refuse or insist that you carry out a survey *before* signing the contract. If serious faults are revealed by the survey the *clause suspensive* should allow you to withdraw from the purchase and have your deposit returned. You may, however, be able to negotiate a satisfactory compromise with the vendor. If a property needs work doing on it to make it habitable, don't accept what you're told regarding the costs of repairs or restoration unless you have a binding quotation (*devis*) in writing from a local builder. One of the most common mistakes foreigners make when buying an old property in France is to underestimate the cost of restoration and modernisation (it bears repeating over and over again!). **You should obtain accurate estimates of renovation and modernisation costs before signing a contract** (see page 165).

Discuss with an 'inspector' exactly what will be included, and most importantly, what will be excluded (you may need to pay extra to include certain checks and tests). A general inspection should include the structural condition of all buildings, particularly the foundations, roofs, walls and woodwork; plumbing, electricity and heating systems; and anything else you want inspected such as a swimming pool and its equipment, e.g. a filter or heating system. A home inspection can be limited to a few items or even a single system only, such as the wiring or plumbing in an old house. You should receive a written report on the structural condition of a property, including anything that could become a problem in the future. Some surveyors will allow you to accompany them and they may produce a video of their findings in addition to a written report.

You may prefer to employ a British surveyor practising in France, who will write a report in English. However, a French surveyor (or other local expert) usually has an more intimate knowledge of local properties and building methods. If you employ a foreign surveyor, you must ensure that he's experienced in the idiosyncrasies of French properties and that he has professional indemnity insurance covering France (which means you can happily sue him if he does a bad job!).

Buying Land: Before buying a home on its own plot of land you should walk the boundaries and look for fences, driveways, roads, and the overhanging eaves of buildings that may be encroaching upon the property. If you're uncertain about the boundaries you should have the land surveyed, which is advisable in any case when buying a property with a large plot of land. When buying a rural property in France, you may be able to negotiate the amount of land you want to be included in the purchase. If a property is part of a larger plot of land owned by the vendor or the boundaries must be redrawn, you will need to hire a land surveyor (*géomètre expert*) to measure the land and draw up a new cadastral plan (*plan cadastral*). You should also check the *Plan d'Occupation des Sols (POS)* to find out what the land can be used for and any existing rights of way (*servitudes*). Since 1998 there has been no VAT on building plots purchased by individuals.

GARAGES & PARKING

A garage or private parking space isn't usually included in the price when you buy a new apartment or townhouse in France, although secure parking is usually available at an additional cost, possibly in an underground garage. Modern single-family homes usually have a garage or a basement (*sous-sol*) that can be used as a garage and cellar. Smaller homes usually have a single garage, while larger properties may have garaging for up to four cars. Parking isn't usually a problem when buying an old home in a rural area, although there may not be a purpose-built garage.

When buying an apartment or townhouse in a modern development, a lock-up garage usually costs an additional 60,000F to 90,000F and even a reserved parking space can cost 20,000F to 50,000F. Note that the cost of a garage or parking space isn't usually recouped when selling, although it makes a property more attractive. The cost of parking is an important consideration when buying in a town or resort in France, particularly if you have a number of cars. It may be possible to rent a garage or parking space, although this can be prohibitively expensive in cities. Bear in mind that in a large development the nearest parking area may be some distance from your home. This may be an important factor, particularly if you aren't up to carrying heavy shopping hundreds of metres to your home and possibly up several flights of stairs.

Note that without a private garage or parking space, parking can be a nightmare, particularly in cities or during the summer in busy resorts or developments. Free on-street parking may be difficult or impossible to find in cities and large towns, and in any case may be inadvisable for anything but a wreck. A lock-up garage is important in areas with a high incidence of car theft and theft from cars (e.g. most cities and popular resorts), and is also useful to protect your car from climatic extremes such as ice, snow and extreme heat.

CONVEYANCING

Conveyancing (the legal term is conveyance, although conveyancing is more widely used) is the legal term for processing the paperwork involved in buying and selling real property and transferring the deeds of ownership. In France, conveyancing is strictly governed by French law and can be performed only by a public notary (*notaire*) authorised by the Ministry of Justice and controlled by the *Chambre des Notaires*. There are around 5,000 *notaires'* offices (*études*) in France and some 7,500 *notaire's*. He (there are few women *notaires*) must follow a strict code of conduct and have a personal insurance covering his professional responsibility and guaranteeing clients against any errors he may make. He also has a financial guarantee covering money temporarily in his safekeeping (such as deposits). A *notaire* represents neither the seller nor the buyer, but the French government, and one of his main tasks is to ensure that all state taxes are paid on the completion of a sale. A *notaire* can act for a client anywhere in France.

Conveyancing includes ensuring that a proper title is obtained; arranging the necessary registration of the title; checking whether the land has been registered at the land registry; verifying that a property belongs to the vendor or that he has legal authority from the owner to sell it; checking that there isn't an outstanding loan larger than the selling price; verifying that there are no pre-emption rights or restrictive covenants over a property (such as rights of way); and checking that there are no plans to construct anything which would adversely affect the enjoyment or use of the property.

Note that a *notaire* checks only planned developments directly affecting a property itself and not those that may affect its value, such as a new railway line or *autoroute* in the vicinity. Obviously a new *autoroute* or railway that disturbs the peace of your home would be something of a disaster, although, on the other hand, an *autoroute* junction or TGV station within a few kilometres may enhance its value. There's no public service in France where you can find out this information, although you can contact the public works department (*Direction Départementale de l'Equipement/DDE*) and check building projects planned for the area. You could also ask the local residents, particularly the local mayor, who usually know of anything planned that would adversely affect a property.

In France, the vendor's *notaire* traditionally acts for both the vendor and buyer, although a buyer can insist on using his own *notaire*. It doesn't cost a buyer any more to engage his own *notaire,* as the two *notaires* work together and share the same fee. This is called a *concurrence* sale, as the two *notaires* are said to be in competition, although only one (the vendor's) can execute the deed. Although some people consider that it's always advisable to instruct your own *notaire*, this is rarely done as a *notaire* must remain strictly impartial (and it isn't encouraged by *notaire*s who don't like sharing their fees). One case where it would be prudent to engage your own *notaire* is when the vendor's *notaire* is also the selling agent.

Don't expect a *notaire* to speak English (few do) or any language other than French or to explain the intricacies of French property law. A *notaire* will rarely point out possible pitfalls in a contract, proffer advice or volunteer any information (as, for example, a real estate agent usually will). If you need additional legal advice, you should employ an experienced lawyer, either locally or in your home country (who must naturally be fluent in French and be an expert in French property law). He must also speak English or a language that you both speak fluently. Employing a lawyer is wise if you don't speak French fluently.

Before hiring a lawyer, compare the fees charged by a number of practises and get quotations in writing. Check what's included in the fee and whether it's 'full and binding' or just an estimate (a low basic rate may be supplemented by much more expensive 'extras'). A lawyer's fees may be calculated as an hourly rate (e.g. 1,000F an hour) or a percentage of the purchase price of a property, e.g. 1 to 2 per cent, with a minimum fee of 4,000F to 8,000F. You could employ a lawyer just to check the preliminary contract (see below) before signing it to ensure that it's correct and includes everything necessary, particularly regarding any necessary conditional clauses (*clauses/conditions suspensives*).

There are two main stages when a *notaire* usually becomes involved in a property purchase. The first is the signing of the preliminary contract (*compromis de vente*) and the second is the completion when the deed of sale (*acte de vente*) is signed. The *notaire* is responsible for ensuring that the sales contract is drawn up correctly and that the purchase price is paid to the vendor. He also witnesses the signing of the deed, arranges for its registration (in the name of the new owner) at the land registry (*cadastre*) and collects any fees and taxes due. Note that the *notaire* doesn't verify or guarantee the accuracy of statements made in a contract or protect you against fraud.

PURCHASE CONTRACTS

The first stage in buying a home in France is the signing of a preliminary contract. There are a number of different types of preliminary contracts depending on whether you're buying an existing (built) property or a new property off-plan, i.e. still to be built or under construction. There are two main types of preliminary contracts used to buy an existing property: a *promesse de vente*, which is common in northern France, and a *compromis de vente*, which is used more in the south. The *compromis* is usually regarded as the more appropriate for individuals and is the most widely used. The most common contract when buying off-plan is a reservation contract (*contrat de réservation*).

Note that you may not be able to dictate the type of contract used, which may vary depending on the particular agent or *notaire*. Agents and *notaires* usually have their own pre-printed contracts, although all contracts should follow a standard design. There are various other contracts including an offer of sale (*l'offre de vente*), an offer of purchase (*l'offre d'achat*), a promise to purchase (*promesse d'achat*) and an exchange of letters (*l'échange de lettres*), **all of which offer little protection to the buyer and should generally be avoided.**

Legal Advice: Note that the preliminary contract is usually binding on both parties and therefore it's important to obtain legal advice before signing it. Although it *isn't* necessary to employ a *notaire* when signing a preliminary contract, it's often advisable as he lends extra legal weight to a deal. **Most experts state that you should have a preliminary contract checked by your legal adviser before signing it.** One of the main reasons to engage a lawyer is to safeguard your interests through the insertion of any necessary conditional clauses (see page 167) in the preliminary contract, which are of little concern to a *notaire* or real estate agent. There are various other reasons to employ a lawyer, for example sometimes the best way to buy a property in France is through a French company such as a *Société Civile Immobilière* (see below) or you may wish to make special provisions regarding inheritance (see **Inheritance & Gift Tax** on page 104). The legal method used to buy French property has important consequences, particularly regarding French inheritance laws and it can be difficult or expensive to correct any errors later.

Buying an Existing Property: With a *compromis de vente*, a buyer is committed from the start and can legally be forced to go through with a purchase. A *promesse de vente* commits the seller to sell at an agreed price, but allows the buyer a period (usually up to three months) during which he can withdraw and forfeit his 10 per cent deposit. The contract includes full details of the property; the price to be paid; how it's to be financed; details of the vendor and buyer; the agent's commission (if applicable) and who will pay it; and the date of completion. Some French agents or *notaires* provide an English translation of a contract, although translations are often so bad as to be meaningless or misleading. You should ensure that you understand *every* clause in the preliminary contract.

Buying Off-Plan: The contract used when buying a new property off-plan is a *contrat de réservation* (or more correctly a *contrat préliminaire*). It's subject to a cooling-off period of seven days from the date of receipt of a registered letter of notification that usually accompanies a copy of the signed contract. The contract contains the timetable for the property's completion; payment dates; the completion date and penalties for non-completion; guarantees for building work; and a copy of the plans and drawings. The floor plan and technical specifications are signed by both parties to ensure that the standard and size of construction is adhered to.

Achat en Viager: Buying a property *achat en viager* usually involves paying a down payment (*bouquet*), e.g. equal to a third of its value, plus an annuity (*rente viagère*) until the death of the owner. It isn't necessary to pay a down payment, although if one isn't paid the annuity payments are higher. The annuity is usually paid in monthly or quarterly payments. The vendor usually remains in the home until his death (*viager occupé*), although he may vacate the property and allow the buyer (*débirentier*) free use of it (called a *viager libre*), in which case he will receive a higher annuity. The rent can be paid to two vendors, e.g. a husband and wife, and can be reduced on the first death or revert totally to the surviving spouse.

It's a gamble on the owner not living too long, in which the buyer usually wins. The annuity paid is based on the life expectancy of the vendor (the greater the life expectancy, the lower the annuity). An *achat en viager* sale permits elderly people to remain in their homes and maintain them in good condition, while at the same time supplementing their incomes, or alternatively allows them to move into a nursing home. It's also a well-known (legal) method of disinheriting children. The buyer must take into account the vendor's age, gender, and mental and physical health. In one famous case, Jeane Calment entered into a *rente viagère* when she was aged 90 and lived to over 120 and was the oldest woman in Europe (the buyer died before she did!).

Buying through a company: Buying a property in France through a French company such as a *Société Civile Immobilière (SCI)* can be beneficial, particularly when two or more people or families are buying between them or when you wish to partially circumvent French inheritance laws. An SCI is a property holding company and cannot trade. When a number of foreigners are buying a property together the SCI can in turn be owned by a company in their home country, thus allowing legal disputes to be dealt with under local law.

The principal advantages of an SCI are that its shares can be simply transferred to new owners and after the company has been established for three years stamp duty is lower than with direct transfers of property. On the death of an owner, shares in an SCI are treated as movable assets and can be bequeathed in accordance with the owner's domicile, thus avoiding the restrictions of French succession law (see **Wills** on page 106). However, French inheritance tax (see page 104) applies to the transfer of shares in an SCI upon death (assuming that the French property represents at least 50 per cent of the SCI's assets). A property owned under an SCI is also subject to French capital gains tax. Note also that if you let a property owned by an SCI, it may be necessary to pay a higher rate of tax on the rental income. Owning French property through an SCI is of little or no benefit to owners resident in France, as many of the advantages don't apply.

If you plan to own a property through an SCI it should be done at the outset, as it will be much more expensive to do it later. The costs of establishing an SCI are around 10,000F to 15,000F in addition to the normal fees. Buying a French property through a foreign or offshore company can result in being hit by various punitive French taxes and it may also incur high management fees. **Before buying a property through an SCI or any other company, it's important to weigh up the long-term advantages and disadvantages and to obtain expert legal advice.**

Conditional Clauses: All preliminary contracts, whether for old or new properties, contain a number of conditional clauses (*clauses/conditions suspensives*) that must be met to ensure the validity of the contract. Conditions usually apply to events out of control of the vendor or buyer, although almost anything the buyer agrees with the vendor can be included in a preliminary contract. If any of the conditions aren't met, the contract can be suspended or declared null and void, and the deposit returned. However, if you fail to go through with a purchase and aren't covered by a clause in the contract, you will forfeit your deposit or could even be compelled to go through with a purchase. Note that if you're buying anything from the vendor such as carpets, curtains or furniture that are included in the purchase price, you should have them listed and attached as an addendum to the contract. Any fixtures and fittings present in a property when you view it (and agree to buy it) should still be there when you take possession, unless otherwise stated in the contract (see also **Completion** on page 169).

There are many possible conditional clauses concerning a range of subjects, including the following:

● being able to obtain a mortgage;

- obtaining planning permission and building permits, e.g. for a septic tank;
- plans to construct anything (e.g. roads, railways, etc.) which would adversely affect the enjoyment or use of the property;
- confirmation of the land area being purchased with a property;
- pre-emption rights or restrictive covenants over a property (such as rights of way);
- dependence on the sale of another property;
- a satisfactory building survey or inspection.

Mortgage Clause: The most common conditional clause states that a buyer is released from the contract should he be unable to obtain a mortgage. This condition is compulsory for all property purchases under the 'Scrivener law' (*Loi Scrivener*). If you don't intend to obtain a loan, you're expected to endorse the contract to this effect in your own handwriting, meaning that you give up your rights under the law. Note, however, that this isn't always wise, even when you have no intention of obtaining a mortgage (you don't have to obtain a mortgage, even if you state that you're going to). If you give up your right to obtain a mortgage and later find that you need one but fail to obtain it, you will lose your deposit. The clause should state the amount, term and interest rate expected or already agreed with a lender, plus the lender's name (if known). If you cannot obtain a mortgage for the agreed amount and terms you won't lose your deposit. You must make an application for the loan within a certain time after signing the contract and have a specified period in which to secure it. Note, however, that if you're unable to obtain a loan for reasons that could have been reasonably foreseen, you can still lose your deposit.

Pre-emption/Business Use: If the plot on which a property is built or the land which is sold with a property is over 2,500m² (0.25 hectares or around half an acre), the *Fédération Nationale des Sociétés d'Aménagement Foncier et d'Etablissement Rural (FNSAFER)* must give permission for the sale. This is usually a formality unless you're buying a farm, a large estate or a vineyard. Note that it's necessary to inform the *notaire* handling the sale if you're planning to operate a commercial business from a property within three years of its purchase, as this will increase the taxes payable on completion.

Deposit: When you sign the preliminary contract you must pay a deposit (*acompte/dépot de garantie*). This is usually 5 per cent when buying a new property off-plan and 10 per cent for an old (existing) property. The safest and fastest method of paying the deposit is usually to make a bank-to-bank transfer from your bank to the *notaire's* or agent's bank account. Note that a real estate agent must be bonded to hold clients' monies (see **Estate Agents** on page 158). If the deposit is described as a *dédit*, the buyer will lose his deposit if he withdraws and equally if the vendor defaults he must pay a penalty equal to the amount of the deposit. If the deposit is described as *acompte*, neither party can withdraw and the sale can be legally enforced. The deposit is refundable under strict conditions only, notably relating to any conditional clauses such as failure to obtain a mortgage, although it can also be forfeited if you don't complete the transaction within the period, e.g. 60 or 90 days, specified in the contract. Note that if you withdraw from a sale after all the conditions have been met, you won't only lose your deposit, but must also pay the real estate agent's commission. **Make sure you know exactly what the conditions are regarding the return or forfeiture of a deposit.**

Civil Status: Once you have signed the preliminary contract, the *notaire* will need to establish your civil status (*état civil*), before processing a sale. This isn't simply to verify your identity and status, but also to satisfy French inheritance law. To do this the *notaire* needs to see your passport, birth certificate, marriage or divorce certificate (or if widowed, a death certificate), and a copy of an electricity or telephone bill verifying your permanent residence. If you have a marriage contract, the *notaire* will require a copy or a certified French translation. If you want the property to be left in its entirety to your surviving spouse, this should be covered in the purchase contract. An unmarried couple must take particular care with regard to inheritance when buying a property jointly in France.

COMPLETION

Completion (or closing) is the name for the signing of the final deed (*acte authentique*), the date of which is usually two or three months after signing the preliminary contract, as stated in the contract (although it may be 'moveable'). Completion involves the signing of the deed of sale, transferring legal ownership of a property, and the payment of the balance of the purchase price plus any other payments due such as the *notaire's* fees, taxes and duties.

When all the necessary documents concerning a purchase have been returned to the *notaire*, he will contact the buyer and request the balance of the purchase price less the deposit and, if applicable, the amount of a mortgage. He will also send you a bill for his fees and all taxes, which must be paid on completion. At the same time the *notaire* should also send you a draft deed of sale (*projet de l'acte de vente*). If he doesn't, you should request one. This should be complete and shouldn't contain any blank spaces to be completed later. If you don't understand the deed of sale, you should have it checked by your legal adviser.

Final Checks: Property is sold subject to the condition that it's accepted in the state it's in at the time of completion, therefore you should be aware of anything that occurs between signing the preliminary contract and completion. Before signing the deed of sale, it's *imperative* to check that the property hasn't fallen down or been damaged in any way, e.g. by a storm or the owners. If you have employed a lawyer or are buying through an agent he should accompany you on this visit. You should also do a final inventory immediately prior to completion (the previous owner should have already vacated the property) to ensure that the vendor hasn't absconded with anything that was included in the price.

You should have an inventory of the fixtures and fittings and anything that was included in the contract or purchased separately, e.g. carpets, light fittings, curtains or kitchen appliances, and check that they are present and in good working order. This is particularly important if furniture and furnishings (and major appliances) were included in the price. You should also ensure that expensive items (such as kitchen apparatus) haven't been substituted by inferior (possibly secondhand) items. Any fixtures and fittings (and garden plants and shrubs) present in a property when you . viewed it should still be there when you take possession, unless otherwise stated in the contract. **Note that unless restrained, some vendors will go to amazing extremes, for example removing not just the electric bulbs, but the bulb-holders, flex and even the ceiling rose!**

If you find anything is missing, damaged or isn't in working order, you should make a note and insist on immediate restitution such as an appropriate reduction in the amount to be paid. In such cases it's normal for the *notaire* to withhold an appropriate amount in escrow from the vendor's proceeds to pay for repairs or replacements. **You should refuse to go through with the completion if you aren't completely satisfied, as it will be difficult or impossible to obtain redress later.** If it isn't possible to complete the sale, you should consult your lawyer about your rights and the return of your deposit and any other funds already paid.

Signing: The final act of the sale is the signing of the deed of sale (*acte de vente*), which takes place in the *notaire's* office (*étude*). Before the deed of sale is signed, the *notaire* checks that all the conditions contained in the preliminary contract have been fulfilled. It's normal for both parties to be present when the deed of sale is read, signed and witnessed by the *notaire*, although either party can give a representative power of attorney (*procuration*). This is quite common among foreign buyers and sellers and can be arranged by your *notaire*. Note, however, that if a power of attorney isn't completed in France it must be signed and authenticated before a public notary abroad. The *notaire* reads through the *acte authentique* and both the vendor and buyer must initial each page and sign the last page after writing in French, *bon pour accord*, which means that they have understood and accept the terms of the document. The *notaire* is supposed to seek the assistance of an English (or other) translator if either party doesn't understand sufficient French, although this is rare.

Payment: The balance of the price after the deposit and any mortgages are subtracted must be paid by banker's draft or bank transfer. The money can be transferred directly to the *notaire's* bank account, which can be done by a bank-to-bank transfer. However, it's important to allow sufficient time for the funds to be transferred. Alternatively you can pay by banker's draft, which is probably the best method as you will have it in your possession (a bank cannot lose it!) and the *notaire* can confirm payment immediately. It also allows you to withhold payment if there's a last minute problem (see **Final Checks** above) that cannot be resolved. Note that when the vendor and buyer are of the same foreign nationality (e.g. British), they can agree that the balance is paid in a currency other than French francs (e.g. £sterling), although the *notaire* must also agree to this. In this case the money should be held by a lawyer in the vendor's and buyer's home country. After paying the money and receiving a receipt, the *notaire* gives you an *attestation de propriété*, which certifies that you're the owner of the property. You will also receive the keys!

Registration: There are no title deeds as such in France and proof of ownership is provided and guaranteed by registration of the property (*titre de propriétaire*) at the land registry (*cadastre*). The land registry's stamp is placed on the deed of sale, a certified copy (*expédition*) of which is given to the buyer by the *notaire* around two months after completion of the sale. If you have a mortgage, the deed is also registered at the *bureau des hypothèques* (office of mortgages). The original deed is retained indefinitely by the *notaire*.

It's a legal requirement in France that properties are insured against third party risks on completion and the *notaire* will ensure that this is done. Note that you will need to transfer services into your name as soon as possible after the deed is signed.

RENOVATION & RESTORATION

Many old properties purchased by foreigners in France are in need of restoration, renovation and modernisation. The most common examples are the many old farmhouses that have been almost totally neglected since they were built in the 18th or

19th centuries and were often abandoned many years ago. In general, the French attitude to old buildings is one of almost total neglect until they are literally in danger of falling down, when complete rebuilding is often necessary. A building sold as requiring renovation in France is usually in need of *substantial* work (rebuilding may be a more accurate description). Partly renovated usually means that part of a building is habitable, which means it at least has sanitation, but the rest is usually in dire need of restoration. The most dilapidated buildings (*ruines*) may consist of just a few walls without a roof.

Restoration: Before buying a property requiring restoration or modernisation, you should consider the alternatives. An extra 100,000F or 200,000F spent on a purchase will usually represent better value for money than spending the money on building work. It's often cheaper to buy a restored or partly restored property than a ruin in need of total restoration, unless you're going to do most of the work yourself. The price of most restored properties doesn't reflect the cost and amount of work that went into them and many people who have restored a ruin would never do it again and advise others against it.

Condition: It's important to ensure that a property has solid foundations and floors, sound walls and a good roof. Obviously sold foundations and floors are essential. Properties that have walls with serious defects are best avoided as it's usually cheaper to erect a new building! Almost any other problem can be fixed or overcome at a price. A sound roof that doesn't leak is desirable as making a building water-proof is the most important priority if funds are scarce. Don't believe a vendor or agent who tells you that a roof or anything else can be repaired or patched up, but obtain expert advice from a local builder. Sound roof timbers are also desirable as they can be expensive to replace.

Old buildings often need a damp-proof course, timber treatment, new windows and doors, a new roof or extensive repairs, a modern kitchen and bathroom, re-wiring and central heating. Electricity and mains water should preferably already be connected as they can be expensive to extend to a property in a remote area. **If a property doesn't have electricity or mains water, it's important to check the cost of extending these services to the property!** Many rural properties get their water from a spring or well, which is usually fine, but you should check the reliability of the water supply as wells can and do run dry! If you buy a waterside property, you should ensure that it has been designed with floods in mind, e.g. with electrical installations above flood level and solid tiled floors.

Septic Tanks: The absence of a septic tank (*fosse septique*) or other waste water system isn't usually a problem, providing the land size and elevation allows for its installation. If there's a stream running through a property it may mean that an expensive *lagunage* system (a series of lakes) needs to be installed to cope with the effluent, which costs three or four times that of a septic tank. If a property already has a septic tank, check that it's in good condition. An old style septic tank (*fosse traditionnelle*) takes bathroom waste only, while new all-purpose septic tanks on a soak-away system (*fosse septique à toutes eaux*) cope with a wide range of waste products. Make sure that a septic tank is large enough for the property in question, e.g. 2,500 litres for two bedrooms and up to 4,000 litres for five bedrooms. Also bear in mind that land drains for a septic tank must be installed a certain minimum distance from the boundaries of a property, e.g. three to five metres. Note that you mustn't use certain cleaning agents such as ammonia in a septic tank as they will destroy it! Specially formulated products are available, including some that will extend its life-span.

Planning Permission & Building Permits: If modernisation of an old building involves making external alterations, such as building an extension or installing larger windows or new doorways, you will need planning permission (*certificat d'urbanisme*) and a building permit (*permis de construire*) from your local town hall. If you plan to do major restoration or building work, you should ensure that a conditional clause (*clause suspensive*) is included in the preliminary contract stating that the purchase is dependent on obtaining planning and building permission (copies of the applications must be sent to the *notaire* handling the sale). If the built area is less than 170m² (1,829ft²) you can make the planning application yourself, but if it exceeds this an architect must make it. **Never start any building work before you have official permission.**

It usually takes a number of months top obtain planning permission and once it's issued and published the public usually have two months in which to lodge an appeal if they have an objection. Planning permission is valid for two years and can be extended for a further year. Technically a new application must be made if work is interrupted for more than one year, although this rule is usually ignored. It's also advisable to obtain permission from your local town hall before demolishing buildings on your land, irrespective of how dilapidated they are. You may be able to sell the building materials or get a builder to demolish them free of charge in exchange for the materials. After restoring a ruin or building a new house a *certificat de conformité* is required to confirm that building work has been carried out according to the planning application.

DIY or Builders? One of the first decisions you need to make regarding restoration or modernisation is whether to do all or most of the work yourself or have it done by professional builders or artisans. A working knowledge of French is essential for DIY, especially the words associated with building materials and measurements (renovating a house in France will also greatly improve your ability to swear in French!). Note that when restoring a period property it's important to have a sensitive approach to restoration. You shouldn't tackle jobs yourself or with friends unless you're sure that you're doing it right. In general you should aim to retain as many of a property's original features as possible and stick to local building materials such as wood, stone and tiles, reflecting the style of the property. When renovations and 'improvements' have been botched, there's often little that can be done except to start again from scratch. It's important not to over-modernise an old property so that its natural, rustic charm and attraction is lost. Note that even if you do much of the work yourself, you will still need to hire artisans for certain jobs. Before starting work and as work is in progress, most people like to have a photographic record of their accomplishments, if only to justify the expense. Note that you must have third party insurance for anyone working on your property.

French or Foreign Builders: When it's a choice between using French craftsmen or foreign builders, most experts recommend using local labour for a number of excellent reasons. French artisans understand the materials and the traditional style of building, are familiar with local planning and building regulations, and usually do excellent work. There are no jobbing builders or jacks of all trades in France, where all artisans have a specialist trade such as a bricklayer, stonemason, joiner, roofer, plasterer, plumber or electrician. If you employ local builders you can virtually guarantee that the result will be *authentique* and it could also save you money. French builders' quotations are binding and their prices are usually reasonable. Finally, bringing in foreign labour won't endear you to the local populace and may even create friction. Never employ 'black' labour (French or foreign) as apart from the lack of insurance there are stiff penalties.

Finding a Builder: When looking for a builder it's advisable to obtain recommendations from local people you can trust, e.g. a real estate agent, *notaire*, local mayor and neighbours. Note, however, that real estate agents or other professionals aren't always the best people to ask as they may receive a commission. Obtain references from previous customers. All qualified artisans living in a commune must be registered at the local town hall (*mairie*) and have a *siret* number (you can verify this via Minitel). Note that it's usually better to use a local building consortium or contractor (*entrepreneur*) rather than a number of independent tradesmen, particularly if you won't be around to supervise them, although it will cost you a bit more. On the other hand, if you do it 'yourself' using local hand-picked craftsmen you can save money and learn a great deal into the bargain.

Quotations: You should obtain written quotations (*devis*) from at least two builders before employing anyone. It's advisable to get a few quotations and offer to pay a fee, e.g. 500F, which should be reimbursed by the builder who gets the job. Note that for quotations to be accurate, you must detail exactly the work that's required, e.g. for electrical work this would include the number of lights, points and switches, and the quality of materials to be used. If you have only a vague idea of what you want, you will receive a vague and unreliable quotation. Make sure that a quotation includes everything you want done and that you fully understand it (if you don't get it translated). Look out for any terms in a quotation allowing for the price to be increased for inflation or a general rise in prices, and check whether it's definitive or provisional, i.e. dependent on further exploratory work. When you accept a quotation you should sign a copy of the *devis* with the builder, which then becomes a fixed price contract if work is started within three months. You should fix a date for completion and if you can get a builder to agree to it, include a penalty for failing to meet it. It's difficult to get French builders to agree to this, but it's worth persevering. Ask for start and finish dates in a quotation. After signing a contract it's usual to pay a deposit, e.g. 10 to 25 per cent, depending on the size of the job.

Supervision: If you aren't on the spot and able to supervise work, you should hire a 'clerk of works' such as a master builder (*maître d'oeuvres*) or an architect to oversee a job, otherwise it could drag on for months (or years) or be left half-finished. This will add around 10 per cent to the total bill, but is usually worth every penny. Many unsupervised French workmen are about as disciplined as French drivers and it isn't uncommon for artisans to work a few hours or a few days and then disappear for weeks or months on end! Be extremely careful whom you employ if you have work done in your absence and ensure that your instructions are accurate in every detail. Make absolutely certain that you understand what has been agreed and if necessary get it in writing (with drawings). It isn't unusual for foreign owners to receive huge bills for work done in their absence that shouldn't have been done at all! **If you don't speak French, it's even more important to employ someone to oversee building works. Progressing on sign language and a few words of French is a recipe for disaster!**

Cost: All building work such as electrical work, masonry and plumbing is costed by the square metre or metre. The cost of total restoration by professional builders varies, but you should expect to pay a minimum of 4,000F a square metre (m²) to bring a ruin to a habitable condition (or around half this for outbuildings). The cost depends on the type of work involved, the quality of materials used and the region. For a property of 100m² you should reckon on a total bill of 400,000F. As a rough guide you should expect the cost of renovating an old 'habitable' building to be at least equal to its purchase price and possibly much more.

How much you spend on restoring a property depends on your purpose and the depth of your pockets. If you're restoring a property as an investment, it's easy to spend more than you could ever hope to recoup when you sell it. On the other hand, if you're restoring a property as a holiday or permanent home, there's no limit to what you can do and how much money you can spend. Keep an eye on your budget (which will inevitably be plus or minus 25 per cent – usually plus!) and don't be in too much of a hurry. Some people take many years to restore a holiday home, particularly when they're doing most of the work themselves. In the last decade many foreigners spent a fortune on renovations, only to find it was impossible to sell and recoup their investment. It also isn't unusual for buyers to embark on a grandiose renovation scheme and run out of money before it's completed and be forced to sell at a huge loss.

It's possible to obtain a mortgage that includes the cost of renovation work, but you must obtain detailed written quotations for a lender. It's also possible to obtain a grant to restore a historic property in some regions (contact the *Conseil Régionale*) or in return for providing low/medium rent apartments for a period of years. If you're renovating a property for a business, e.g. *gîtes*, it may be advantageous to buy it through a French company, which will enable you to recover your VAT (TVA). Note that if you buy an old house and completely renovate it, e.g. retaining only the roof and external walls, thus transforming it into a 'new' house, then you may be liable for TVA. Therefore you should, if possible, retain a small part of the existing internal structure.

It's important to ensure that you pay for work on time, because if you get a reputation as a late payer (or not paying at all) you will soon find that you cannot get anyone local to work for you. However, you should make sure that a job's completely finished (including repairing any damage done by workmen) before paying bills. Never pay a builder in advance, particularly a large sum, as it's possible that he will disappear with your money (it happens, particularly when employing foreign, non-registered builders). It's best to pay one month in arrears, which most builders will agree to. On the other hand, if you want a job doing while you're away you will need to pay a builder a sum in advance or get someone local to supervise his work and pay him regularly, otherwise he's unlikely to finish the job. Cash deals are often negotiated without TVA, although you should bear in mind that if you don't have a legitimate bill you won't be able to offset the cost of work against rental income or capital gains tax when you sell, and you also won't have a guarantee against faulty workmanship.

Guarantees: All work done by French and foreign builders registered in France is covered by insurance which guarantees work for from one to ten years (*garantie décennale*), as when buying a new property, even if a builder goes out of business before the guarantee period has expired. A 10-year guarantee is provided for building work such as brick and stone work. A two-year guarantee of 'perfect functioning' is provided for all systems (such as plumbing and electrical installations) and a one-year guarantee is given for minor defects that may appear after completion of building work, such as cracking due to shrinkage after concrete dries out.

Swimming Pools: It's common for foreign buyers to install a swimming pool at a home in France, which if you're letting, will greatly increase your rental prospects and the rent you can charge. Many self-catering holiday companies won't take on properties without a pool. There are many swimming pool installation companies in France or you can even buy and install one yourself. Above ground pools are the cheapest but they are unsightly and are only advisable as a stop-gap or for those who really cannot afford anything better. Expect to pay around 16,000F for an 8 x 4 metre above ground pool. A better option is a liner pool which can be installed by anyone with basic DIY skills (for information contact JW Green Swimming Pools on UK 01902-27709). A liner pool costs around 80,000F fully installed. A conventional pool measuring 8 x 4 metres (with a simple but effective step/filter unit) can be purchased from the French company Desjoyeaux for around 80,000F including installation. A saline water option costs a bit more, but gives a better quality of water and provides lower maintenance costs.

A concrete fully-tiled pool of 8 x 4 metres costs from around 120,000F installed including filtration and heating, and can be almost any shape. Note that you need planning permission (*Déclaration de Travaux Exemptés de Permis de Construire*) to install a pool and should apply a few months in advance. Pools require regular maintenance and cleaning. If you have a holiday home in France or let a property, you will need to employ someone to maintain your pool (you may be able to get a local family to look after it in return for using it). See also **Swimming Pools** on page 175).

DIY & Building Supplies: There's a wide choice of DIY equipment and building supplies in France, although they can be more expensive than in some other countries, e.g. French paint is expensive and not particularly good, although imported paint is also available. Ask your neighbours about where to buy fittings and materials, as they usually know the best places locally. There are many DIY hypermarkets and superstores in France, which in addition to stocking most DIY requirements also have a wide range of tools and machinery for hire. National chains include Mr. Bricolage, Bricorama, Leroy Merlin, Maison de Bricolage, Castorama (who publish a comprehensive 500-page catalogue), Lapeyre, similar to Castorama but with a more limited range of products, and Kilatou, who hire all kinds of DIY equipment and also produce a catalogue. Most DIY stores stock a large selection of goods (and keep most items in stock), accept credit cards and have helpful staff. Look out for special promotions and even if something appears not to be on offer it's worthwhile asking, as offers aren't always advertised.

DIY stores are relatively expensive for some items and it's also worth checking trade suppliers such as Menuiseries Lapeyre. Most towns have a hardware store (*quincaillerie*) that's handy for tools and small items. Secondhand stores such as the ubiquitous *trocs* are good for plumbing parts and porcelain (bidets can be picked up for around 60F), doors and mantlepieces. It's also possible to buy reclaimed materials such as floor tiles, old doors and tiles (e.g. from Spain). Information about French architectural salvage yards can be obtained for 10F per department from Salvo, rue de la Gare, 52700 Manois, Haute-Marne (or Salvo, PO Box 1295, Bath BA1 3TJ, UK, ☎ 016686-494).

Further Reading: No-one attempting DIY in France should be without the *Oxford-Duden Pictorial French-English Dictionary* or the *Harraps French Visual Dictionary*. A good French/English architecture and building dictionary is the *Dictionnaire d'Architecture et de Construction* by J R Forbes (Lavoisier). There are also a number of books on the market for those brave enough to attempt their own renovations, such as *Buying and Restoring Old Property in France* by David Everett (Robert Hale). If your French is up to it, *Tout Le Bricolage* (Le Livre de Poche) comprises a series of six books covering all aspects of DIY with well-illustrated, step-by-step instructions. An excellent French DIY magazine is *Maison et Travaux*. *Bon courage!*

See also **Buying an Old Home** on page 151, **Inspections & Surveys** on page 161, **Wiring** on page 185, **Water** on page 187 and **Heating & Air-Conditioning** on page 189. The Service Directory in **Appendix E** contains the names of several building companies and professionals doing business in France.

MOVING HOUSE

After finding a home in France it usually takes just a few weeks to have your belongings shipped from within continental Europe. From anywhere else it varies considerably, e.g. around four weeks from the east coast of America, six weeks from the US west coast and the Far East, and around eight weeks from Australasia. Customs clearance is no longer necessary when shipping your household effects from one European Union (EU) country to another. However, when shipping your effects from a non-EU country to France, you should enquire about customs formalities in advance. If you fail to follow the correct procedure you can encounter numerous problems and delays and may be charged duty or fined. The relevant forms to be completed by non-EU citizens depend on whether your French home will be your main residence or a second home. Removal companies usually take care of the paperwork and ensure that the correct documents are provided and properly completed (see **Customs** on page 203).

It's advisable to use a major shipping company with a good reputation. For international moves it's best to use a company that's a member of the International Federation of Furniture Removers (FIDI) or the Overseas Moving Network International (OMNI), with experience in France. Members of FIDI and OMNI usually subscribe to an advance payment scheme providing a guarantee. If a member company fails to fulfil its commitments to a client, the removal is completed at the agreed cost by another company or your money is refunded. Some removal companies have subsidiaries or affiliates in France, which may be more convenient if you encounter problems or need to make an insurance claim.

You should obtain at least three written quotations before choosing a company, as costs vary considerably. Moving companies should send a representative to provide a detailed quotation. Most companies will pack your belongings and provide packing cases and special containers, although this is naturally more expensive than packing them yourself. Ask a company how they pack fragile and valuable items, and whether the cost of packing cases, materials and insurance (see below) are included in a quotation. If you're doing your own packing, most shipping companies will provide packing crates and boxes. Shipments are charged by volume, e.g. the square metre in Europe and the square foot in the USA. You should expect to pay from 20,000F to 40,000F to move the contents of a three to four-bedroom house within Western Europe, e.g. from London to the south of France. If you're flexible about the delivery date, shipping companies will quote a lower fee based on a 'part load', where the cost is shared with other deliveries. This can result in savings of 50 per cent or more compared with an individual delivery. Whether you have an individual or shared delivery, obtain the maximum transit period in writing, otherwise you may need to wait months for delivery!

Be sure to fully insure your belongings during removal with a well established insurance company. Don't insure with a shipping company that carries its own insurance as they usually fight every centime of a claim. Insurance premiums are usually 1 to 2 per cent of the declared value of your goods, depending on the type of cover chosen. It's prudent to make a photographic or video record of valuables for insurance purposes. Most insurance policies provide cover for 'all-risks' on a replacement value basis. Note that china, glass and other breakables can usually be included in an 'all-risks' policy only when they're packed by the removal company. Insurance usually covers total loss or loss of a particular crate only, rather than individual items (unless they were packed by the shipping company). If there are any breakages or damaged items, they must be noted and listed before you sign the delivery bill (although it's obviously impractical to check everything on delivery). If you need to make a claim, be sure to read the small print, as some companies require clients to make a claim within a few days, although seven is usual. Send a claim by registered mail. Some insurance companies apply an 'excess' of around 1 per cent of the total shipment value when assessing claims. This means that if your shipment is valued at 200,000F and you make a claim for less than 2,000F, you won't receive anything.

If you're unable to ship your belongings direct to France, most shipping companies will put them into storage and some allow a limited free storage period prior to shipment, e.g. 14 days. **If you need to put your household effects into storage, it's imperative to have them fully insured as warehouses have been known to burn down!** Make a complete list of everything to be moved and give a copy to the removal company. Don't include anything illegal (e.g. guns, bombs or drugs) with your belongings as customs checks can be rigorous and penalties severe. Provide the shipping company with *detailed* instructions of how to find your French address from the nearest *autoroute* (or main road) and a telephone number where you can be contacted.

After considering the shipping costs, you may decide to ship only selected items of furniture and personal effects and buy new furniture in France. If you're importing household goods from another European country, you can rent a self-drive van or truck. If you plan to transport your belongings to France personally, check the customs requirements in the countries you must pass through. Most people find it isn't advisable to do their own move unless it's a simple job, e.g. a few items of furniture and personal effects only. It's no fun heaving beds and wardrobes up stairs and squeezing them into impossible spaces. If you're taking pets with you, you may need to ask your vet to tranquillise them, as many pets are frightened (even more than people) by the chaos and stress of moving house.

Bear in mind when moving home that everything that can go wrong often does, so allow plenty of time and try not to arrange your move from your old home on the same day as the new owner is moving in. That's just asking for fate to intervene! **Last but not least, if your French home has poor or impossible access for a large truck you must inform the shipping company (the ground must also be firm enough to support a heavy vehicle).** Note also that if furniture needs to be taken in through an upstairs window, you may need to pay extra. See also **Customs** on page 203 and the **Checklists** on page 206.

MOVING IN

One of the most important tasks to perform after moving into a new home is to make an inventory of the fixtures and fittings and, if applicable, the furniture and furnishings. When you have purchased a property, you should check that the previous owner hasn't absconded with any fixtures and fittings which were included in the price or anything that you specifically paid for, e.g. carpets, light fittings, curtains, furniture, kitchen appliances, garden ornaments, plants or doors (see **Completion** on page 169). It's common to do a final check or inventory when buying a new property, which is usually done a few weeks before completion.

When moving into a long-term rental property it's necessary to complete an inventory (*inventaire détaillé/état des lieux*) of its contents and a report on its condition. This includes the condition of fixtures and fittings, the state of furniture and furnishings, the cleanliness and state of the decoration, and anything that's damaged, missing or in need of repair. An inventory should be provided by your landlord or agent and may include every single item in a furnished property (down to the number of teaspoons). The inventory check should be carried out in your presence, both when taking over and when terminating a rental agreement. If an inventory isn't provided, you should insist on one being prepared and annexed to the lease. If you find a serious fault after signing the inventory, send a registered letter to your landlord and ask for it to be attached to the inventory.

The inventory can be drawn up by a *huissier* (for around 1,000F), who's an official (similar to a bailiff) authorised to prepare factual legal documents. If the inventory is prepared by a *huissier* you have a better chance of resolving any disputes as his evidence is indisputable in a court of law. An inventory should be drawn up both when moving in (*état des lieux d'entrée*) and when vacating (*état des lieux de sortie*) a rented property. If the two inventories don't correspond, you must make good any damages or deficiencies or the landlord can do so and deduct the cost from your deposit. Although French landlords are generally no worse than those in most other countries, some will do almost anything to avoid repaying a deposit. Note the reading on your utility meters (e.g. electricity, gas, water) and check that you aren't overcharged on your first bill. The meters should be read by utility companies before you move in, although you may need to organise it yourself.

It's advisable to obtain written instructions from the previous owner concerning the operation of appliances and heating and air-conditioning systems; maintenance of grounds, gardens and lawns; care of special surfaces such as wooden or marble floors; and the names of reliable local maintenance men who know a property and are familiar with its quirks. Check with your local town hall regarding local regulations about such things as rubbish collection, recycling and on-road parking.

HOME SECURITY

When moving into a new home it's often wise to replace the locks (or lock barrels) as soon as possible, as you have no idea how many keys are in circulation for the existing locks. This is true even for new homes, as builders often give keys to sub-contractors. In any case it's advisable to change the external locks or lock barrels periodically if you let a home. If they aren't already fitted, it's advisable to fit high security (double cylinder or dead bolt) locks. Modern properties are usually fitted with special high security locks that are individually numbered. Extra keys for these locks cannot be cut at a local hardware store and you need to obtain details from the previous owner or your landlord. Many modern developments and communities have security gates and caretakers.

In areas with a high risk of theft (e.g. some parts of Paris and the French Riviera), your insurance company will insist on extra security measures such as two locks on external doors (one a five-lever mortise deadlock), internal locking shutters, and security bars or metal grilles on windows and patio doors. A policy may specify that all forms of protection on doors must be employed when a property is unoccupied, and that all other forms (e.g. shutters) must also be used after 2200 and when a property is left empty for two or more days.

You may wish to have a security alarm fitted, which is usually the best way to deter thieves and may also reduce your household insurance (see page 57). It should include external doors and windows, internal infra-red security beams, and may also include a coded entry keypad (that can be frequently changed and is useful for clients if you let) and 24-hour monitoring. (If money is no object, you can install closed circuit TV cameras and monitor your home from abroad via the Internet.) With a monitored system, when a sensor (e.g. smoke or forced entry) detects an emergency or a panic button is pushed, a signal is sent automatically to a 24-hour monitoring station. The duty monitor will telephone to check whether it's a genuine alarm (a code must be given) and if he cannot contact you someone will be sent to investigate.

You can deter thieves by ensuring that your house is well lit at night and not conspicuously unoccupied. External security 'motion detector' lights (that switch on automatically when someone approaches); random timed switches for internal lights, radios and televisions; dummy security cameras; and tapes that play barking dogs (etc.) triggered by a light or heat detector may all help deter burglars. In remote areas it's common for owners to fit two or three locks on external doors, alarm systems, grilles on doors and windows, window locks, security shutters and a safe for valuables. The advantage of grilles is that they allow you to leave windows open without inviting criminals in (unless they are *very* slim). You can fit UPVC (toughened clear plastic) security windows and doors, which can survive an attack with a sledge-hammer without damage, and external steel security blinds (that can be electrically operated), although these are expensive. A dog can be useful to deter intruders, although he should be kept inside where he cannot be given poisoned food. Irrespective of whether you actually have a dog, a warning sign with a picture of a fierce dog may act as a deterrent. If not already present, you should have the front door of an apartment fitted with a spy-hole and chain so that you can check the identity of a visitor before opening the door. **Remember, prevention is better than cure as stolen property is rarely recovered.**

Holiday homes are particularly vulnerable to thieves and in some areas they are regularly ransacked. No matter how secure your door and window locks, a thief can usually obtain entry if he's sufficiently determined, often by simply smashing a window or even breaking in through the roof or by knocking a hole in a wall! In isolated areas thieves can strip a house bare at their leisure and an un-monitored alarm won't be a deterrent if there's no-one around to hear it. If you have a holiday home in France, it isn't advisable to leave anything of real value (monetary or sentimental) there. If you vacate your home for an extended period, it may be obligatory to notify a caretaker, landlord or insurance company, and to leave a key with the caretaker or landlord in case of emergencies. If you have a robbery, you should report it immediately to your local *gendarmerie*, where you must make a statement (*plainte*). You will receive a copy, which is required by your insurance company if you make a claim.

When closing up a property for an extended period, e.g. over the winter, you should ensure that everything is switched off and that it's secure (see **closing a property for the winter** on page 196). Another important aspect of home security is ensuring that you have early warning of a fire, which is easily accomplished by installing smoke detectors. Battery-operated smoke detectors can be purchased for under 50F and should be tested weekly to ensure that the batteries aren't exhausted.

You can also fit an electric-powered gas detector that activates an alarm when a gas leak is detected.

ELECTRICITY

Electricity throughout most of France is supplied by the state-owned *Électricité de France (EDF)*, although there are local electricity companies in some areas. EDF is combined with *Gaz de France* (GDF) and the two companies are often referred to as EDF-GDF. Unlike other western countries, France generates some 75 per cent of its electricity from nuclear power, with the balance coming mostly from various hydro-electric schemes. This ensures that France's electricity is among the cheapest in Europe and it supplies electricity to its neighbours for less than they can produce it themselves. Due to the moderate cost of electricity and the high degree of insulation in new homes, electric heating is more common in France than in other European countries.

Connection: The first thing to check before moving into a home in France is whether there are any light fittings. When moving house, some people remove not just the bulb, but bulb-holders, flex and even the ceiling rose! You must usually apply to your local EDF office to have your electricity connected and to sign a contract specifying the power supply (see page 182) installed and the tariff required. To have your electricity connected, you must prove that you're the owner by producing an *attestation* or a lease if you're renting. You must also show your passport or residence permit (*carte de séjour*). If you wish to pay your bill by direct debit from a bank or post office account, don't forget to take along your account details (*relevé d'identité bancaire*).

When moving house, most people simply tell the EDF the day they are leaving (although EDF requests two weeks notice) and EDF assumes that someone else is taking over the property. To ensure your electricity supply is connected and that you don't pay for someone else's electricity, you should contact your local EDF office and ask them to read the meter (*relevé spécial*) before taking over a property. If the property has an existing electricity supply, you must pay a registration (*mise en service*) fee of around 75F. New residents don't usually pay a deposit, although non-residents may be required to pay one. When payable, the deposit is refundable against future bills.

EDF publish a useful free booklet entitled *EDF répond à vos questions* (EDF answers your questions) available from any EDF office. Your local electricity board may also have a booklet (*livret de l'usager de l'électricité*) explaining the electricity supply and apparatus. If you have any questions regarding the electricity supply in France contact Electricité de France, 2, rue Louis Murat, 75008, France (☎ 01.40.42.22.22).

Plugs, Fuses & Bulbs

Depending on where you have come from, you may need new plugs (*fiches*) or a lot of adapters. Plug adapters for imported lamps and other electrical apparatus may be difficult to obtain in France, so it's wise to bring some with you, plus extension cords and multi-plug extensions that can be fitted with French plugs. France has some nine different plug configurations with two, three, four or five contact points (including earths), and amp ratings of 6, 16 or 20 amps. However, most French plugs have two round pins, possibly with a female socket (*prise*) in the plug forming a 'third' earth pin. Small low-wattage electrical appliances up to six amps, such as table lamps, small TVs and computers, don't require an earth. Plugs with an earth must be used for high-wattage appliances up to 16 amps such as fires, kettles, washing machines, refrigerators and cookers. These plugs must be used with corresponding two-pin female/third-pin male sockets, although they fit ordinary two-pin sockets.

Electrical appliances that are earthed have a three-core wire and must never be used with a two-pin plug without an earth socket. Note that many French sockets aren't earthed and many electrical appliances are operated without an earth, with the exception of washing machines, dishwashers and dryers. French plugs aren't fitted with fuses. **Always make sure that a plug is correctly and securely wired, as bad wiring can be fatal (and is also a fire hazard).** In modern installations, fuses (*fusibles*) are of the resetting pop-out type or earth trip system. When there's a short circuit (*court-circuit*) or the system has been overloaded, a circuit breaker (*disjoncteur*) is tripped and the power supply is cut. Before reconnecting the power, switch off any high-power appliances such as a washing machine or dishwasher. Make sure you know where the trip switch is located and keep a torch handy so that you can find it in the dark (see **Power Supply** below).

Electric light bulbs in France are either of the Edison type with a bayonet or a screw fitting. Therefore if you have lamps requiring bayonet bulbs, these can be purchased in France. You can also buy adapters to convert from one to the other. Bulbs for non-standard electrical appliances, i.e. appliances that weren't made for the French market, such as refrigerators and sewing machines, may not be available in France, so bring some spares with you.

Power Supply

The electricity supply in France is delivered to homes at 380/440 volts through three separate phases (not one as in some countries) and is then shared across the three phases at 220/240 volts with a frequency of 50 hertz (cycles). Some appliances such as large immersion heaters or cookers draw power from all three phases. Older buildings may still have 110/120 volt supplies, although these have been converted to 220/240 in most areas. In many rural areas the lights often flicker and occasionally go off and come back on almost immediately (just long enough to crash your computer!). If you live in an area with an unstable electricity supply, it's prudent to obtain a power stabiliser for a computer or other vital equipment to prevent it powering off when the power drops. If you use a computer, it's also advisable to fit an uninterrupted power supply (UPS) with a battery backup which allows you time (around five minutes) to save your work and shut down your computer after a power failure. Power cuts are fairly frequent in some areas, particularly during thunderstorms, and you should keep torches, candles and preferably a gas lamp handy.

If the power keeps tripping off when you attempt to use a number of high-powered appliances simultaneously, it probably means that the power supply of your property is too low to operate all the appliances simultaneously. This is a common problem in France. If this is the case, you must ask EDF to uprate the power supply to your property. If you have an integrated electrical heating system, you can have a gadget called a *délesteur* installed. This momentarily cuts off convectors, under-floor heating and water-heater (etc.) when the system is overloaded when other high-consumption appliances are in use, but without noticeable temperature fluctuations. It may therefore be possible to avoid a higher supply rating that could save you up to 40 per cent on your standing charge. The power setting is usually shown on your meter (*compteur*). The possible ratings are 3, 6, 9, 12, 15, 18, 24, 30 and 36Kva or KW. The three lower rates (3, 6 and 9KW) don't cater for electric heating, which needs a power supply of 12KW to 18KW (if you have numerous high-wattage electrical appliances and electrical heating you may need the maximum 36KW supply).

To calculate the power supply required, you need to list all the electrical appliances you have (plus any you intend installing, such as an electric shower or dishwasher) and the power consumption of each. Add the power consumption of the appliances you're likely to operate simultaneously to obtain the total kilowatt power supply required. If you have appliances such as a washing machine, dishwasher, water heater and electric heating in an average sized house (e.g. two to three bedrooms), you will probably need an 18KW supply. Your standing charge (*abonnement*) depends on the power rating (*puissance*) of your supply. Unless you use very little or a great deal of electricity, the most appropriate rating is 18KW operating under the Tempo tariff (see **Tariffs** below). When buying electrical appliances in France, the label PROMETELEC (*Association pour le développement et l'amélioration des installations intérieures*) indicates that they are safe. The safety of electrical materials is usually indicated by the French safety standards association's initials 'NF' (*normes françaises*). EDF-GDF publish a number of leaflets detailing their services and tariffs including one in French and English (*Le Service du Gaz et de l'Électricité*).

Converters & Transformers

Electrical equipment rated at 110 volts AC (for example, from the USA) requires a converter or a step-down transformer (*transformateur*) to convert it to 240 volts AC, although some electrical appliances (electric razors, hair dryers) are fitted with a 110/240 volt switch. Check for the switch, which may be inside the casing, and make sure that it's switched to 240 volts *before* connecting it to the power supply. Converters can be used for heating appliances, but transformers are required for motorised appliances. Total the wattage of the devices you intend to connect to a transformer and make sure that its power rating *exceeds* this sum.

Generally small, high-wattage, electrical appliances, such as kettles, toasters, heaters, irons, etc., need large transformers. Motors in large appliances such as cookers, refrigerators, washing machines, dryers and dishwashers, need replacing or fitting with a large transformer. In most cases it's simpler to buy new appliances in France, which are of good quality and reasonably priced. Note also that the dimensions of imported cookers, microwave ovens, refrigerators, washing machines, dryers and dishwashers, may differ from those in France, and may not fit into a French kitchen.

An additional problem with some electrical equipment is the frequency rating, which in some countries, e.g. the USA, is designed to run at 60 Hertz (Hz) and not France's 50Hz. Electrical equipment *without* a motor is generally unaffected by the drop in frequency to 50Hz (except TVs, see page 69). Equipment with a motor may run okay with a 20 per cent drop in speed; however, automatic washing machines, cookers, electric clocks, record players and tape recorders are unusable in France if not designed for 50Hz operation. To find out, look at the label on the back of the equipment. If it says 50/60Hz it should be okay. If it says 60Hz, you might try it anyway, **but first ensure that the voltage is correct as outlined above.** Bear in mind that the transformers and motors of electrical devices designed to run at 60Hz will run hotter at 50Hz, so you should ensure that equipment has sufficient space around it for cooling.

Tariffs

EDF offers two domestic tariffs: Blue Tariff (*tarif bleu*) divided into two options, normal tariff (*option base*) and reduced tariff (*option heures creuses*), and *Tempo*. It is worth noting that EDF in common with many European countries is reducing the price of electricity on an annual basis.

Blue Tariff: With the normal tariff (*option base*) there's no difference between day and night rates and the meter has just one dial. This system isn't recommended unless you use little or no electricity! The standing charge per year (1999) is from 129F (3KW power supply) to 4,650.72F a year (36KW power supply). There is also the possibility of paying the standing charge monthly. The price per kWh is 0.6441F for a 3KW supply and 0.5311F above this.

With the reduced rate tariff (*option heures creuses*), you can select your own reduced rate period, e.g. from 2230 to 0630, or 0230 to 0730 *and* 1330 to 1630 for a maximum of eight hours daily. The low night tariff is generally used to heat hot water and charge night storage heaters. You can have relays installed by EDF to switch on your immersion water heater, tumble dryer or dish washer during the cheap period. The meter has two dials, one for normal tariff, marked *heures pleines* (HP) with an image of the sun on it, and one for night tariff marked *heures creuses* (HC) with an image of the moon on it. Your bill will show your day-time and night-time consumption separately. The standing charge per year is from 588.96F (6KW power supply) to 7428.12F a year (36KW power supply). The off-peak tariff doesn't apply to a 3KW supply. The price per kWh is 0.3242F off-peak (*creuses*) and 0.5311F at peak rate (*pleines*).

Tempo: The Tempo tariff (*option tempo*) is designed to encourage users to conserve electricity during severe weather when demand is at its highest. It allows you to use off-peak rates throughout the year with the exception of peak demand days. Under the Tempo scheme, the year is divided into three periods, blue (*bleu*) for 300 days, white (*blanc*) for 43 days and red (*rouge*) for 22 days of the year. Within these periods the day is also divided into peak and off rate consumption like the *option heures creuses.* The standing charge per year is from 907.44F (9KW power supply) to 3117.72F a year (36KW power supply). There's no monthly payment option for the tempo tariff, which applies only to power supplies rated at 9, 12, 15, 18 and 36KW, in homes with a viable alternative to electrical heating. The *bleu* rate per kWh is 0.2198F off-peak and 0.2753F peak. The *rouge* rate per kWh is 0.4532F off-peak and 0.5394F peak. For the remaining 22 'peak days' (*jour rouge*) you're required to pay around *four* to *eight* times the normal off-peak rate for your electricity, i.e. 0.8416F per kWh off-peak and 2.3182F peak. The 22 peak days are selected by EDF between 1st November and the 31st March and are determined by the meteorological centre in Toulouse.

You can have a special light and/or buzzer installed by an electrician giving you a 30-minute warning of the start of the higher rate. You can also have your heavy consumption appliances connected to a remote control switch (*Télécommande*) so that they switch off automatically during the high rate period and switch on again when the period ends. There's no charge for switching to the Tempo scheme and a special meter is installed free of charge, although you must pay for the installation of the warning light or buzzer and the remote control switch. There's also a lower standing charge under the Tempo scheme. Obviously if you have a second home in France that's unoccupied during the winter, you should choose the Tempo tariff.

Electricity Bills

You're billed for your electricity every two or four months, depending on your electricity company and the size of your bills. A number of bills (*facture*) received throughout the year, e.g. alternate bills, are estimated. Bills include a standing charge (*abonnement*), value added tax (TVA) and local taxes (*taxes locales*). TVA is levied at 20.6 per cent on the standing charge and 19.5 per cent on the total power consumption. Local taxes (*taxes commune/département*) are around 12 per cent and where applicable are levied before TVA is added.

All your utility bills (plus telephone) can be paid by direct debit (*prélèvement automatique*) from a bank or post office account. It's also possible to pay a fixed amount each month by standing order based on your estimated usage. At the end of the year you receive a bill for the amount owing or a rebate of the amount overpaid. These methods of payment are preferable, particularly if you spend a lot of time away from home or you're a non-resident. If you don't pay a bill on time, interest (*majoration*) can be charged at 1½ times the current interest rate and if your bills still aren't paid after a certain period your electricity company can cut your service. If you're a non-resident, you can have your bills sent to an address outside France.

Meters: Meters are usually installed in a box on an outside wall of a property. However, if your meter isn't accessible or a house isn't permanently occupied, make sure you leave the keys with a neighbour or make special arrangements to have your meter read, which is done every four months. If your meter cannot be read, you will receive an estimate based on your previous bills, although it *must* be read at least once a year.

Wiring

If you buy an old rural property, particularly a ruin in a remote area, you may find that it has no electricity supply. **Note that if a rural property has no electricity supply, the cost of installing it may be prohibitive and must be investigated before signing a contract.** If a property has no electricity supply you must pay to have it connected from the nearest point, which can cost tens of thousands of francs just to get power to a property. If a property is located in a natural park you may have to pay to have an underground supply, as pylons and poles are being gradually replaced in areas of natural beauty. EDF will give you a quotation for extending the service to your property from the nearest point, to which you must add the cost of wiring, e.g. around 20,000F for a two to three-bedroom house.

If this proves prohibitive you could install a small generator (which must be securely protected against theft, particularly if you have a holiday home) or a solar power system. A solar power system can be used to provide electricity in a remote rural home where the cost of extending electricity is prohibitive. The cost is around

30,000F for a modest installation sufficient to operate around eight lights and a small refrigerator. Gas bottles can be used to provide energy for cooking and hot water.

The electrical system in older properties is often eccentric and may even be dangerous, with exposed sockets and bare wires evident. One of the most important tasks after buying a property is to check that the electrical system is in good condition and adequate to meet your needs (see **Power Supply** on page 182). You can get an EDF representative to check the wiring in a property. Make sure you have sufficient power points fitted, as even in new properties it's common for developers not to install sufficient points (although it's possible to run up to around five separate, low-wattage appliances from one socket via a multi-plug connector).

It's essential to use a qualified French electrician for electrical work (look under *Électricité générale* in the Yellow Pages). Apart from the danger of electrocuting yourself, homes in France are wired differently from those in many other countries (it *doesn't* use a ring main system, which is prohibited). French regulations regarding the fittings and appliances in bathrooms are specific and no electric switches or outlets must be placed within 2.25m (7½ft) of a bath or shower. The electricity supply to a new property or a property that has been rewired will be connected by EDF only on receipt of a certificate (*certificat/attestation de conformité*) approved by the Electricity Users Safety Commission (*Comité National pour la Sécurité des Usagers de l'Électricité*/CONSUEL). This can be arranged by a French builder or a registered electrician.

GAS

Mains gas (*gaz de ville*) in France is available only in towns and cities and is supplied by the state-owned *Gaz de France (GDF)*, part of the same company as *Électricité de France (EDF)*. If you buy a property without a mains gas supply, a new connection (*raccordement*) within 35 metres of the nearest supply will cost around 5,500F for tariffs *base* and B0 (see below), providing of course mains gas is available in the area. Contact *Gaz de France* for an accurate estimate. When moving into a property with mains gas, you must contact GDF to have the gas switched on and/or have the meter read, and to have the account switched to your name. This can usually be done at the same time as you arrange for your electricity supply (see page 181). If you're taking over a property with an existing gas supply, there's a registration fee (*mise en service*) of around 75F.

Billing: As with most utilities in France, you're billed every two months and if your electricity is supplied by EDF, your gas is included on the same bill as your electricity. As with other utility bills, gas bills can be paid by direct debit (*prélèvement automatique*) from a French bank or post office account or a fixed amount can be paid each month. Meters are read every four or six months.

Tariffs: As with electricity, you can choose the gas tariff that best suits your requirements. There are four standing charge rates depending on the amount of gas you use: Base (less than 1,100 kWh a year), B0 (between 1,100 and 7,300 kWh), B1 (between 7,300 and 17,000 kWh) and 3GB (between 17,000 and 30,000 kWh). The *base* rate is for those who cook by gas only, the BO rate for cooking plus hot water and the other rates are necessary for homes with gas central heating. The cubic metres of gas you use are converted to kilowatt hours for invoicing. In apartment buildings where gas is used only for cooking and apartments are owned *en copropriété*, a standard charge for gas may be included in your service charge. As with heating and hot water charges, this isn't advisable if you own a holiday home in France.

Bottled Gas: Most rural homes have cookers and possibly water heaters that use bottled gas. Cookers often have a combination of electric and (bottled) gas rings (you can choose the mix). If your gas rings are sparked by electricity, keep some matches handy for power cuts. Check when moving into a property that the gas bottle isn't empty. Keep a spare bottle or two handy and make sure you know how to change bottles (get the previous owner or the real estate agent to show you). A bottle used just for cooking will last an average family around six weeks. Note that the rubber cover over the gas outlet turns clockwise, in contrast to most other threaded devices.

Bottled gas is more expensive than mains gas. You can buy it at most petrol stations and super/hypermarkets, but should trade in an empty bottle for a new one, otherwise it's much more expensive. An exchange bottle costs around 130F. If you need to buy new gas bottles, a retailer will ask you to register and pay a bottle deposit. Some village shops also sell bottled gas. Some houses keep their gas bottles outside, often under a lean-to. If you do this you must buy propane gas rather than butane, as it can withstand a greater range of temperatures than butane, which is for internal use only. Ignore those who say this doesn't matter on the Côte d'Azur, as even there temperature variations can be huge (it even snows occasionally!).

Gas central heating is common in France, although in rural areas the gas supply comes from a gas tank (*citerne*) installed on the property, rather than a mains supply. Tanks are hired from gas suppliers such as Total and Antargaz, who will install a tank free of charge in return for a contract to provide gas for a fixed period. Note that having a gas tank on your property will increase your insurance premiums.

WATER

Mains water in France is supplied by a number of private companies, the largest of which are Vivendi, Lyonnaise des Eaux, Cise (group St Gobaun) and Saur (group Bouygues), who between them supply some three-quarters of the water in France. Most properties in France are metered, where you pay only for the water you use. If you need to have a water meter installed, there's a small non-refundable charge. When moving into a new house, ask the local water company to read your meter. It's usual to have a contract for a certain amount of water and if you exceed this amount you incur a higher charge. There's no flat fee (*forfait*), which has been abolished, although 'special charges' may be levied.

Cost: The price of water in France varies considerably from region to region, depending on its availability or scarcity, and is among the most expensive in the world. In the most expensive towns water can cost as much as 30F per cubic metre, although the national average is around 13F per cubic metre or 16.50F when a town employs a private company to provide the service. Note that if you have a

septic tank (*fosse septique*) as opposed to mains drainage (*tout à l'égout*), your water bill will be much lower, e.g. 3F to 4F per cubic metre. You're billed by your local water company annually or every six months and can pay by direct debit. If an apartment block is owned *en copropriété*, the water bill for the whole block is usually divided among the apartments according to their size. Hot water may be charged by adding an amount per cubic metre consumed by each apartment to cover the cost of heating the water, or may be shared among apartments in proportion to their size.

Reliability: Water shortages are rare in towns (although they do occur occasionally), but are fairly common in some rural areas during long hot summers, when the water may periodically be switched off. It's possible to have a storage tank installed for emergencies and you should also keep an emergency supply for watering the garden or recycle your house water. Always confirm that a property has a reliable water source.

Wells: Beware of the quaint well (*puits*) or spring (*source*) as they can dry up, particularly in parts of central and southern France. If a property gets its water from a spring or well (possibly on a neighbour's land) make sure that there's no dispute about its ownership and your rights to use it, e.g. that it cannot be stopped or drained away by your neighbours. If necessary, this should be made a condition of a purchase contract (see page 165). Note, however, that well water is usually excellent (and free), although you may need a pump (manual or electric) to bring it to the surface.

Mains Connection: If you own a property in or near a village, you can usually be connected to a mains water system. Note, however, that connection can be expensive as you must pay for digging the channels required for pipes. Obtain a quotation (*devis*) from the local water company for the connection of the supply and the installation of a water meter. Expect the connection to cost at least 5,000F, depending on the type of terrain and soil (or rock!) which must be dug to lay pipes. If you're thinking of buying a property and installing a mains water supply, obtain an estimate before signing the purchase contract.

Water Heaters: If you need to install a hot water boiler or immersion heater, make sure that it's large enough for the size of property, e.g. one room studio (100 litres), two rooms (150 litres), three to four rooms (200 litres) and five to seven rooms or two bathrooms (300 litres). Many holiday homes have quite small water boilers which are often inadequate for more than two people. If you need to install a water heater or a larger water heater, you should consider the merits of both electric and bottled gas heaters. An electric water boiler with a capacity of 75 litres (sufficient for two people) usually takes between one and two hours (in winter) to heat water to 40 degrees.

A gas, flow-through water heater is more expensive to purchase and install than an electric water boiler, but you get unlimited hot water immediately whenever you want it and there are no standing charges. A gas heater should have a capacity of 10 to 16 litres per minute if it's to be used for a shower. There's usually little difference in quality between different priced heaters, although a gas water heater with a permanent flame may use up to 50 per cent more gas than one without it. A resident family with a constant consumption is usually better off with an electric heater operating on a reduced tariff, while non-residents using a property for short periods will find a self-igniting gas heater more economical. A solar power system can also be used to provide hot water (see page 190).

Security Measures: Before moving into a new home you should check where the main stop-valve or stopcock is located so that you can turn off the water supply in an emergency. If the water stops flowing for any reason, you should ensure that all taps are turned off to prevent flooding when the supply starts again. Note that in community properties, the tap to turn the water on or off is usually located outside the building. When leaving a property empty for an extended period, particularly during the winter when there's the possibility of freezing, you should turn off the mains stopcock, switch off the system's controls and drain the pipes, toilets (you can leave salt in the toilet bowls to prevent freezing) and radiators. It's also advisable to have your cold water tank and the tank's ball valves checked periodically for corrosion, and to check the hosing on appliances such as washing machines and dishwashers. It can be expensive if a pipe bursts and the leak goes undiscovered for a long time!

Quality: When water isn't drinkable it's marked 'undrinkable' (*eau non potable*), for example in trains. Note that water from wells and springs isn't always safe to drink. You can have well or spring water analysed by the public health department (*Département de l'Action Sanitaire et Sociale*) or the local water authority (*compagnie des eaux/syndicat de gestion des eaux*). It's possible to install filtering, cleansing and softening equipment to improve water quality, but you should obtain independent advice before installing a system as not all equipment is equally effective. Note that while boiling water will kill any bacteria, it won't remove any toxic substances contained in it. Although mains tap water in France is usually excellent, many French people consider it undrinkable and drink bottled water (when not drinking wine!). In general, water is hard in France with the exception of Brittany, Normandy, parts of southwest France and the area around Grenoble. You can use a water softener to soften hard water and a filter to prevent the furring of pipes, radiators and appliances. Water in France may be fluoridated, depending on the area.

HEATING & AIR-CONDITIONING

Central heating systems in France may be powered by oil, gas, electricity, solid fuel (usually wood) or even solar power. Whatever form of heating you use, it's essential to have good insulation, without which up to 60 per cent of heating is lost through the walls and roof. Insulation is given a high priority in France, particularly in new homes, and there are statutory maximum room temperatures of 19°C in living rooms and bathrooms and 18°C in bedrooms. Some 65 per cent of French homes have central heating, which is essential if you wish to let your home during winter. Many people keep their central heating on a low setting during the winter (which can be controlled via a master thermostat) during short absences to prevent freezing.

Solid Fuel: Some six million rural homes rely solely on wood-burning stoves or fireplaces for their heating and hot water, particularly in rural areas. Stoves come in a huge variety of sizes and styles and can be purchased secondhand from *brocantes* (see page 63). Most people burn wood (which should have been seasoned for at least two years) rather than coal or coke. It's an inexpensive fuel in France costing from around 100F to 150F per cubic metre (*stère*) uncut, although it can cost much more to have it delivered cut and dried (which is preferable as it can be very tough). You can also collect it free if you live in the country. The main disadvantages are the chores of collecting and chopping wood, cleaning the grate and lighting fires. Smoke can also be a problem. Note that an open fireplace (*cheminée*) can be wasteful of heat and fuel. An enclosed hearth with a glass door (*insert*) is more effective and often has the advantage of a hot-air chamber that warms other parts of a home, plus less heat wastage, a reduced fire hazard, and less ash and dust.

Electric: Electric central heating is the most common form in France, particularly in modern homes with good insulation and a permanent system of ventilation, and is inexpensive to run using off-peak storage heaters. A thermostatically controlled system is called integral electric heating. Electric central heating isn't recommended for old properties with poor insulation. If you install an electric central heating system you must usually uprate your electricity supply (see **Power Supply** on page 182) to cope with the extra demand. Note that some stand-alone electric heaters are expensive to run and are best suited to holiday homes.

Gas: Gas central heating is popular in towns with mains gas and is the cheapest to run. Gas is clean, economical and efficient, and the boiler is usually fairly small and can be wall-mounted. In rural areas where there's no mains gas, you can have a gas tank (*citerne*) installed on your property. You will need space for the tank, which must be installed at least three metres from the house. Tanks can be hired from gas suppliers such as Total and Antargaz and refilled on demand. Note that gas tanks are expensive to install (along with all the necessary piping), the system needs regular maintenance and having a gas tank on your property will increase your household insurance.

Oil: Oil-fired central heating isn't common in France due to the high cost of heating oil (*mazout* often referred to as fuel or *fioul*) and the problems associated with storage and deliveries. As with gas, you need space to install the storage tank. If you have a large tank of 2,000 litre capacity or larger it must be buried in your garden or stored in a separate location sheltered from frost and away from the house. A smaller tank can be located in your home, but will need to be refilled more often.

Solar Power: A solar power system can be used to supply all your energy needs, although in France it's usually combined with an electric or gas heating system, as solar power cannot usually be relied upon year-round for heating and hot water. The main drawback is the high cost of installation, which varies considerably depending on the region and how much energy you require. It must be installed by an expert. The advantages are no running costs, silent operation, maintenance free and no electricity bills. A system should last 30 years (it's usually guaranteed for ten years) and can be uprated to provide more power in the future. Solar power can also be used to heat a swimming pool. Continuous advances in solar cell and battery technology are expected to dramatically increase the efficiency and reduce the cost of solar power, which is forecast to become the main source of energy worldwide in the next century. A solar power system can also be used to provide electricity in a remote rural home, where the cost of extending electricity is prohibitive.

The Costs: The cost of heating a property varies depending on a number of factors, not least the fuel used, the size of your home and the length of time your heating is switched on. The French Agency for Energy Control (*Agence Française pour la Maîtrise de L'Énergie*, 27, rue Louis Vicat, F-75737 Paris 15 Cedex, ☎ 01.47.65.20.20) will provide a thermal diagnosis (*diagnostic thermique*) for a fee of around 2,000F. This is basically a study of the heating requirements and the cost of heating a property, taking into account the current insulation and equipment installed. The inspector will produce a report (*dossier*) detailing the most effective means of insulating and heating your home and a number of cost estimates.

Humidifiers: Note that central heating dries the air and may cause your family to develop coughs. Those who find the dry air unpleasant can purchase a humidifier to add moisture to the air. Humidifiers that don't generate steam should be disinfected occasionally with a special liquid available from pharmacies, (to prevent nasty diseases). The French commonly use humidifiers, ranging from simple water containers hanging from radiators, to expensive electric or battery-operated devices.

Air-Conditioning: In some regions of France summer temperatures are often above 30°C (86°F) and although properties are usually built to withstand the heat, you may wish to install air-conditioning (*climatisation*). Note, however, that there can be negative effects if you suffer from asthma or respiratory problems. You can choose between a huge variety of air-conditioners, fixed or moveable, indoor or outdoor installation, and high or low power. An air-conditioning system with a heat pump provides cooling in summer and economical heating in winter. Some air-conditioners are noisy, so check the noise level before buying one. Many people fit inexpensive ceiling fans for extra cooling in the summer.

PROPERTY INCOME

Many people planning to buy a holiday home in France are interested in owning a property that will provide them with an income to cover the running costs and help with mortgage payments (or to supplement a pension). The most common examples are holiday letting for owners of second homes and *gîtes*, and bed and breakfast accommodation for residents. Owning and operating a furnished cottage (e.g. a *gîte*) or bed and breakfast accommodation (*chambre d'hôte*) isn't usually considered a commercial activity by the French authorities, providing you don't set up a trading company or register as a business. Operating on a self-employed basis rather than trading through a company usually means lower taxes and social security payments. However, a property with six or more rooms to let is classed as a commercial business and is more expensive to establish and operate. Always obtain professional advice before buying a commercial property.

Note that you're highly unlikely to meet your mortgage payments and running costs from rental income. Buyers who over-stretch their financial resources often find themselves on the rental treadmill, constantly struggling to find sufficient income to cover their running costs and mortgage payments. It's difficult to make a living providing holiday accommodation or bed & breakfast in most areas, as the season is too short and there's too much competition (the market is saturated in most regions). If you're planning on holiday lets, don't overestimate the length of the season, which varies depending on the region. In some areas it's as long as 16 weeks, while in others it's only ten weeks. The letting season is longest in southern France, particularly on the Côte d'Azur, although in some areas such as the major cities or ski resorts, properties have year-round letting potential.

In the early '90s many overseas buyers lost their French homes after they defaulted on their mortgage payments, often because rental income failed to meet expectations. Note that buying property in France (and in most other countries) isn't a good investment compared with the return on income that can be achieved by investing elsewhere. **Most experts recommend that you don't purchase a home in France if you need to rely on rental income to pay for it.**

Gîtes: A *gîte* can refer to anything from one or two spartan outhouses converted to self-catering accommodation to a large luxury property with a number of self-contained apartments and cottages. *Gîtes* aren't considered a commercial activity and therefore it isn't necessary to register them as a business. Existing tax legislation in France favours anything to do with the tourist industry and in particular *gîtes*. If you intend to live in France, then it makes sense to have a number of units, thus reducing costs and sharing the cost of installing amenities such as a swimming pool. Note, however, that an established *gîte* business with a good income costs anything between one and two million francs. It's possible to undertake a course in establishing and operating a *gîte* such as those held by Tony and Patricia Smith in Languedoc (☎ 05.67.38.06.12).

Before establishing a *gîte*, obtain legal advice and contact your town hall regarding local regulations. If you're buying a property with the express intention of setting up *gîtes*, make sure that permission will be granted before you buy or make it a condition of purchase (see **Purchase Contracts** on page 165). Grants are available to set up *gîtes* (and other holiday accommodation) in certain areas, e.g. from the *Fédération Nationale des Gîtes de France*, but you must apply *before* starting work. Note that there's a time limit of two years for the completion of work associated with a grant from *Gîtes de France*. Grants are conditional on the quality of restoration or conversion and the accommodation provided (properties are assessed annually). The minimum grant is usually equal to around 30 per cent of the cost of work (up to a maximum of 30,000F) excluding taxes, which may be paid only on completion, although 50 per cent is sometimes paid halfway through a project. Note that a grant from *Gîtes de France* is conditional on the property being available to rent by them for a period of ten years and if you sell within this period or the property isn't made available, you must repay the grant. You must also bear in mind that if you let your *gîte* under the banner of *Gîtes de France* or a similar organisation, you may need to wait a long time to get paid. See also **Renovation & Restoration** on page 170.

Bed & Breakfast (B&B): No authorisation is required to offer B&B, although it must be registered as a commercial entity with the local trade registry (*Registre du Commerce*). The most common B&B accommodation in France is a *chambre d'hôte*, which provides the option of an evening meal, usually taken with the family. Note that if alcohol is to be served with the evening meal (mandatory in France!), a licence is required from the local town hall. Grants are available for creating or renovating rooms as *chambre d'hôte* accommodation. If you operate a *Gîtes de France* approved *chambre d'hôte*, food must be French and include regional dishes. Running a *chambre d'hôte* with a number of rooms isn't a part-time activity, at least not in the summer, and it's generally vital that one of the owners speaks good French, otherwise you will have to rely on foreign guests. It may be worthwhile having an entry in one or more of the many French bed & breakfast directories, such as those listed in **Appendix B**. Jennifer Jane Viner (☎ 05.67.39.87.15) in the Languedoc runs courses in setting up a bed and breakfast (*chambre d'hôte*) business in France. See also **Starting a Business** on page 21.

Location/Swimming Pools: If an income from your French property has a high priority, you should buy a property with this in mind. To maximise rental income, a property should be located as close as possible to the main attractions and/or a beach, be suitably furnished and professionally managed. A swimming pool is obligatory, as properties with pools are much easier to let than those without (unless a property is situated on a beach, lake or river). It's usually necessary to have a private pool with a single-family home, but a shared pool is sufficient for an apartment or townhouse. You can also charge a higher rent for a property with a pool and you may be able to extend the season even further by installing a heated or indoor pool. Some private letting agencies won't handle properties without a pool. Note that there are strict regulations (*Direction Département des Affaires Sanitaires et Sociales/DDASS*) regarding pools used by the public, which includes pools at private homes that are let for holidays. Regulations include all aspects of a pool's construction and operation including filtration, drainage, water quality and surrounds. Make sure you understand the regulations before installing a pool or letting a property.

Rents: Rental rates vary considerably depending on the time of year, area, size and quality. A house sleeping six in an average area can be let for around 2,000F to 2,500F a week in high season. At the other extreme, a luxury property in a popular area with a pool and accommodation for 8 to 12 can be let for between 10,000F and 20,000F a week in the high season. The high season generally includes the months of July and August and possibly the first two weeks of September. The mid season usually comprises June, September and October (and possibly Easter), when rents are usually around 25 per cent lower than the high season; the rest of the year is the low season. For long lets in the low season, a house sleeping six usually rents for around 1,000F a week (4,000F a month) in most regions, with the tenant paying for all services.

Furnishings & Keys: If you let a property, don't fill it with expensive furnishings or valuable personal belongings. While theft is rare, items will certainly get damaged or broken over a period of time. When furnishing a property that you plan to let, you should choose hard-wearing, dark-coloured carpets that won't show the stains, and buy durable furniture and furnishings. Simple inexpensive furniture is best in a modest *gîte*, as it will need to stand up to hard wear. Small two-bedroom properties usually have a settee (e.g. a 'clic-clac') in the living room that converts into a double bed. Properties should be well-equipped with cooking utensils, crockery and cutlery, and it's also advisable to provide bed linen and towels. You may also need a cot or high chair for young children. Depending on the price and quality of a property, your guests may also expect central heating, a washing machine, dishwasher, microwave, covered parking, a barbecue and garden furniture. Some owners provide bicycles, and badminton and table tennis equipment. It isn't usual to have a telephone in rental homes, although you could install a credit card telephone or a phone that will receive incoming calls only.

You will need several sets of spare keys, which will inevitably get lost at some time. If you employ a management company, their address should be on the key fob and not the address of the house. If you let a home yourself, you can use a 'keyfinder' service, whereby lost keys can be returned to the keyfinder company by anyone finding them. You should ensure that you get 'lost' keys returned, otherwise you may need to change the locks (in any case it's advisable to change the external locks periodically if you let a home). You don't need to provide clients with keys to all the external doors, only the front door (the others can be left in your home). If you arrange your own lets, you can mail keys to clients in your home country, otherwise they can be collected from a caretaker in France. It's also possible to install a security key-pad entry system.

Letting Agents: If you're letting a second home, the most important decision is whether to let it yourself or use a letting agent (or agents). If you don't have much spare time you're better off using an agent, who will take care of everything and save you the time and expense of advertising and finding clients. An agent will charge commission of between 20 and 40 per cent of gross rental income, although some of this can be recouped through higher rents. If you want your property to appear in an agent's catalogue, you must contact him the summer prior to the year in which you wish to let it (the deadline is usually September). Note that although self-catering holiday companies may fall over themselves to take on a luxury property on the Côte d'Azur, the top letting agents turn down as many as nine out of every ten properties they're offered.

Most agents don't permit owners to use a property during the peak letting season (July and August) and may also restrict their use at other times. There are numerous self-catering holiday companies including Allez France (☎ UK 01903-742345), Bowhills (☎ UK 01489-877627), Crystal Holidays (☎ UK 0181-240 3331), Interhome (☎ UK 0181-891 1294) and Vacances en Campagne (☎ UK 01798-869433) in Britain, plus the main ferry companies. Many French real estate agents also act as letting agents for property owners and some specialise in long-term winter lets. Note that when letting an apartment, you may be required to notify the community's *syndic* (see page 152). Check before buying an apartment that letting is permitted. You must also notify your insurance company if a property is to be let.

Take care when selecting a letting agent, as a number have gone bust in recent years owing customers tens of thousands of francs. Make sure that your income is kept in an escrow account and paid regularly, or even better, choose an agent with a bonding scheme who pays you the rent *before* the arrival of guests (some do). It's absolutely essential to employ an efficient, reliable and honest company, preferably long-established. Anyone can set up a holiday letting agency and there are many 'cowboy' operators. Ask a management company to substantiate rental income claims and occupancy rates by showing you examples of actual income received from other properties. Ask for the names of satisfied customers and check with them.

Other things to ask a letting agent include who they let to; where they advertise; whether they have contracts with holiday and travel companies; whether you're expected to contribute towards marketing costs; and whether you're free to let the property yourself and use it when you wish. The larger companies market homes via newspapers, magazines, overseas agents, colour brochures and the Internet, and have representatives in many countries. Management contracts usually run for a year. A management company's services should include arranging routine and emergency repairs; reading meters (if electricity is charged extra); routine maintenance of house and garden, including lawn cutting and pool cleaning; arranging cleaning and linen changes between lets; advising guests on the use of equipment; and providing guest information and advice (possibly 24-hours in the case of emergencies). Agents may also provide someone to meet and greet clients, hand over the keys and check that everything is in order. The actual services provided will usually depend on whether a property is a basic *gîte* or a luxury villa costing tens of thousands of francs a week. A letting agent's representative should also make periodic checks when a property is empty to ensure that it's secure and that everything is in order.

Doing Your Own Letting: Some owners prefer to let a property to family, friends, colleagues and acquaintances, which allows them more control (and *hopefully* the property will be better looked after). In fact, the best way to get a high volume of lets is usually to do it yourself, although many owners use a letting agency in addition to doing their own marketing in their home country. If you wish to let a property yourself, there's a wide range of French and foreign newspapers and magazines in which you can advertise, e.g. *Dalton's Weekly* and newspapers such as the *Sunday Times* in Britain. Many of the English-language newspapers & magazines listed in **Appendix A** (such as *France* and *Living France*) also include advertisements from property owners. You will need to experiment to find the best publications and days of the week or months to advertise.

There are also companies that produce directories of properties let directly by owners such as Bonnes Vacances (☎ UK 01306-876876), Lets Direct (☎ UK 01489-878612) and Private Villas (☎ UK 01564-794011) in Britain. You pay for the advertisement but handle bookings yourself. French regional tourist agencies can put you in touch with French letting agents. You can also advertise among friends and colleagues, in company and club magazines (which may even be free), and on notice boards in companies, stores and public places. The more marketing you do, the more income you're likely to earn. It also pays to work with other local people in the same business and send surplus guests to competitors (they will usually reciprocate). It isn't necessary to just advertise locally or stick to your home country and you can also extend your marketing abroad (you can also advertise via the Internet). It's necessary to have a telephone answering machine and a fax machine.

To get an idea of the rent you should charge, simply ring a few letting agencies and ask them what it would cost to rent a property such as yours at the time of year you plan to let. They are likely to quote the highest possible rent you can charge. You should also check the advertisements in newspapers and magazines. Set a realistic rent as there's a lot of competition. Add a returnable deposit (e.g. 1,000F) as security against loss (e.g. of keys) or breakages, although this cannot be more than 25 per cent of the rental fee or be requested more than six months in advance. A deposit should be refundable only up to six weeks before a booking. It's normal to have a minimum two-week rental period in July and August. You will need to have a simple agreement form that includes the dates of arrival and departure and approximate times. Note that if you plan to let to non-English speaking clients, you must have a letting agreement in French or other foreign languages.

If you plan to let a home yourself, you will need to decide how to handle enquiries about flights and car rentals. It's easier to let clients do it themselves, but you should be able to offer advice and put them in touch with airlines, ferry companies, travel agents and car rental companies (see page 44). You will also have to decide whether you want to let to smokers or accept pets or young children (some people don't let to families with children under five years of age due to the risks of bed-wetting). It's best to provide linen (some agents provide a linen hire service), which is usually expected, although electricity may or may not be included in the rental fee.

It's advisable to produce a coloured brochure containing external/internal pictures (or a single colour brochure with coloured photographs glued to it, although this doesn't look so professional); important details; the exact location; local attractions; details of how to get there (with a small map); and the name, address and telephone number of your local caretaker or letting agent. You should enclose a stamped, addressed envelope when sending out leaflets. It's necessary to make a home look as attractive as possible in a brochure without distorting the facts or misrepresentation (you can be fined heavily for this in France). Advertise honestly and don't over-sell your property. **Finally keep detailed records and ensure that you never double book!**

Local Information: You should also provide an information pack for clients explaining how things work (such as heating and air-conditioning); what not to do; where to shop; recommended restaurants; local emergency numbers and health services such as doctors, hospitals and dentists; and assistance such as a general repairman, plumber, electrician and pool maintenance. If you allow young children and pets, you should make a point of emphasising any dangers, such as falling in the pool. It's also beneficial to have a visitor's book where your clients can write their comments and recommendations. If you want to impress your guests you may wish to arrange for fresh flowers, fruit, a good bottle of wine and a grocery pack to greet them on their arrival (you can allow for this in the rent if it's a relatively inexpensive abode). It's little touches like this that ensure repeat business and recommendations. If you go 'the extra mile' it will pay off in recommendations and you may even find after your first year or two that you rarely need to advertise. Many people return to the same property each year and you should do an annual mail-shot to previous clients and send them some brochures. **Word-of-mouth advertising is the cheapest and always the best.**

Caretaker: If you have a second home in France, you will find it beneficial or even essential to employ a local caretaker, irrespective of whether you let it. You may also need to employ a gardener. You can have your caretaker prepare the house for your family and guests as well as looking after it when it isn't in use. If you have a holiday home in France it's advisable to have your caretaker check it periodically (e.g. fortnightly) and to give him authority to authorise minor repairs. If you let a property yourself, your caretaker can arrange for (or do) cleaning, linen changes, maintenance and repairs, gardening and the payment of bills. If you employ a caretaker or housekeeper (*femme de ménage*) you should expect to pay at least the minimum wage, possibly plus social security costs.

Increasing Rental Income: It's possible to increase rental income outside the high season by offering special interest or package holidays, which could be done in conjunction with other local businesses in order to broaden the appeal and cater for larger parties. These may include activity holidays such as golf, tennis, cycling or hiking; cooking, gastronomy and wine tours/tasting; and arts & crafts such as painting, sculpture, photography and writing courses. You don't need to be an expert or conduct courses yourself, but can employ someone to do it for you.

Long-Term Lets: Long-term lets can be anything from one to six months and usually exclude the high season. Most people who let year round have low, medium and high season rates. Rates are naturally much lower for winter lets, when you shouldn't expect to earn more than around 750F to 1,000F a week (3,000F to 4,000F a month) in most regions for a *gîte* sleeping six. The tenant usually pays for the running costs, including utilities. Note that central heating is essential if you want to let long-term. If you let a property long-term, you should be aware that there are separate laws governing unfurnished accommodation, furnished accommodation and holiday lettings, i.e. furnished lets of less than six months (see **Renting** on page 136).

Closing a property for the winter: Before closing up a property for the winter, you should turn off the water at the mains and drain all pipes (see also **Security Measures** on page 188), remove the fuses (except the one for a dehumidifier if you leave it on while you're away), empty the food cupboards and the refrigerator/freezer, disconnect gas cylinders and empty dustbins. You should also leave the interior doors open and a few small windows with grilles or secure shutters open to provide some ventilation. Many people keep their central heating on a low setting during the winter (which can be controlled via a master thermostat) when they are absent to prevent freezing. Lock the doors and shutters and secure anything of value against theft or leave it with a neighbour. Check whether any essential work needs to be done before you leave and if necessary arrange for it to be done in your absence. Most importantly leave a set of keys with a neighbour and have a caretaker check your home periodically.

See also **Renting** on page 136 **and Taxation of Property Income** on page 97.

SELLING A HOME

Although this book is primarily concerned with buying a home in France, you may wish to sell your French home at some time in the future. Before offering your home for sale, it's advisable to investigate the state of the property market. For example unless you're forced to sell, it definitely isn't advisable during a property slump when prices are depressed. It may be wiser to let your home long-term and wait until the market has recovered. It's also unwise to sell in the early years after purchase, when you will probably make a loss unless it was an absolute bargain. Having decided to sell, your first decision will be whether to sell it yourself (or try) or use the services of a real estate agent. Although the majority of properties in France are sold through real estate agents, a large number of owners also sell their own homes. If you need to sell a property before buying a new one, this must be included as a conditional clause (see page 167) in the purchase contract for a new home. Note that when selling a property in France the vendor chooses the *notaire* who performs the completion.

Price: It's important to bear in mind that (like everything) property has a market price and the best way of ensuring a quick sale (or any sale) is to ask a realistic price. In recent years prices have plummeted and in some regions buyers have dried up, and some properties have remained on the market for years largely because owners have asked absurd prices. If your home's fairly standard for the area you can find out its value by comparing the prices of other homes on the market, or those that have recently been sold. Most agents will provide a free appraisal of a home's value in the hope that you will sell it through them. However, don't believe everything they tell you as they may over-price it simply to encourage you. You can also hire a professional appraiser to determine the market value. Note that you should be prepared to drop the price slightly (e.g. 5 or 10 per cent) and should set it accordingly, but shouldn't grossly over-price a home as it will deter buyers. Don't reject an offer out of hand unless it's ridiculously low, as you may be able to get the prospective buyer to raise his offer. When selling a second home in France, you may wish to include the furnishings (plus major appliances) in the sale, particularly when selling a relatively inexpensive property with modest furnishings. You should add an appropriate amount to the price to cover the value of the furnishings, or alternatively you could use them as an inducement to a prospective buyer at a later stage, although this isn't usual in France.

Presentation: The secret to selling a home quickly lies in its presentation (assuming that it's competitively priced). First impressions (both exteriors and interiors) are vital when marketing your home and it's important to make every effort to present it in its best light and make it as attractive as possible to potential buyers. It may pay to invest in new interior decoration, new carpets, exterior paint and landscaping. A few plants and flowers can do wonders. Note that when decorating a home for resale, it's important to be conservative and not to do anything radical (such as install a red or black bathroom suite); white is a good neutral colour for walls, woodwork and porcelain.

It may also pay you to do some modernisation such as installing a new kitchen or bathroom, as these are of vital importance (particularly kitchens) when selling a home. Note, however, that although modernisation may be necessary to sell an old home, you shouldn't overdo it as it's easy to spend more than you could ever hope to recoup in the sale price. If you're using an agent, you can ask him what you should do (or need to do) to help sell your home. If your home is in poor repair this must be reflected in the asking price and if major work is needed that you cannot afford, you should obtain a quotation (or two) and offer to knock this off the asking price. Note that you have a duty under French law to inform a prospective buyer of any defects which aren't readily apparent and which materially affect the value of a property. There are also special disclosure requirements for apartments and other community properties (see page 152).

Selling Your Home Yourself: While certainly not for everyone, selling your own home is a viable option for many people and is particularly recommended when you're selling an attractive home at a *realistic* price in a favourable market. It may allow you to offer it at a more appealing price, which could be an important factor if you're seeking a quick sale. How you market your home will depend on the type of home, the price, and the country or area from where you expect your buyer to come. For example, if your property isn't of a type and style and in an area desirable to local inhabitants, it's usually a waste of time advertising it in the local press.

Advertising is the key to selling your home. The first step is to get a professional looking 'for sale' sign made (showing your telephone number) and erect it in the garden. Do some market research into the best newspapers and magazines for advertising your property, and place an advertisement in those that look most promising. If you own a property in an area popular with foreign buyers, it may be worthwhile using an overseas agent (see below) or advertising in foreign newspapers and magazines, such as the English-language publications listed in Appendix A.

You could also have a leaflet printed (with pictures) extolling the virtues of your property, which you could drop into local letter boxes or have distributed with a local newspaper (many people buy a new home in the immediate vicinity of their present home). You may also need a 'fact sheet' printed if your home's vital statistics aren't included in the leaflet mentioned above and could offer a finder's fee (e.g. 5,000F) to anyone finding you a buyer. Don't omit to market your home around local companies, schools and organisations, particularly if they have many itinerant employees. Finally, it may help to provide information about local financing sources for potential buyers. With a bit of effort and practice you may even make a better job of marketing your home than an agent! Unless you're in a hurry to sell, set yourself a realistic time limit for success, after which you can try an agent. When selling a home yourself, you will need to obtain legal advice regarding contracts and to engage a *notaire* to hold the deposit and complete the sale.

Using An Agent: Most owners prefer to use the services of an agent or *notaire*, either in France or in their home country, particularly when selling a second home. If you purchased the property through an agent, it's often advisable to use the same agent when selling, as he will already be familiar with it and may still have the details on file. You should take particular care when selecting an agent as they vary considerably in their professionalism, expertise and experience (the best way to investigate agents is by posing as a buyer). Note that many agents cover a relatively small area, so you should take care to choose one who regularly sells properties in your area and price range.

Agents' Contracts: Before offering a property for sale, a French agent must have a signed authorisation, called a sales mandate (*mandat de vente*), from the owner of the property. There are generally two types of mandate, an ordinary or non-exclusive mandate (*mandat simple*), which means that you reserve the right to deal with other agents and to negotiate directly with private individuals. An exclusive mandate (*mandat exclusif*) gives a single agent the exclusive right to sell a property, although you can reserve the right to find a private buyer. An agent's fees are usually one or two percentage points lower with an exclusive mandate than with a non-exclusive mandate. **Note that if you sign a contract without reserving the right to find your own buyer, you must still pay the agent's commission even if you sell your home yourself.** Make sure that you don't sign two or more exclusive mandates to sell your home. Check the contract and make that sure you understand what you're signing.

An agent with an exclusive mandate has the authority to sign a sales contract on behalf of the vendor. Therefore before signing a contract to sell a property yourself, you must ensure that any other agents to whom you have given a mandate haven't found a buyer and signed a contract on your behalf. Notify all agents with a non-exclusive mandate by registered letter when a property has been sold. Mandates are for a limited period only, usually three months, and can be extended for further three-month periods up to one year, when they usually terminate. It's usually possible to terminate the contract after three months by giving written notice by registered mail two weeks before the end of the three-month period. Note that you must still pay an agent's fee if you sell to someone introduced by him within one year of the expiry of a *mandat*. Contracts state the agent's commission, what it includes, and most importantly, who must pay it. **Generally you shouldn't pay any fees unless you require extra services and you should never pay commission before a sale is completed.**

Agents' Fees: When selling a property in France, the agent's commission (5 to 10 per cent of the sale price) is usually paid by the vendor and included in the purchase price (see **Estate Agents** on page 158). Foreign agents who work with French agents share the standard commission, so you pay no more by using a foreign agent. Note that when a *notaire* is the selling agent, his seller's commission *isn't* included in the asking price and is paid by the buyer.

Capital Gains Tax (CGT): Non-residents must pay capital gains tax on the profit made on the sale of a home in France if it hasn't been owned for 22 years (see page 103). Where applicable, CGT is withheld by the *notaire* handling the sale. Before a sale the *notaire* prepares a form (Cerfa 2090) calculating the tax due and appoints an agent (*agent fiscal accredité*) or guarantor to act on the vendor's behalf concerning tax. If the transaction is straightforward, the local tax office may grant a dispensation (*dispense*) of the need to appoint a guarantor, providing the *notaire* applies before completion of the sale. If you obtain a dispensation, the proceeds of the sale can be released to you in full after CGT has been paid.

As when buying a home in France, you must be very, very careful who you deal with when selling a home. Never agree to accept part of the sale price under the table, as if the buyer refuses to pay the extra money there's nothing you can do about it (at least legally). If you do decide to accept part of the price 'under the table', make sure that it's paid in cash *before* you sign the final deed (see **Avoiding Problems** on page 128). Note also that it can take some weeks before you receive the proceeds from the sale of a property in France, although a phone call to the *notaire* or bank involved can usually speed things up.

5.

ARRIVAL & SETTLING IN

On arrival in France, your first task will be to negotiate immigration and customs. Fortunately this presents few problems for most people, particularly European Union (EU) nationals after the establishment of 'open' EU borders on 1st January 1993. However, with the exception of EU nationals and visitors from a number of other countries, all others wishing to enter France require a visa (see page 18).

France is a signatory to the Schengen agreement (named after a Luxembourg village on the Moselle River where the agreement was signed) which came into effect on 1st January 1995 and introduced an open-border policy between member countries. These now comprise Austria, Belgium, France, Germany, Greece, Iceland, Italy, Luxembourg, the Netherlands, Portugal, Spain and Sweden. Under the agreement, immigration checks and passport controls take place when you first arrive in a member country, after which you can travel freely between member countries. However, France invoked a special 'safeguard' clause in the agreement to preserve frontier controls because of fears over illegal immigration and cross-border drug trafficking. France still carries out checks for drugs at some of its borders (particularly with Spain) and it's common for foreign motorists to be stopped by 'flying' customs officials (*douane volante*) anywhere in France.

In addition to information about immigration and customs, this chapter also contains checklists of tasks to be completed before or soon after arrival in France and when moving house, plus suggestions for finding local help and information.

IMMIGRATION

When you arrive in France from another EU country, there are usually no immigration checks or passport controls, which take place when you arrive in an EU country from outside the EU. If you're a non-EU national and arrive in France by air or sea from outside the EU, you must go through immigration (*police des frontières*) for non-EU citizens. If you have a single-entry visa it will be cancelled by the immigration official. **If you require a visa to enter France and attempt to enter without one, you will be refused entry.** Some people may wish to get a stamp in their passport as confirmation of their date of entry into France. If you're a non-EU national coming to France to work, study or live, you may be asked to show documentary evidence.

Immigration officials may ask non-EU visitors to produce a return ticket, proof of accommodation, health insurance and financial resources, e.g. cash, traveller's cheques and credit cards. The onus is on visitors to show that they are genuine and that they won't violate French immigration laws. Immigration officials aren't required to prove that you will breach the immigration laws and can refuse you entry on the grounds of suspicion only. Young people may be liable to interrogation, particularly long-haired youths with 'strange' attire. It's advantageous to carry international credit and charge cards, a return or onward travel ticket, a student identity card, and a letter from an employer or college stating that you're on holiday.

French immigration officials are usually polite and efficient, although they are occasionally a little over zealous in their attempts to exclude illegal immigrants, and some racial groups (e.g. Africans and Arabs) may experience harassment and persecution.

CUSTOMS

The Single European Act, which came into effect on 1st January 1993, created a single trading market and changed the rules regarding customs (*douanes*) for EU nationals. The shipment of personal (household) effects to France from another EU country is no longer subject to customs formalities, although an inventory must be provided. Note, however, that those arriving in France from outside the EU (including EU citizens) are still subject to customs checks and limitations on what may be imported duty-free. There are no restrictions on the import or export of French or foreign banknotes or securities, although if you enter or leave France with 50,000F or more in cash or negotiable instruments, you must make a declaration to French customs.

If you require general information about French customs regulations or have specific questions contact the *Centre Renseignement des Douanes*, 238, quai de Bercy, 75572 Paris Cedex 12 (☎ 01.40.01.02.06). Information about duty-free allowances can be found on page 65 and pets on page 66.

Visitors

Visitors' belongings aren't subject to duty or VAT when they are visiting France for up to 90 days. This applies to the importation of private cars, camping vehicles (including trailers or caravans), motorcycles, aircraft, boats and personal effects. Goods may be imported without formality providing their nature and quantity doesn't imply any commercial aim. All means of transport and personal effects imported duty-free mustn't be sold or given away in France and must be exported before the expiration of the 90-day period.

If you enter France by road you may drive (at a walking pace) through the border without stopping. However, any goods and pets that you're carrying must fall within the exemptions and mustn't be the subject of any prohibition or restriction (see page 204). Customs officials can still stop anyone for a spot check, e.g. to check for drugs or illegal immigrants. Occasionally (although rarer nowadays) you will come across an obstructive customs officer who will insist on inspecting everything in your car, which is often pure obstruction as they usually aren't looking for anything. However, if you enter France from Spain, particularly if you're a single male in an old car, your vehicle is likely to be searched and be 'inspected' by a drugs 'sniffer' dog.

If you arrive at a seaport by private boat there are no particular customs' formalities, although you must show the boat's registration papers if asked. If you arrive at a river port or land border with a boat, you may be asked to produce registration papers for the boat *and* its out-board motor(s). A foreign-registered boat may remain in France for a maximum of six months in a calendar year, after which it must be exported or permanently imported (and duty and tax paid). Foreign-registered vehicles and boats mustn't be lent or hired to anyone while in France.

Non-EU Residents

If you're a non-EU resident planning to take up permanent or temporary residence in France, you're permitted to import your furniture and personal effects free of duty. These include vehicles, mobile homes, pleasure boats and aircraft. However, to qualify for duty-free importation, articles must have been owned and used for at least six months. Value Added Tax (VAT) must be paid on items owned for less than six months that weren't purchased within the EU. If goods were purchased within the EU, a VAT receipt must be produced.

To import personal effects, an application must be made to the *Direction Régionale des Douanes* in the area where you will be resident. Customs clearance can be carried out by a customs office in an internal town in France, rather than at the border, in which case you should obtain a certificate (*carte de libre circulation*) proving that you have declared your belongings on entry into France and are entitled to travel with them.

All items should be imported within one year of the date of your change of residence, either in one or a number of consignments, although it's best to have one consignment only. After one year's residence in France, you must pay French VAT (TVA) on further imports from outside the EU, except in certain exceptional circumstances such as property resulting from an inheritance. A complete inventory of items to be imported (even if they're imported in a number of consignments) must be provided for customs officials, together with proof of residence in your former country and proof of settlement in France. If there's more than one consignment, subsequent consignments should be cleared through the same customs office.

If you use a removal company to transport your belongings to France, they will usually provide the necessary forms and take care of the paperwork. Keep a copy of forms and communications with customs officials, both French customs officials and those in your previous or permanent country of residence. You should have an official record of the export of valuables from any country in case you wish to re-import them later.

Prohibited & Restricted Goods

When entering France certain goods are subject to special regulations and in some cases their import (and export) is prohibited or restricted. This applies in particular to animal products; plants (see below); wild fauna and flora and products derived from them; live animals; medicines and medical products (except for prescribed drugs and medicines); firearms and ammunition; certain goods and technologies with a dual civil/military purpose; and works of art and collectors' items. If you're unsure whether any goods yo're importing fall into the above categories, you should check with French customs.

To import certain types of plants into France, you must obtain a phytosanitary health certificate (*certificats sanitaires*). Information can be obtained from the *Service de la Protection des Végétaux*, 175, rue du Chevaleret, 75646 Paris Cedex 13 (☎ 01.45.84.13.13) or your country's customs department. There's usually a limit on the number of plants that can be imported into France. However, as plants can be imported as part of your personal effects, they won't usually be subject to any controls.

If you make it through customs unscathed with your car loaded to the gunnels with illicit goods, don't be too quick to break out the champagne in celebration. France has 'flying' customs officials (*douane volante*) with the power to stop and search vehicles at random anywhere within its borders (they often stop vehicles at *autoroute* toll gates and roundabouts on national highways).

RESIDENCE PERMIT

All foreigners (legally) residing in France for longer than 90 days must register with the local authorities and obtain a residence permit. Whether you're an employee, student, or a non-employed resident, you must usually register within one week of taking up residence in France. EU nationals who visit France with the intention of finding employment or starting a business have three months in which to find a job and apply for a residence permit. Once employment has been found, an application must be made for a residence permit. If you don't have a regular income or adequate financial resources, your application will be refused. Failure to apply for a residence permit before three months have expired is a serious offence and may result in a fine. For further information see **Residence Permit** on page 18.

FINDING HELP

One of the biggest difficulties facing new arrivals in France is how and where to find help with day-to-day problems, for example finding accommodation, schooling, insurance and so on. **This book was written in response to this need.** However, in addition to the comprehensive information provided herein, you will also need detailed *local* information. How successful you are at finding help depends on your employer, the town or area where you live (e.g. residents of Paris are better served than those living in rural areas), your nationality, French proficiency and your sex (women are better served than men through numerous women's clubs).

There's an abundance of information available in French, but little in English and other foreign languages. An additional problem is that much of the available information isn't intended for foreigners and their particular needs. You may find that your friends and colleagues can help, as they can often offer advice based on their own experiences and mistakes. **But take care!** Although they mean well, you're likely to receive as much false and conflicting information as accurate (it may not necessarily be wrong, but may be invalid for your particular situation).

Your local community is usually an excellent source of reliable information, but you need to speak French to benefit from it. Your town hall (*mairie*) is often the local registry of births, deaths and marriages; passport office; land registry; council office; citizens advice bureau; and tourist office. Some companies employ staff to help new arrivals or contract this job out to a relocation consultant. However, most French employers are totally unaware of (or disinterested in) the problems and difficulties faced by foreign employees and their families.

An organisation of particular interest to foreigners moving to France is the 'National Union for Welcome in French Towns' (*Union Nationale des Accueils des Villes Françaises/AVF*). The AVF is a national organisation comprising over 600 local volunteer associations who provide a welcome for individuals and families, and help them settle into their new environment. Each association operates an information centre where information and advice is available free of charge. The address of local associations in France can be found via Minitel (3615 AVF-ACCUEIL) terminals at any post office. Foreigners planning to move to France can obtain information about particular areas from the *Union Nationale des AVF*, Relations Internationales, Secrétariat Administratif, 20, rue du 4 Septembre, 75002 Paris (☎ 01.40.17.02.36). Write to them indicating the town, department and region where you're planning to live and the reason for moving to France, e.g. work, retirement, study or training.

There's a wealth of valuable information and expatriate organisations in major French cities, particularly in Paris, where foreigners are well-served by English-speaking clubs and organisations. Contacts can be found through many expatriate magazines and newspapers. In Paris, the American Church (65, quai d'Orsay, 75007 Paris, ☎ 01.40.62.05.00), runs an annual newcomer's orientation series in October called 'Bloom Where You Are Planted'. The programme is designed to help foreigners adjust to life in France and consists of seminars on topics such as overcoming culture shock, survival skills, personal and professional opportunities, networking, enjoying France/food, fashion, travel and wine. The Women's Institute for Continuing Education (20, bd du Montparnasse, 75015 Paris, ☎ 01.45.66.75.50) also operate a 'Living in France' programme for newcomers, as do expatriate clubs and organisations throughout France.

Note that in France it isn't what you know, but who you know that can make the difference between success or failure. String-pulling or the use of contacts is widespread in France and is invaluable when it comes to breaking through the numerous layers of bureaucracy, when a telephone call on your behalf from a French neighbour or colleague can work wonders. In fact any contact can be of help, even a professional acquaintance, who may not even charge you for his time.

Most consulates provide their nationals with local information including details of lawyers, interpreters, doctors, dentists, schools, and social and expatriate organisations. The British Community Committee publishes a free *Digest of British and Franco-British Clubs, Societies and Institutions*, available from British consulates in France (see **Appendix A**).

Finally, you should buy a copy of *Living and Working in France* (Survival Books) written by your author David Hampshire (there's an order form on page 240), which contains essential information about life in France for both visitors and residents.

CHECKLISTS

Before Arrival

The checklists on the following pages list tasks which you need (or may need) to complete before and after arrival in France, and when moving your home permanently to France.

- Check that your and your family's passports are valid.

- Obtain a visa, if necessary, for you and all your family members (see page 18). Obviously this *must* be done before arrival in France.

- Arrange health and travel insurance for yourself and your family (see pages 53 and 59). This is essential if you aren't already covered by an international health insurance policy and won't be covered by French social security.

- If you don't already have one, it's advisable to obtain an international credit or charge card, which will prove invaluable in France.

- If necessary, obtain an international driver's licence.

- Open a bank account in France (see page 84) and transfer funds. You can open an account with many French banks from abroad, although it's best done in person in France.

- It's advisable to obtain some French francs before arriving in France as this will save you having to queue to change money on arrival (and you will probably receive a better exchange rate).

- If you plan to become a permanent resident you may also need to do the following:

  - Arrange schooling for your children.

  - Organise the shipment of your personal and household effects.

  - Obtain as many credit references as possible, for example from banks, mortgage companies, credit card companies, credit agencies, companies with which you have had accounts, and references from professionals such as lawyers and accountants. These will help you to establish a credit rating in France.

If you're planning to become a permanent resident don't forget to take all your family's official documents with you. These may include birth certificates; driving licences; marriage certificate, divorce papers or death certificate (if a widow or widower); educational diplomas and professional certificates; employment references and curriculum vitaes; school records and student ID cards; medical and dental records; bank account and credit card details; insurance policies (plus records of no-claims' allowances); and receipts for any valuables. You also need the documents necessary to obtain a residence permit plus certified copies, official translations and numerous passport-size photographs (students should take at least a dozen).

After Arrival

The following checklist contains a summary of the tasks to be completed after arrival in France (if not done before arrival):

- On arrival at a French airport or port, have your visa cancelled and your passport stamped, as applicable.

- If you aren't taking a car with you, you may wish to rent (see page 44) or buy one locally. Note that it's practically impossible to get around in rural areas without a car.

- Open a cheque account (see page 84) at a local bank and give the details to any companies that you plan to pay by direct debit or standing order (such as utility and property management companies).

- Arrange whatever insurance is necessary such as health, car, household and third party liability.

- Contact offices and organisations to obtain local information (see page 205).

- Make courtesy calls on your neighbours and the local mayor within a few weeks of your arrival. This is particularly important in villages and rural areas if you want to be accepted and become part of the local community.

- If you plan to become a permanent resident in France, you will need to do the following within the next few weeks (if not done before your arrival):

- apply for a residence permit at your local mairie or préfecture within one week of your arrival;
- apply for a social security card from your local social security office;
- find a local doctor and dentist;
- arrange schooling for your children.

Moving House

When moving permanently to France there are many things to be considered and a 'million' people to be informed. Even if you plan to spend just a few months a year in France, it may still be necessary to inform a number of people and companies in your home country. The checklists below are designed to make the task easier and help prevent an ulcer or a nervous breakdown (providing of course you don't leave everything to the last minute). See also **Moving House** on page 176 and **Moving In** on page 178.

● If you live in rented accommodation you will need to give your landlord notice (check your contract).

● If you own your home, arrange to sell or rent it well in advance of your move.

● Inform the following:

- Your employer, e.g. give notice or arrange leave of absence.
- Your local town hall or municipality. You may be entitled to a refund of your local taxes.
- If it was necessary to register with the police in your home country, you should inform them that you're moving abroad.
- Your electricity, gas, water and telephone companies. Contact companies well in advance, particularly if you need to get a deposit refunded.
- Your insurance companies (for example health, car, home contents and private pension); banks, post office (if you have a post office account), stockbroker and other financial institutions; credit card, charge card and hire purchase companies; lawyer and accountant; and local businesses where you have accounts.
- Your family doctor, dentist and other health practitioners. Health records should be transferred to your new doctor and dentist, if applicable.
- Your children's schools. Try to give a term's notice and obtain a copy of any relevant school reports or records from your children's current schools.
- All regular correspondents, subscriptions, social and sports clubs, professional and trade journals, and friends and relatives. Give them your new address and telephone number and arrange to have your mail redirected by the post office or a friend.
- If you have a driving licence or car you will need to give the local vehicle registration office your new address abroad and, in some countries, return your car's registration plates.

- Return any library books or anything borrowed.

- Arrange shipment of your furniture and belongings by booking a shipping company well in advance (see page 176). Major international moving companies usually provide a wealth of information and can advise on a wide range of matters concerning an international relocation. Find out the exact procedure for shipping your belongings to France from your local French embassy or consulate.

- Arrange to sell anything you aren't taking with you (e.g. house, car and furniture). If you're selling a home or business, you should obtain expert legal advice as you may be able to save tax by establishing a trust or other legal vehicle. Note that if you own more than one property, you may have to pay capital gains tax on any profits from the sale of second and subsequent homes.

- If you have a car that you're exporting to France, you will need to complete the relevant paperwork in your home country and re-register it in France after its arrival. Contact your local French embassy or consulate for information.

- Arrange inoculations and shipment for any pets that you're taking with you (see page 66).

- You may qualify for a rebate on your tax and social security contributions. If you're leaving a country permanently and have been a member of a company or state pension scheme, you may be entitled to a refund or may be able to continue payments to qualify for a full (or larger) pension when you retire. Contact your company personnel office, local tax office or pension company for information.

- It's advisable to arrange health, dental and optical check-ups for your family before leaving your home country (see page 50). Obtain a copy of all health records and a statement from your private health insurance company stating your present level of cover.

- Terminate any outstanding loan, lease or hire purchase contracts and pay all bills (allow plenty of time as some companies are slow to respond).

- Check whether you're entitled to a rebate on your road tax, car and other insurance. Obtain a letter from your motor insurance company stating your no-claims' discount.

- Check whether you need an international driving licence or a translation of your foreign driving licence(s) for France. Note that some foreigners are required to take a driving test in France in order to buy and register a car.

- Give friends and business associates an address and telephone number where you can be contacted in France.

- If you will be living in France for an extended period (but not permanently), you may wish to give someone 'power of attorney' over your financial affairs in your home country so that they can act for you in your absence. This can be for a fixed period or open-ended and can be for a specific purpose only. **Note, however, that you should take expert legal advice before doing this!**

- Allow plenty of time to get to the airport, register your luggage, and clear security and immigration.

Bon Voyage!

APPENDICES

APPENDIX A: USEFUL ADDRESSES

Embassies

Foreign embassies are located in the capital Paris and many countries also have consulates in other cities (British provincial consulates are listed on page 215). Embassies and consulates are listed in the Yellow Pages under *Ambassades, consulats et autres représentations diplomatiques*. Note that many countries have more than one office in Paris. Before writing or calling you should telephone to confirm that you have the correct address. A selection of embassies are listed below:

Albania: 131, rue Pompe, 16e (☎ 01.45.53.51.32).

Algeria: 50, rue Lisbonne, 8e (☎ 01.53.93.20.20).

Angola: 19, av Foch, 16e (☎ 01.45.01.58.20).

Argentina: 6, rue Cimarosa, 16e (☎ 01.45.53.22.25).

Armenia: 9 rue Viète, 17e (☎ 01.42.12.98.00)

Australia: 4, rue Jean Rey, 15e (☎ 01.40.59.33.00).

Austria: 6, rue Fabert, 7e (☎ 01.45.56.97.86).

Bahrain: 3015 pl Etats-Unis, 16e (☎ 01.47.23.48.68).

Bangladesh: 5, sq Pétrarque, 16e (☎ 01.45.53.41.20).

Belgium: 9, rue Tilsitt, 17e (☎ 01.44.09.39.39).

Benin: 87, av Victor Hugo, 16e (☎ 01.45.00.98.82).

Bolivia: 12, av Président Kennedy, 16e (☎ 01.42.24.93.44).

Bosnia Herzegovenia: 194 rue Courcales, 17e (☎ 01.42.67.34.22)

Brazil: 34 Cours Albert 1er, 8e (☎ 01.45.61.63.00).

Brunei Darussalam: 4, rue Logelbach, 17e (☎ 01.42.67.49.47).

Bulgaria: 1, av Rapp, 7e (☎ 01.45.51.85.90).

Cambodia: 4 rue Adolphe Yvon, 16e (☎ 01.45.03.47.20)

Cameroon: 73, rue Auteuil, 16e (☎ 01.47.43.98.33).

Canada: 35, av Montaigne, 8e (☎ 01.44.43.29.16).

Central African Republic: 30, rue Perchamps, 16e (☎ 01.42.24.42.56).

Chad: 65, rue Belles Feuilles, 16e (☎ 01.45.53.36.75).

Chile: 2, av La Motte Picquet, 7e (☎ 01.44.18.59.60).

China: 11, av George V, 8e (☎ 01.47.23.36.77).

Colombia: 22, rue Elysée, 8e (☎ 01.42.65.46.08).

Comoros: 20, rue Marbeau, 16e (☎ 01.40.67.90.54).

Congo: 37 bis, rue Paul Valéry, 16e (☎ 01.45.00.68.57).

Costa Rica: 78, av Emile Zola, 15e (☎ 01.45.78.96.96).

Cote d'Ivoire: 102, av Raymond Poincaré, 16e (☎ 01.53.64.62.62).

Croacia: 79, av Georges Manbel, 16e (☎ 01.53.70.02.80)

Cyprus: 23, rue Galilée, 8e (☎ 01.47.20.86.28).

Czech Republic: 15, av Charles Floquet, 7e (☎ 01.40.65.13.00).

Cuba: 16, rue Presles, 15e (☎ 01.45.67.55.35).

Denmark: 77, av Marceau, 16e (☎ 01.44.31.21.21).
Djibouti: 26, rue Emile Menier, 16e (☎ 01.47.27.49.22).
Ecuador: 34, av Messine, 8e (☎ 01.42.56.22.59).
Egypt: 56, av Léna, 16e (☎ 01.53.67.88.30).
El Salvador: 12, rue Galilée, 16e (☎ 01.47.20.42.02).
Estonia: 14, bd Montmartre, 9e (☎ 01.48.01.00.22).
Ethiopia: 35, av Charles Floquet, 7e (☎ 01.47.83.83.95).
Finland: 2, rue Fabert, 7e (☎ 01.44.18.19.28).
Gabon: 26 bis, av Raphaël, 16e (☎ 01.44.30.22.60).
Gambia: 17, rue St Lazare, 8e (☎ 01.42.94.09.30).
Germany: 13, av F.D. Roosevelt, 8e (☎ 01.53.83.45.00).
Ghana: 8, villa Said, 16e (☎ 01.45.00.09.50).
Greece: 17, rue Auguste Vacquerie, 16e (☎ 01.47.23.72.28).
Guatemala: 73, rue Courcelles, 8e (☎ 01.42.27.78.63).
Guinea: 51, rue Faisanderie, 16e (☎ 01.47.04.81.48).
Guinea-Bissau: 94, rue St. Lazare, 9e (☎ 01.45.26.18.51).
Haiti: 10, rue Théodule Ribot, 17e (☎ 01.47.63.47.78).
Honduras: 8, rue Crevaux, 16e (☎ 01.47.55.86.43).
Hungary: 5 bis, sq Avenue Foch, 16e (☎ 01.45.00.41.59).
Iceland: 8, av Kléber , 16 (☎ 01.44.17.32.85).
India: 15, rue Alfred Dehodencq, 16e (☎ 01.40.58.70.70).
Indonesia: 49, rue Cortambert, 16e (☎ 01.45.03.07.60).
Iran: 4, av Léna, 16e (☎ 01.40.69.70.00).
Ireland: 41, rue Rude, 16e (☎ 01.44.17.67.00).
Israel: 3, rue Rabelais, 8e (☎ 01.40.76.55.00).
Italy: 51, rue Varenne, 7e (☎ 01.49.54.03.00).
Jamaica: 60, av Fich, 16e (☎ 01.45.00.62.25).
Japan: 7 av Hoche, 8e (☎ 01.48.88.62.00).
Kenya: 3, rue Cimarosa, 16e (☎ 01.45.53.35.00).
Korea: 125, rue Grenelle, 7e (☎ 01.47.53.01.01).
Kuwait: 2, rue Lubeck, 16e (☎ 01.47.23.54.25).
Laos: 74, av Raymond Poincaré, 16e (☎ 01.45.53.02.98).
Latvia: 6, Villa Saïd, 16e (☎ 01.53.64.58.10).
Lebanon: 42, rue Copernic, 16e (☎ 01.40.67.75.75).
Liberia: 12, pl Général Catroux, 17e (☎ 01.47.63.58.55).
Libya: 2, rue Charles Lamoureux, 16e (☎ 01.45.53.40.70).
Lithuania: 14, bd Montmartre, 9e (☎ 01.48.01.00.33).
Luxembourg: 33, av Rapp, 7e (☎ 01.45.55.13.37).
Madagascar: 4, av Raphaël, 16e (☎ 01.45.04.62.11).
Malawi: 20, rue Euler, 8e (☎ 01.40.70.18.46).
Malaysia: 32, rue Spontini, 16e (☎ 01.45.53.11.85).
Mali: 89, rue Cherche Midi, 6e (☎ 01.45.48.58.43).

Malta: 92, av Champs Elysées, 8e (☎ 01.45.62.53.01).
Mexico: 9, rue Longchamp, 16e (☎ 01.42.61.51.80).
Monaco: 22, bd Suchet, 16e (☎ 01.45.04.74.54).
Morocco: 35, rue Le Tasse, 16e (☎ 01.45.20.69.35).
Mozambique: 82, rue Laugier, 17e (☎ 01.47.64.91.32).
Myanmar: 60, rue Courcelles, 8e (☎ 01.42.25.56.95).
Nepal: 45 bis, rue Acacias, 17e (☎ 01.46.22.48.67).
Netherlands: 7, rue Eblé, 7e (☎ 01.40.62.34.66).
New Zealand: 7 ter, rue Léonard de Vinci, 16e (☎ 01.45.00.24.11).
Nicaragua: 34, av Bugeaud, 16e (☎ 01.44.05.90.42).
Niger: 154, rue Longchamp, 16e (☎ 01.45.04.80.60).
Nigeria: 173, av Victor Hugo, 16e (☎ 01.47.04.68.65).
Norway: 28, rue Bayard, 8e (☎ 01.53.67.04.00).
Oman: 50, av Léna, 16e (☎ 01.47.23.01.63).
Pakistan: 18, rue Lord Byron, 8e (☎ 01.45.62.23.32).
Panama: 145, av Suffren, 15e (☎ 01.47.83.23.32).
Paraguay: 1, rue St Dominique, 7e (☎ 01.42.22.85.05).
Peru: 50, av Kléber, 16e (☎ 01.53.70.42.00).
Poland: 1, rue Talleyrand, 7e (☎ 01.45.51.49.12).
Portugal: 3, rue Noisiel, 16e (☎ 01.47.27.35.29).
Qatar: 57, quai Orsay, 7e (☎ 01.45.51.90.71).
Romania: 3, rue Exposition, 7e (☎ 01.45.51.42.46).
Russia: 40, bd Lannes, 16e (☎ 01.45.04.05.50).
Rwanda: 12, rue Jadin, 17e (☎ 01.42.27.36.31).
San Marino: 21, rue Auguste Vacquerie, 16e (☎ 01.47.23.78.05).
Saudi Arabia: 5, av Hoche, 8e (☎ 01.47.66.02.06).
Senegal: 14, av Robert Schuman, 7e (☎ 01.47.05.39.45).
Seychelles: 51, rue Mozart, 16e (☎ 01.42.30.57.47).
Sierra Leone: 16, av Hoche, 8e (☎ 01.42.56.14.73).
Singapore: 12, sq Avenue Foch, 16e (☎ 01.45.00.33.61).
Somalia: 26, rue Dumont d'Urville, 16e (☎ 01.45.00.76.51).
South Africa: 59, quai Orsay, 7e (☎ 01.53.59.23.23).
Spain: 22, av Marceau, 8e (☎ 01.44.43.18.00).
Sri Lanka: 15, rue Astorg, 8e (☎ 01.42.66.35.01).
Sudan: 56, av Montaigne, 8e (☎ 01.42.25.55.73).
Sweden: 17, rue Barbet de Jouy, 7e (☎ 01.44.18.88.00).
Switzerland: 142, rue Grenelle, 7e (☎ 01.49.55.67.00).
Syria: 20, rue Vaneau, 7e (☎ 01.47.05.92.73).
Tanzania: 13, av Raymond Poincare, 16e (☎ 01.53.70.63.66).
Thailand: 12, rue Lord Byron, 8e (☎ 01.42.89.89.44).
Togo: 15, rue Madrid, 8e (☎ 01.44.70.04.39).
Tunisia: 25, rue Barbet de Jouy, 7e (☎ 01.45.55.95.98).

Turkey: 16, av Lamballe, 16e (☎ 01.45.24.52.24).
Uganda: 13, av Raymond Poincaré, 16e (☎ 01.53.70.62.70).
United Arab Emirates: 3, rue Lota, 16e (☎ 01.45.53.94.04).
United Kingdom: 35, rue Fauberg St. Honoré, 8e (☎ 01.44.51.31.02).
United States of America: 2, rue St Florentin, 1e (☎ 01.43.12.23.47).
Uruguay: 15, rue Le Sueur, 16e (☎ 01.45.00.81.37).
Venezuela: 11, rue Copernic, 16e (☎ 01.45.53.29.98).
Vietnam: 62, rue Boileau, 16e (☎ 01.44.14.64.00).
Yemen: 25, rue Georges Bizet, 16e (☎ 01.47.23.61.76).
Yugoslavia (Republic of): 54, rue Faisanderie, 16e (☎ 01.40.72.24.24)
Zaire: 32, cours Albert, 1er, 8e (☎ 01.42.25.57.50).
Zambia: 34, av Messing, 8e (☎ 01.45.61.05.08).
Zimbabwe: 5, rue Tilsitt, 8e (☎ 01.53.81.90.10).

British Provincial Consulates

Biarritz, British Consulate (Hon.), 7, av Edouard VII, Barclays Banks SA, 64202 Biarittz Cedex (☎ 05.59.24.21.40).
Bordeaux, British Consulate-General, 353, bd du Président Wilson, BP 91, 33073 Bordeaux Cedex (☎ 05.57.22.21.10).
Boulogne-sur-Mer, British Consulate (Hon.), c/o Cotrama, Tour Administrative, Hoverport, 62200 Boulogne-sur-Mer (☎ 03.21.87.16.80).
Calais, British Consulate, c/o P&O European Ferries, 41, place d'Armes, 62100 Calais (☎ 03.21.96.33.76).
Cherbourg, British Consulate (Hon.), c/o P&O European Ferries, Gare Maritime, 50101 Cherbourg (☎ 02.33.44.20.13).
Dinard, British Consulate (Hon.), La Hulotte, 8, bd des Maréchaux, 35800 Dinard (☎ 02.99.46.26.64).
Dunkerque, British Consulate (Hon.), c/o L. Dewulf, Cailleret & Fils, 11, rue des Arbres, BP 1502, 59383 Dunkerque (☎ 03.28.66.11.98).
Le Havre, British Consulate (Hon.), c/o Lloyds Register of Shipping, 124, bd de Strasbourg, 76600 Le Havre (☎ 02.35.42.27.47).
Lille, British Consulate-General, 11, square Dutilleul, 59800 Lille (☎ 03.20.12.82.72).
Lyon, British Consulate-General, 24, rue Childebert, 69288 Lyon Cedex 1 (☎ 04.72.77.81.70).
Marseille, British Consulate-General, 24, av du Prado, 13006 Marseille (☎ 04.91.15.72.10). Also deals with **Monaco**.
Nantes, British Consulate (Hon.), L'Aumarière, 44220 Couëron (☎ 02.40.63.16.02).
Nice, British Consulate (Hon.), 8, rue Alphonse Kerr, 06000 Nice (☎ 04.93.82.32.04). Also deals with **Monaco**.
Toulouse, British Consulate (Hon.), c/o Lucas Aerospace, Victoria Center, 20, chemin de Laporte, 31300 Toulouse (☎ 05.61.15.02.02).

English-Language Newspapers & Magazines

Blue Coast, 32, rue Maréchal Joffre, 06000 Nice, France. Monthly magazine.

Boulevard, Mediatime France SA, 68, rue des Archives, 75003 Paris, France. Paris lifestyle magazine.

France Magazine, Dormer House, Stow-on-the-Wold, Glos. GL54 1BN, UK. Monthly lifestyle magazine.

France-USA Contacts, FUSAC, 3 rue La Rochelle, 75014 Paris, France. Free weekly magazine.

French Property News, 2A Lambton Road, London SW20 0LR, UK. Monthly property newspaper.

Focus on France, Outbound Publishing, 1 Commercial Road, Eastbourne, East Sussex BN21 3XQ, UK.

Living France, 79 High Street, Olney MK46 4EF, UK. Monthly lifestyle/property magazine.

The News, Brussac, 3, chemin La Monzie, 24000 Perigueux, France. Monthly newspaper.

Paris Free Voice, 65, quai d'Orsay, 75007 Paris, France. Free weekly newspaper.

The Riviera Reporter, 56, chemin de Provence, 06250 Mougins, France. Monthly free magazine.

Miscellaneous

Alliance Française, 101, blvd Raspail, 75270 Paris Cedex 06 (☎ 01.45.44.38.28).

Association Nationale pour l'Information sur le Logement, 2, blvd. St. Martin, 75010 Paris (☎ 01.42.02.05.50).

Automobile Club de France, 6-8, Place de la Concorde, 75008 Paris (☎ 01.42.65.34.70).

British Association of Removers (BAR) Overseas, 3 Churchill Court, 58 Station Road, North Harrow, Middx. HA2 7SA, UK (☎ 0181-861 3331).

British Business Centre, BP 21, 14700 Falaise (☎ 03.31.40.05.77).

Centre d'Échanges Internationaux, 104, rue de Vaugirard, 75006 Paris (☎ 01.45.49.26.25).

Centre Française de Londres, 61/69 Chepstow Place, London W2 4TR, UK (☎ 0171-792 0337).

Centre d'Information des Notaires, 1, blvd. de Sébastopol, 75005 Paris (☎ 01.44.82.24.00).

Centre des Impôts de Non-Résidents, 9, rue d'Uzès, 75094 Paris Cedex 02.

Centre National de Documentation sur l'Enseignement Privé, 20, rue Faubert, 75007 Paris (☎ 01.47.05.32.68).

Centre Nationale pour l'Aménagement des Structures des Expositions, 7, rue Ernest Renan, BP 1, 92136 Issy les Moulineaux Cedex (☎ 01.46.48.40.00).

Centre Renseignements Douaniers, 23, rue de l'Université, 75007 Paris (☎ 01.40.24.65.10).

Chambre de Commerce Française de Grande Bretagne, Knightsbridge House, 197 Knightsbridge, London SW7 1RB, UK (☎ 0171-304 4040).

Chambres des Experts Immobiliers, c/o FNAIM, 129, rue du Fauberg St-Honoré, 75008 Paris (☎ 01.42.25.24.26).

Commission de Contrôle des Assurances, 54, rue de Châteaudun, 75436 Paris Cedex 09 (☎ 01.40.82.20.20).

Compagnie Nationale des Experts Immobiliers, 18, rue Volney, 75002 Paris (☎ 01.42.96.18.46).

Confédération Nationale des Experts Agricoles et Fonciers et des Experts Forestiers (CNEAFF), 6, rue St. Didier, 75116 Paris (☎ 01.47.27.00.89).

Conseil Supérieur du Notariat, 31, rue du Général Foy, 75008 Paris (☎ 01.44.90.30.00).

Délégation à l'Aménagement du Territoire et à l'Action Régionale (DATAR), 21-24 Grovenor Place, London SW1X 7HU, UK (☎ 0171-235 5140) and 1, avenue Charles Floquet, 75007 Paris (☎ 01.47.83.61.20 or 01.40.65.12.34).

Electricité de France, 2, rue Louis Murat, 75008 Paris (☎ 01.40.42.22.22).

Fédération Nationale des Agents Immobiliers et Mandataires (FNAIM), 129, rue du Fauberg St. Honoré, 75008 Paris (☎ 01.44.20.77.00).

Fédération Nationale des Gîtes de France, 35, rue Godot-de-Mauroy, 75439 Paris Cédex 09 (☎ 01.47.42.20.20).

Fédération Nationale des Société d'Aménagement Foncier et d'Etablissement Rural (FNSAFER), 3, rue de Turin, 75008 Paris (☎ 01.42.93.66.06)

Federation of Overseas Property Developers, Agents and Consultants (FOPDAC), PO Box 3524, London NW5 1DQ, UK (☎ 0181-744 2362).

French Government Tourist Office, 178 Piccadilly, London W1V 0AL, UK (☎ 0171-491 7622/0891-244123).

Institut de Langue Française, 15, rue Arsène Houssaye, 75008 Paris (☎ 01.42.27.14.77).

Ministry of Agriculture, Fisheries & Food (MAFF), Animal Health (International Trade) Division B, Hook Rise South, Tolworth, Surbiton, Surrey KT6 7NF, UK (☎ 0181-330 4411).

Office du Tourisme, 127, av des Champs-Elysées, 75008 Paris (☎ 01.49.52.53.54).

Order des Avocats à la Cour de Paris, Palais de Justice, 4, blvd du Palais, 75001 Paris (☎ 01.44.32.48.48).

De Particulier à Particulier, 8, rue du Général Delastraint, 75016 Paris (☎ 01.46.51.01.11).

Touring Club de France, 14 ave. de la Grand Armée, 75017 Paris (☎ 01.43.80.68.58).

Union Nationale des AVF, Relations Internationales, Secrétariat Administratif, 20, rue du 4 Septembre, 75002 Paris (☎ 01.40.17.02.36).

APPENDIX B: FURTHER READING

The books listed below are just a small selection of the many books written for those planning to buy a home or work in France. Note that some titles may be out of print, but may still be obtainable from bookshops and libraries. Books prefixed with an asterisk (*) are recommended by the author.

Property & Business

Buying and Renovating Property in France, J. Kater Pollock (Flowerpoll)
*Buying & Restoring Old Property in France, David Everett (Robert Hale)
Buying and Selling Residential Property in France (French Chamber of Commerce)
*Can We Afford The Bidet?, Elizabeth Morgan (Lennard)
*English-French Building and Property Dictionary, J. Kater Pollock (Flowerpoll)
*French Country, Buchholz & Skolnik (Aurum Press)
*The French Farmhouse, Elsie Burch Donald (Little, Brown & Co.)
French Housing, Laws & Taxes, Frank Rutherford (Sprucehurst)
French Real Property and Succession Law, Henry Dyson (Robert Hale)
The French Room, Elizabeth Wilhide (Conran Otopus)
French Style, Suzanne Slesin and Stafford Dliff (Thames and Hudson)
The French Touch, Daphné de Saint Sauveur (Thames & Hudson)
A Guide to Renovating Your Home in France, Janine Paul (199 Amyand Park Road, Twickenham, Middx. TW1 3HN).
At Home in France, Christopher Petkanas (Weidenfeld & Nicolson)
*At Home in France, Jane Hawking (Allegretto)
Letting French Property Successfully, Stephen Smith & Charles Parkinson (PFK Publishing)
Maison Therapy, Alastair Simpson (New Horizon)
The Most Beautiful Villages of the Dordogne, James Bentley
*One Foot in France, Roger Pilkington
Plat du Jour, Tom Higgins (Aurum Press)
Really Rural, Marie-France Boyer (Thames & Hudson)
Setting Up a Small Business in France (French Chamber of Commerce)
*Traditional Houses of Rural France, Bill Laws (BCA)
The Villages of Northern France, Andrew Sanger & John Miller (Le Shuttle/ Pavilion)

Accommodation/Self-Catering

Alistair Sawday's French Bed & Breakfast (Alistair Sawday Publishing)
Bed & Breakfast of Character and Charm in France (Fodor's Rivages)
Bed & Breakfast France (B&B France, ☎ UK 01491-578803)
*Café Couette (available from FGTOs)

Chambre d'Hôtes de Prestige (Gîtes de France)
Chambre d'Hôtes et Table d'Hôtes (Gîtes de France)
*Charming Small Hotel Guides: France Bed & Breakfast, Paul Wade & Kathy Arnold (Duncan Peterson)
*French Country Welcome (Gîtes de France)
French Entrée Bed and Breakfast in France, Patricia Fenn & Rosemary Gower-Jones (Quiller Press)
*Gîtes de France Official Handbook (Gîtes de France)
*The Gîtes Guide (FHG Publications)
Gîtes et Refuges en France (Éditions Créer)
*The Good Hotel Guide: France, Hilary Rubenstein (Papermac)
Guide to Hotels and Country Inns of Character and Charm in France (Rivages)
*Karen Brown's French Country Bed & Breakfast (Travel Press)
*Michelin Green Guide - Camping and Caravanning (Michelin)
*Michelin Red Guide (Michelin)
*Self-Catering France, John P. Harris and William Hedley (Collins)

Living & Working in France

*A Bull by the Back Door, Anne Loader (Léonie Press)
The Dreamer's Guide to Living in France, John Hodgkinson (Breese Books)
*The Duck With a Dirty Laugh, Anne Loader (Léonie Press)
*An Englishman in the Midi, John P. Harris (BBC)
French Dirt, Richard Goodman (Pavilion Books)
French or Foe, Polly Platt (Culture Crossings)
Home and Dry in France, George East (La Puce Publications)
*A House in the Sunflowers, Ruth Silvestre (WH Allen)
Living as a British Expatriate in France (French Chamber of Commerce)
**Living and Working in France, David Hampshire (Survival Books)
Long Stays in France, Dorothy Phillpotts and Rosalind Mazzawi (David & Charles)
*More From an Englishman in the Midi, John P. Harris (BBC)
*A Normandy Tapestry, Alan Biggins (Kirkdale Books)
Paradise Found, Jim Keeble (Carnell)
*Perfume from Provence, Lady Fortescue (Black Swan)
*René & Me, George East (La Puce Publications)
*Some of My Best Friends are French, Colin Corder (Shelf Publishing)
*Sunset House, Lady Fortescue (Black Swan)
To Live in France, James Bentley
*Toujours Provence, Peter Mayle (Pan)
*Understanding France, John P. Harris (Papermac)
*A White House in Gascony, Rex Grixell (Victor Gollancz)
*A Year in Provence, Peter Mayle (Pan)

APPENDIX C: MAP OF REGIONS & DEPARTMENTS

The map opposite shows the 22 regions and 95 departments of France, which are listed below. The departments are (mostly) numbered alphabetically from 01 to 89. Departments 91 to 95 come under the Ile-de-France region, which also includes Ville de Paris (75), Seine-et-Marne (77) and Yvelines (78), shown in detail opposite. A map of France showing the major cities and geographical features is on page 6.

01 Ain	33 Gironde	65 Hautes-Pyrénées
02 Aisne	34 Hérault	66 Pyrénées-Orientales
03 Allier	35 Ille-et-Vilaine	67 Bas-Rhin
04 Alpes-de-Hte-Provence	36 Indre	68 Haut-Rhin
05 Hautes-Alpes	37 Indre-et-Loire	69 Rhône
06 Alpes-Maritimes	38 Isère	70 Haute-Saône
07 Ardèche	39 Jura	71 Saône-et-Loire
08 Ardennes	40 Landes	72 Sarthe
09 Ariège	41 Loir-et-Cher	73 Savoie
10 Aube	42 Loire	74 Haute-Savoie
11 Aude	43 Haute-Loire	75 Paris
12 Aveyron	44 Loire-Atlantique	76 Seine-Maritime
13 Bouches-du-Rhône	45 Loiret	77 Seine-et-Marne
14 Calvados	46 Lot	78 Yvelines
15 Cantal	47 Lot-et-Garonne	79 Deux-Sèvres
16 Charente	48 Lozère	80 Somme
17 Charente-Maritime	49 Maine-et-Loire	81 Tarn
18 Cher	50 Manche	82 Tarn-et-Garonne
19 Corrèze	51 Marne	83 Var
20 Corse	52 Haute-Marne	84 Vaucluse
21 Côte-d'Or	53 Mayenne	85 Vendée
22 Côtes-d'Armor	54 Meurthe-et-Moselle	86 Vienne
23 Creuse	55 Meuse	87 Haute-Vienne
24 Dordogne	56 Morbihan	88 Vosges
25 Doubs	57 Moselle	89 Yonne
26 Drôme	58 Nièvre	90 Territoire de Belfort
27 Eure	59 Nord	91 Essonne
28 Eure-et-Loir	60 Oise	92 Hauts-de-Seine
29 Finistère	61 Orne	93 Seine-Saint-Denis
30 Gard	62 Pas-de-Calais	94 Val-de-Marne
31 Haute-Garonne	63 Puy-de-Dôme	95 Val-d'Oise
32 Gers	64 Pyrénées-Atlantiques	

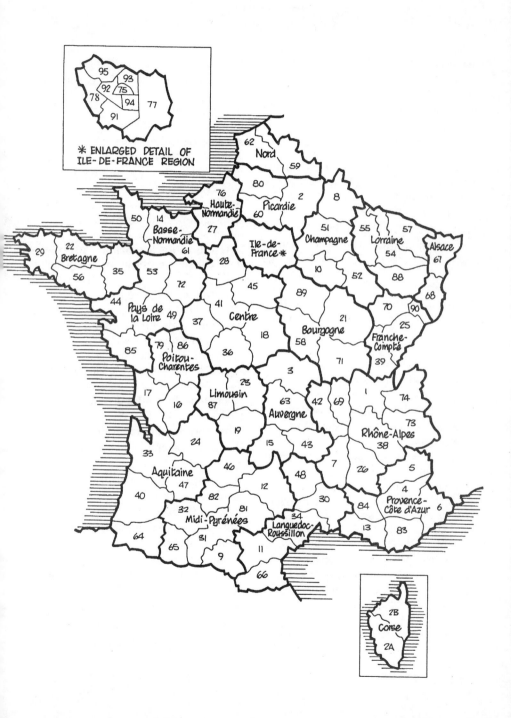

APPENDIX E: GLOSSARY

Abonnement: Standing charge, e.g. for electricity, gas, telephone or water services.

Achat en Viager: Buying a property by paying a life annuity with the vendor as naméd beneficiary.

Acompte: Deposit (non-refundable). If a deposit is described as *acompte* neither party can withdraw and the sale can be legally enforced.

Acquéreur: The buyer.

Acte: Legal document or deed.

Acte authentique: The final contract (authentic deed or document) for the purchase of a property drawn up, verified and stamped by a notary.

Acte en main: The total cost of a property including agent's and notary's fees.

Acte de vente: Deed of sale or conveyance document.

Administration Fiscale: Tax authorities.

Agent immobilier: Real estate agent.

Aggrandissement: Extension or enlargement.

Aménagé/aménageable: Converted/convertible.

Amortissement: Amortisation. The gradual process of systematically reducing debt in equal payments (as in a mortgage) comprising both principal and interest, until the debt is paid in full.

Appartement: Apartment or flat.

Appartement bourgeois: Spacious (usually 19th century) apartment with separate servant's quarters (*chambre de bonne*).

Appartement de standing: A luxury (usually modern) apartment. Also called a *grand standing*.

Appentis: Lean-to.

Are: 100 square metres.

Arrhes: Deposit (refundable).

Arrière-pays: Hinterland, i.e. not by the sea.

Arrondissement: Administrative districts in Lyon and Paris.

Ascenseur: Lift or elevator.

Assurance multirisques habitation: Fully comprehensive (all-risk) household insurance policy.

Atelier: Workshop.

Attestation d'acquisition: Proof of purchase.

Attestation de conformité aux règles de sécurité: Certificate of safety standards.

Attestation de propriété: Proof of ownership of a property.

Attribution de juridiction: The formal signing of a purchase contract.

Authentique: Authentic, i.e. a document signed in the presence of a notary and authenticated by him.

Avec tout le confort: With all mod. cons.

Avec travaux: For renovation.

Avocat: Lawyer or solicitor.

Bail: Lease.

Bailleur: Lessor, e.g. the owner or landlord of a property.

Balcon: Balcony.

Ballon (à eau chaude): Hot water tank or immersion heater.

Banlieue: Suburb.

Bastide: Square or fortified stone house.

Bâtiment: Building.

Bergerie: Sheepfold or sheep pen.

Biens mobiliers: Movable property.

Bilan (de santé immobilier): Survey (house).

Bi-propriété: Shared ownership.

Bois/Boiserie: Wood/woodwork.

Bon état: Good condition.

(au) Bord de la Mer: By the sea.

Bourg: Small town or large village.

Bricolage: Building, repairs and do-it-yourself (DIY) supplies.

Brique: Brick.

Buanderie: Wash house, laundry or utility room.

Bûcher: Woodshed.

Bureau: Study.

Bureau de vente: Sales office.

Cabinet: A small room.

Cabinet WC: Toilet.

Cadastre: Land registry/land registration.

(à la) Campagne: In the country.

Carré: Square (measurement); a *mètre carré* is a square metre.

Caution: Guarantee or security deposit.

Cave: Cellar.

Cave voûtée: Vaulted cellar.

Cellier: Storeroom or cellar.

Centre foncier: Land office.

Centre des impôts: Tax office. Also called a *bureau des impôts* or *hôtel d'Impôts*.

Certificat d'Urbanisme: Town planning permit.

Cession: Transfer of ownership or rights, including property.

Chai: Wine cellar or vat room.

Chambre (à coucher): Bedroom.

Chambres d'Hôte: Bed and breakfast establishment.

Chantier: Builder's yard.

Charges: Utilities such as electricity, gas, water, insurance, maintenance and other services.

Chartreuse: Monastery or large manor house.

Château: Large country mansion, manor house, fort or castle.

Chaudière: Boiler (water heater).

Chauffage (central): Heating (central).

Chauffage collectif: Communal or shared heating, e.g. in an apartment block.

Chauffe-eau: A gas water heater or hot water tank.

Chaume: Thatch.

Chaumière: Thatched cottage.

Cheminée: Fireplace or chimney.

Citerne à eau: Water tank.

Citerne à gaz: Gas tank, e.g. for central heating.

Clause particulière: Special condition.

Clause pénale: A penalty clause in a sales contract.

Clauses suspensives: A conditional clause in a contract which must be met to ensure its validity.

Climatisation: Air-conditioning.

Colombage: A half-timbered house common in Normandy.

Colombier: Pigeon House or dovecote.

Comble: Loft.

Commission compris (C/C): Commission included, e.g. the sale price of a property including the agent's commission.

Commission non compris: Commission not included.

Communauté: Joint estate of a husband and wife.

Communauté universelle: A marriage *régime* where all assets are owned jointly.

Commune: Town, village, district or parish.

Compromis de vente: Preliminary contract of sale for a property.

Comptable: Accountant.

Comptant: Payable in cash without a loan.

Compte séquestre: A deposit held in a special escrow account pending fulfilment of certain conditions.

Compteur: Meter (electricity/gas/water).

Concierge: Caretaker or porter of an apartment block.

Concurrence: A *concurrence* (competition) sale is where two notaries are involved, although only one can execute the deed. The notary who doesn't execute the deed (*reçoit l'acte*) is said to be in *concurrence*.

Conditions particulières: Special conditions, e.g. in an insurance policy.

Conditions suspensives: Special conditions in a contract which allow one or both parties to declare the contract null and void if they aren't met.

Congélateur: Freezer.

Conseil juridique: Professional legal adviser.

Conseiller fiscal: Financial or tax adviser.

Conservateur des hypothèques: District land register.

Constat d'huissier: A statement of fact prepared by a *huissier* (bailiff) which is irrefutable in a court of law.

Constructible: Land that's available for building purposes.

Contrat: Contract.

Contrat préliminaire: Preliminary contract. Same as a *contrat de réservation*.

Contrat de réservation: Promissory contract to buy a property off-plan before it's built.

Convention: Agreement.

Copropriété: Co-ownership of communal property, equivalent to a US condominium.

Copropriété financière: Co-owner finance.

Corps de bâtiments: Group of buildings.

Cour: Yard or courtyard.

Cour de ferme: Farmyard.

Cuisine: Kitchen.

Cuisine américaine: Modern fitted kitchen possibly with a dining area.

Cuisine meublée: Kitchen with fixed cooker, refrigerator, etc.

Cuisinière: Cooker/stove.

Cuve: Tank, e.g. for gas or oil.

Date de livraison prévue: Estimated date of completion.

Débarras: Box room or small store room.

Décennale: Ten-year warranty provided by a registered builder.

Déclaration de sincérité: Formal acceptance of purchase price.

Décorée: Decorated and fitted out ready for occupation.

Dédit: Penalty provided for in a contract should either party default. If a deposit is described as a *dédit* the buyer will lose his deposit if he withdraws. If the seller withdraws he must repay the deposit and a penalty equal to the same sum.

Délabré: Dilapidated or tumbledown.

Déménagement: Moving house.

Demeure: Any dwelling, but it normally refers to a grand country house with extensive grounds.

Dépannage: Emergency repair service.

Département: Administrative area roughly equivalent to a British county or an American state.

Dépendance: Outbuilding.

Dépôt de garantie: The deposit paid when buying or renting a property.

Dernière étage: Top floor.

(à) Deux étages: Two storey.

Devis: A written quotation, e.g. for work to be done on a house.

Direction Départementale de l'Équipement (DDE): Departmental surveyors, land planning and public works department.

(à) Discuter: To be discussed or negotiated.

Disjoncteur: Electricity overload trip switch or circuit breaker.

Domaine: A country estate with a stately home.

Domicile fiscal: Main residence for tax purposes.

Donation de jouissance: Legal document to safeguard the rights of the surviving joint owner of a property.

Donation entre époux: Gift between spouses, whereby a surviving spouse is given a life interest in a property in priority to children or parents.

Douche: Shower.

Droit de passage: Right of way.

Droit de Préemption: Mandate to make enquiries for buyer.

Droits de donation: Gift tax.

Droits d'enregistrement: Stamp duty on a property purchase which is paid by the buyer.

Droits de passage: Right of way.

Droits de succession: Inheritance tax.

Duplex: An apartment or maisonette on two floors.

Durée: Duration or period of a mortgage.

Durée initiale: The initial duration of a lease for rented property.

Eau chaude collective: Shared hot water supply, e.g. in an apartment block.

Eaux usées: Drain or waste water.

Échange de lettres: Exchange of letters (type of property purchase contract).

Écurie: Stable.

Emoluments d'actes: Fixed scale of fees for a notary's standard services.

Emoluments de négociation: Fees for introducing the buyer.

Emprunt: Loan.

Engagement: Commitment, usually of vendor.

Enregistrement: Stamp duty.

Entrée: Hallway.

Entreprenuer: Building consortium or contractor.

Entretien: Maintenance.

Escalier: Stairway.

Étable: Stable or cowshed.

Étage: Floor or storey.

Étang: Lake or pond.

État hypothécaire: Land registry search.

Étude: A notary's office or practise.

Expédition: A certified copy of the title deed of a property.

Expert de bâtiment: Surveyor.

Expert géomètre: Land surveyor.

Expertise: Survey or valuation.

Facture: Bill.

Fenêtre: Window.

Fenêtre en baie: Bay window.

Ferme: Farm.

Fermette: Small farm or smallholding.

FNAIM: The initials of the *Fédération Nationale des Agents Immobiliers et Mandataires*, the main French national association of real estate agents.

FNSAFER: See SAFER.

Forfait: Fixed price or contract with an all-in price.

Fosse septique: Septic tank.

Fosse septique à toutes eaux: An all-purpose septic tank which can handle a wide range of waste products.

Fosse traditionelle: Traditional septic tank taking bathroom waste only.

Four: Oven.

Four à pain: Bread oven or bakehouse.

Foyer principal: Main or principal home.

Frais: Fees.

Frais d'acte: The notary's fees for producing a deed plus stamp duty, land registry fees and other relevant disbursements.

Frais compris: Fees included.

Frais de dossier: The arrangement fee charged by a bank for establishing a mortgage.

Frais de notaire: Same as *frais d'acte*.

Garantie d'achèvement: Guarantee of completion of a property purchased off plan.

Gardien/gardienne: Guardian (male/female) or caretaker.

Gaz en boutelle: Bottled gas.

Gaz de ville: Mains gas.

Gentilhommière: Small manor house, originally a gentleman's country seat.

Gîte: Self-catering accommodation.

Grange: Barn.

Grenier: Attic or loft.

Gros oeuvre: Shell or basic structure of a house.

Habitation: Dwelling.

Hameau: Hamlet.

Hectare: 10,000m² or 2.471 acres.

Honoraires: A notary's fee which isn't fixed by an official scale.

Hors frais/taxes: Fees (*frais*) or taxes aren't included.

Hôtel de ville: Town hall in cities and large towns. See also *Mairie*.

Hôtel particulier: Elegant townhouse or mansion, sometimes better described as a palace.

Huissier: An officer of the court who's roughly equivalent to a bailiff and serves writs and court orders and prepares statements of fact (*constat d'huissier*) which are irrefutable in a court of law.

Hypothèque: A mortgage or loan on a property.

Immeuble: Apartment block or a legal term for immovable property.

Immobilier: Real estate agent.

Impôt: Tax.

Impôts locaux: Local property taxes.

Impôt sur la fortune: Wealth tax.

Impôt sur les plus-values: Capital gains tax.

Impôt sur le revenu: Income tax.

Indemnité de l'immobilisation: Down payment on a preliminary contract of sale, usually 10 per cent of the price.

Indivis/Indivision: Joint ownership of a property or tenancy in common.

Inscription: Registered charge.

Installation: Fixture or fitting.

Installation électrique: Wiring.

Interdiction: A restriction on a vendor assigning rights to a third party.

Inventaire détaillé/état des lieux: A detailed inventory of the contents and condition of a rented property.

Jardin/Jardinier: Garden/gardener.

Jouissance: Possession (or taking possession) or tenure.

Jouissance libre: Vacant possession.

Jumelle: Semi-detached house.

Laverie: Laundry room.

Living: Living room.

Location: Tenancy.

Location vente: Renting a property while buying some of the equity value.

Locataire: Tenant.

Logement: Lodging, accommodation.

Logis: Manor house.

Lotissement: Housing estate.

(à) Louer: To rent, hire or let.

Loyer: Rent/rental.

Lucarne: Dormer window or skylight.

Maçon: Builder such as a bricklayer or stone mason.

Maçonnerie: Brick or Stone work.

Mainlevée: Release or withdrawal of mortgage or charge.

Maison: House.

Maison à étage: A two-storey house.

Maison d'amis: Second or holiday home.

Maison bourgeoise: Large period house designed for the professional classes during the 19th century.

Maison de campagne: House in the country.

Maison de caractère: House of character, often with a dovecote or pigeon tower.

Maison en carré: House built around a courtyard.

Maison de chasse: Hunting lodge, usually located on the edge of a forest.

Maison de maître: Gentleman's mansion or imposing house, usually a few centuries old.

Maison mitoyenne: Semi-detached house.

Maison neuve: New house.

Maison paysanne: Farmhouse.

Maison secondaire: Second or holiday home.

Maison de viticulteur: Winegrower's house.

Maisonette: Cottage.

Maire: Mayor.

Mairie: Town hall or office of the mayor in small towns and villages. See also *Hôtel de ville*.

Maître: Title used when addressing a *notaire*.

Maître d'oeuvres: Master builder, clerk of works or project manager.

Mandat/Mandataire: Mandate or power of attorney document. The representative or proxy who's given a power of attorney.

Mandat exclusif: An exclusive mandate, e.g. for a real estate agent to sell a property.

Mandat de recherche: An agreement with an agent to find a property.

Mandat simple: A non-exclusive mandate, e.g. for a real estate agent to sell a property, which means that the vendor reserves the right to deal with other agents and to negotiate directly with private individuals.

Mandat de vente: Sales mandate.

Manoir: Manor house.

Marchands de biens: Property developers and speculators.

Marquise: Porch.

Mas: A Provençal style farmhouse, usually L-shaped, often used to refer to any house built in the Mediterranean style.

Mazet: Small stone hut.

Menuisier: Carpenter or joiner.

Mètre carré: A square metre.

Meublé: Furnished. Unfurnished is *non-meublé*.

Meubles: Furniture.

Mode de paiement: Method of payment.

(à la) Montagne: In the mountains.

Montant: Amount (of money) to be paid.

Moquette: Fitted carpet.

Moulin: Watermill.

Moulin à vent: Windmill.

Multipropriété: The most common term for timesharing.

Multirisques d'habitation: Fully comprehensive (all-risk) household insurance.

Mur: Wall.

Mur mitoyen: A party wall shared with another property.

Nantissement: Collateral or security for a loan.

Net vendeur: The amount the vendor receives, excluding any agent's fees.

Non-meublé: Unfurnished.

Notaire: Notary. The legal professional who handles the conveyancing for all property sales in France (similar to a British solicitor or an American property lawyer).

Nouvelle propriété: Sale-and-leaseback.

Nu-propriétaire: Rights of owner set aside during a tenant's lifetime.

Off-plan: Buying a property off plans or drawings before it's built. Also called 'on plan'.

Offre d'achat/Offre de vente: A formal offer to purchase (sell) a property.

Offre préalable: A conditional offer, e.g. of a mortgage from a bank.

On plan: See *Off-plan*.

Organisme prêteur: Lender.

Paiement comptant: Paid in cash.

Pailler: Barn for storing straw.

Palier: Landing (stairs).

Parcelle: Plot of land.

Parquet: Wooden Floor.

Parties communes: Communal or shared parts of a building or development, e.g. foyers, lifts and hallways.

Parties privatives: Private areas of a shared building or development, e.g. an apartment.

Pavillon: Small detached cottage or house, usually located on the outskirts of a town or village.

Pays: A country or the countryside.

Pelouse: Lawn.

Pépinière: Garden centre.

Période d'anticipation: The period before completion of a property purchased off-plan, during which interest is paid on a monthly basis on the amount advanced by the bank only (plus insurance).

Permis de construire: Building permit.

Perron: Flight of steps in front of a mansion.

Pièce: A room.

Pièce de garantie: The amount of the financial guarantee of a bonded real estate agent, which must be displayed in his office.

Pierre (du pays): Stone (local).

Pierres apparentes: Exposed stone-work, e.g. the outer surface of a wall.

Pigeonnier: Pigeon tower.

Pignon: Gable.

Piscine: Swimming pool.

Plage: Beach.

Plain-pied: Single storey.

Plan d'amortissement: Schedule for paying off a mortgage.

Plan cadastral: Cadastral plan showing the dimensions of a property's land area.

Plan de financement: Plan or schedule of purchase payments, e.g. in stages when buying a new property.

Plancher: Wooden floor.

Pleine propriété: Freehold.

Plomberie: Plumbing.

Plombier: Plumber.

Plus-values: Capital gains.

Portes-fenêtres à la française: French windows.

Potager: Kitchen garden.

Poubelle(s): Dustbin or rubbish can.

Poutre: Beam (wooden).

Pouvoir: Given power to act, e.g. power of attorney.

Prélèvement automatique: Direct debit.

Presbytère: Presbytery or vicarage.

Prêt: Loan.

Prêt immobilier: Mortgage.

Prêt relais: Bridging loan.

Prix déclaré: The price of a property declared to the authorities.

Prix demandée: The asking price.

Prix fermé: Fixed price (non-negotiable).

Procuration: Power of attorney. Also known as a *mandat* or *pouvoir*.

Projet d'acte: A draft conveyance deed.

Promesse d'achat: Preliminary or promissory contract to buy a property.

Promesse de vente: Preliminary or promissory contract to sell a property.

Promesse unilatérale de vente: A property that's rented with a promise to sell at an agreed price in the future with part of the rent going towards the purchase price.

Promoteur: Property developer.

Propriétaire: Owner.

Propriété: Property.

Propriété à restaurer: Property for restoration.

Propriété en ruines: Property in ruins.

Propriétés baties: Developed or built property.

Publicité foncière: Obligatory registration of a property at the land registry.

Puisard: Cesspool or sump.

Puissance: Electricity power rating (in kilowatts).

Puits: Well.

Quartier: Neighbourhood.

Quincaillerie: Hardware store or iron-monger's.

Quittance: Receipt.

Ramoneur: Chimney sweep.

Rangement: Storage area.

Ravalement: Restoration.

Réalisation: To carry out or fulfil an agreement.

Réduit: Box room.

Réfection: Reconstruction.

Réfrigérateur: Refrigerator (often shortened to *frigo*).

Règlement de copropriété: The document containing the rules and regulations of a *copropriété* building.

Remise des clefs: Handing over the keys to a new owner.

Rénovation: Renovation.

Rente viagère: Buying a property (usually) with a down payment (e.g. a third of its value) plus an annuity until the death of the owner. The vendor may or may not remain in the property until his death.

Représentative accrédité: A guarantor for capital gains tax purposes.

Réservoir: Water tank.

Résidence principal: Main or principal home.

Résidence secondaire: Second or holiday home.

Responsabilité civile propriétaire: Third party liability of homeowners for which insurance is mandatory.

Restaurer: To restore (a building).

Révision de loyer: A revision or review of the rent payable on a property.

Renouvellement: The renewal of a rental contract (lease).

Rez-de-chaussée: Ground floor.

Ruine: Ruin or run-down property. A property in need of restoration, renovation and modernisation is referred to as a *propriété en ruines* or a *propriété à restaurer*.

SAFER: *Société d'Aménagement Foncier et d'Établissement Rural.* Also referred to as the *Fédération Nationale des Société d'Aménagement Foncier et d'Etablissement Rural (FNSAFER)*

Saisie-arrêt: Distraint or attachment.

Saisie-exécutions: Distraint for sale by court order.

Salle: Room.

Salle d'eau: Shower room.

Salle de bains: Bathroom.

Salle de douches: Shower room.

Salle à manger: Dining room.

Salle de séjour: Living room.

Salon: Sitting room, lounge or drawing room.

Sanitaire: Bathroom or plumbing.

Sanitation: Sanitation or main drainage.

Sans travaux: Ready to occupy.

Séjour: Living room.

Séjour principal: Main or principal residence.

Séparation des biens: Separation of property. A marriage *régime* where each spouse retains legal ownership of his or her own assets.

Service du cadastre: Land registry or cadastral survey.

Servitudes: Building regulations, rights of way or easements.

SNPI: *Syndicate National des Professionnels Immobiliers,* a professional association of estate agents.

Société Civile Immobilière (SCI): A civil real estate company that holds voting shares in a property.

Sol: Ground.

Source: Spring (a *sourcier* is a water diviner).

Sous-seing: Preliminary contract.

Sous-sol: Basement often used as a garage or cellar.

Studio: A one-roomed apartment or bedsitter.

Surface habitable: Habitable area excluding terraces, balconies, cellars, store rooms, etc.

Syndicat (des copropriétaire): The committee appointed to manage a *copropriété* (condominium) development.

Système de chauffage: Heating system.

Tapis: Carpet or rug. A fitted carpet is a *moquette.*

Taxe d'habitation: Dwelling or local property tax based on occupancy (not ownership) of a property.

Taxes (impôt) foncière: Local property tax (rates) levied on real property owners. The tax is split into two amounts: one for the building (*taxe foncière bâtie*) and a smaller one for the land (*taxe foncière non bâtie*).

Témoin: Show apartment or house (*appartement/maison témoin*).

Terrain: Grounds or land.

Terrain à bâtir: Building site for sale.

Terrasse: Terrace.

Testament: Will.

Titre de propriété: Title deed.

Toilettes: Toilet or lavatory (public).

Toit/Toiture: Roof/roofing.

Toit en terrasse: Flat roof.

Tontine: Ownership in joint tenancy under which the assets pass to the survivor. A *clause tontine* can be included in a property purchase contract (*acte de vente*).

Tout à l'égout: Mains drainage system.

Toutes taxes: Including taxes.

Travaux: Building works.

Trésor Public: Public treasury or treasurer's department.

Triplex: Maisonette on three floors.

TVA: *Tax sur la Valeur Ajouté* or value added tax. *TVA mmobilière* is payable on property less than five years old.

Urbanisme: Town planning.

Urgence: Emergency.

Usufruct/Usufruit: Legal term for a life interest in a property.

Valeur cadastrale: Assessment of a property's value for land tax purposes.

Valeur vénale: Market value.

Vendeur: Vendor or seller.

Vente en l'état futur d'achèvement: Buying a property off-plan (on plan) before it's built.

Vente à réméré: Sale which is subject to a right of repurchase.

Vente sous conditions suspensives: Sale subject to special conditions, e.g. the sale of an existing property.

Vente à tenure: Sale of usufruct.

Véranda: Conservatory, sun-room or extension.

Verger: Orchard.

Vieille maison: An old house.

Villa: A (usually modern) detached house with garden.

Ville: Town.

Volet (roulant): Shutter (roller).

APPENDIX F: SERVICE DIRECTORY

This **Service Directory** is to help you find local businesses and services in France and the UK, serving residents and visitors in France. Note that when calling France from abroad, you must dial the international access number (e.g. 00 from the UK) followed by 33 (the country code for France, **shown in the telephone numbers listed below**), the area code and the subscriber's number. Please mention *Buying a Home in France* when contacting companies.

AGENTS (PROPERTY)

KBM Consultancy, No 4 Carpenters Buildings, The Avenue, Cirencester, Gloucester GL7 1EJ, UK (☎ 01285-656700, fax: 01285-657090, e-mail: karen@kbm-europe.co.uk). Contact: Karen Mulcahy. Family-run business specialising in helping families to find their holiday 'home from home'. **See advertisement on page 113.**

Regent St. Properties, Suite 401, 302 Regent Street, Mayfair, London W1R 6HH, UK (☎ 020-8289 9697/020-7580 4242, fax: 020-7580 4729). Contact: Patrick O'Connell. Specialising in properties in Brittany, Normandy and Provence (£50,000 - £250,000). Resident agent available. Research undertaken for your ideal home.

Vivre en France, 4 Raleigh House, Admirals Way, London E14 9SN, UK. (☎ 020-7515 8660, fax: 020-7538 0895, e-mail: info@vefuk.com). Contact: Monique Scholfield (head of sales). Whatever your budget VEF has something to offer you. Winners of 'The Best Estate Agent of the Year' award – we can offer you something wonderful!

LEGAL SERVICES

John Howell & Co., 17 Maiden Lane, Covent Garden, London WC2E 7NA, UK (☎ 020-7420 0400, fax: 020-7836 3626, e-mail: info@europelaw.com). Contact: John Howell (principal). The only firm of English solicitors dealing exclusively with French, Spanish and Portuguese work. **See advertisement on page 129.**

Penningtons, Bucklersbury House, 83 Cannon Street, London EC4N 8PE, UK (☎ 020-7457-3000/01256-406300, fax: 020-7457-3240, e-mail: brookscm@penningtons. co.uk). Contact: Charles Brooks (partner, solicitor/avocat). Advice on French property, inheritance, wills and related subjects available from English lawyers qualified in French law.

Graham Platt, 150 Roundhay Road, Leeds LS8 5LD, UK (☎ 0113-2496 496, fax: 0113-2480 466, e-mail: gpavocat@aol.com). Contact: Graham Platt (partner). Be warned *un homme averti en vaut deux*. Speak to Graham before you sign up. **See advertisement on page 165.**

Sean O'Connor & Co., 2 River Walk, Tonbridge, Kent TN9 1DT, UK (☎ 01732-365378, fax: 01732-360144, e-mail: seanoconnorco@compuserve.com). Contact: Sean O'Connor (solicitor). Heavy legal jargon is our business. We understand it fully. Spot on. Alert.

Simone Paissoni, Solicitor, 22, avenue Notre Dame, 06000 Nice, France (☎ +33 04.93.62.94.95, fax: +33 04.93.62.95.96, e-mail: spaissonirad@magic.fr). Contact:

Simone Paissoni. English qualified solicitor will assist clearly and comprehensibly with all aspects of property ownership/acquisition.

Taylors Solicitors & Notaries Public. The Red Brick House, 28/32 Trippet Lane, Sheffield S14 EL (☎ 0114-2766767, fax; 0114-2731287, e-mail: Taylors FPD@AOL.com. Contact: Susan Smith (Partner). Advice on French property matters including inheritance and wills.

MORTGAGES

Conti Financial Services, 204 Church Road, Hove, Sussex BN3 2DJ. (☎ 01273-772811, fax: 01273-321269, email: enquiries@conti-financial.com, internet: www. conti-financial.com). Contact: Simon Conn (proprietor). Specialising in arranging finance in over 20 Countries including Western Europe, USA, Australia, Canada and South Africa.

MFS Partners, Grosvenor House, 47 Alma Road, Plymouth, Devon PL3 4HE. (☎ 01752-664777, fax: 01752-201341, email: mfspartners@zetnet.co.uk). Contact: Marcus Connell (senior partner). French mortgages are different – Find out how! Ring for free leaflet or further advice.

REMOVALS

Delahaye Moving Ltd., 27 Wates Way, Mitcham, Surrey CR4 4HR, UK (☎ 020-8687 0400, fax: 020-8687 0404, e-mail: mail@delahayemoving.co.uk). Contact: Mr. F. P. Delahaye. Family business. International removals, storage and shipping. Personalised and effortless from start to finish.

The Old House (Removals & Warehousing) Ltd., 1/2/3 Pelham Yard, High Street, Seaford, East Sussex BN25 1PQ, UK (☎ 01323-892934/020-8947 1817, fax 01323-894474, email; amsmoves@cs.com). Contact: Mr. Peter Barrett (managing director). Fully bonded member of B.A.R. Overseas. Moving to France over 35 years . Full and part loads. Free quotations and advice. **See advertisement on page 177.**

INDEX

ORDER FORM – ALIEN'S/BUYING A HOME SERIES

Qty.	Title	Price (incl. p&p)*			Total
		UK	Europe	World	
	The Alien's Guide to America	Autumn 2001			
	The Alien's Guide to Britain	£5.95	£6.95	£8.45	
	The Alien's Guide to France	£5.95	£6.95	£8.45	
	Buying a Home in Abroad	£11.45	£12.95	£14.95	
	Buying a Home in Britain	£11.45	£12.95	£14.95	
	Buying a Home in Florida	£11.45	£12.95	£14.95	
	Buying a Home in France	£11.45	£12.95	£14.95	
	Buying a Home in Greece/Cyprus	£11.45	£12.95	£14.95	
	Buying a Home in Ireland	£11.45	£12.95	£14.95	
	Buying a Home in Italy	£11.45	£12.95	£14.95	
	Buying a Home in Portugal	£11.45	£12.95	£14.95	
	Buying a Home in Spain	£11.45	£12.95	£14.95	
	Rioja and its Wines	£11.45	£12.95	£14.95	
				Total	

Order your copies today by phone, fax, mail or e-mail from: Survival Books, PO Box 146, Wetherby, West Yorks. LS23 6XZ, United Kingdom (☎/🖷 +44-1937-843523, ✉ orders@survivalbooks.net, 🖳 www.survivalbooks.net). If you aren't entirely satisfied, simply return them to us within 14 days for a full and unconditional refund.

Cheque enclosed/please charge my Delta/Mastercard/Switch/Visa* card

Card No. _ _ _ _   _ _ _ _   _ _ _ _   _ _ _ _

Expiry date _____   **Issue number (Switch only)** _____

Signature _____   **Tel. No.** _____

NAME _____

ADDRESS _____

_____

* **Delete as applicable (prices include postage – airmail for Europe/World)**

ORDER FORM – LIVING AND WORKING SERIES

Qty.	Title	Price (incl. p&p)*			Total
		UK	Europe	World	
	Living & Working in Abroad	Spring 2001			
	Living & Working in America	£14.95	£16.95	£20.45	
	Living & Working in Australia	£14.95	£16.95	£20.45	
	Living & Working in Britain	£14.95	£16.95	£20.45	
	Living & Working in Canada	£14.95	£16.95	£20.45	
	Living & Working in France	£14.95	£16.95	£20.45	
	Living & Working in Germany	£14.95	£16.95	£20.45	
	Living & Working in Ireland	Spring 2001			
	Living & Working in Italy	£14.95	£16.95	£20.45	
	Living & Working in London	£11.45	£12.95	£14.95	
	Living & Working in N. Zealand	£14.95	£16.95	£20.45	
	Living & Working in Spain	£14.95	£16.95	£20.45	
	Living & Working in Switzerland	£14.95	£16.95	£20.45	
				Total	

Order your copies today by phone, fax, mail or e-mail from: Survival Books, PO Box 146, Wetherby, West Yorks. LS23 6XZ, United Kingdom (☎/🖷 +44-1937-843523, ✉ orders@survivalbooks.net, 🖳 www.survivalbooks.net). If you aren't entirely satisfied, simply return them to us within 14 days for a full and unconditional refund.

Cheque enclosed/please charge my Delta/Mastercard/Switch/Visa* card

Card No. __ __ __ __   __ __ __ __   __ __ __ __   __ __ __ __

Expiry date _____   **Issue number (Switch only)** _____

Signature _____   Tel. No. _____

NAME _____

ADDRESS _____

_____

* **Delete as applicable (prices include postage – airmail for Europe/World).**

THE ALIEN'S GUIDE TO FRANCE

Here at last is a guide for visitors to France who are mystified and maybe a little daunted by all those funny little foibles and idiosyncrasies which make the French so endearingly FRENCH!

This book will help you avoid the newcomer's most serious gaffes and help you appreciate more fully the rich *bouillon* of the French *joie de vivre*. Vital topics covered include:

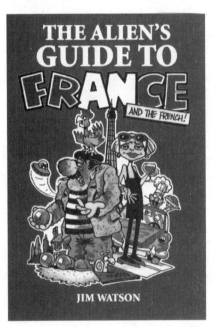

- All you need to know about French wine
- History without mystery
- Useful sign language
- French culture for barbarians
- French cuisine and eating anything
- Basic French etiquette
- French cars and driving badly
- Regional characters
- Shopping 'til you're dropping
- Sensitive areas
- And much, much more

So straighten your beret, slip into a little black dress and cast off the corset of timidity – with a copy of this book in your pocket you can visit France with poise and confidence, secure in the knowledge that you too can live the life *au français*.

***The Alien's Guide to France* is required reading for all visitors to France – whatever planet you are from!**

Order your copies today by phone, fax, mail or e-mail from: Survival Books, PO Box 146, Wetherby, West Yorks. LS23 6XZ, United Kingdom (☎/🖷 +44-1937-843523, ✉ orders@survival books.net, 🖳 www.survivalbooks.net).

LIVING AND WORKING IN FRANCE

Living and Working in France is essential reading for anyone planning to spend some time in France including holiday-home owners, retirees, visitors, business people, migrants, students and even extraterrestrials! It's packed with over 450 pages of important and useful information designed to help you **avoid costly mistakes and save both time and money.** Topics covered include how to:

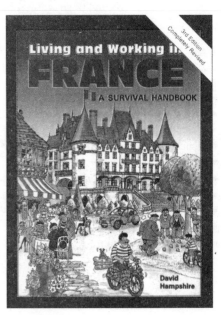

- find a job with a good salary & conditions
- obtain a residence permit
- avoid & overcome problems
- find your dream home
- get the best education for your family
- make the best use of public transport
- endure motoring in France
- obtain the best health treatment
- stretch your French francs further
- make the most of your leisure time
- enjoy the French sporting life
- find the best shopping bargains
- insure yourself against most eventualities
- use post office & telephone services
- do numerous other things not listed above

Living and Working in France is the most comprehensive and up-to-date source of practical information available about everyday life in France. It isn't, however, a boring text book, but an interesting and entertaining guide written in a highly readable style.

Buy this book and discover what it's <u>really</u> like to live and work in France.

Order your copies today by phone, fax, mail or e-mail from: Survival Books, PO Box 146, Wetherby, West Yorks. LS23 6XZ, United Kingdom (☎/🖷 +44-1937-843523, ✉ orders@survival books.net, 🖳 www.survivalbooks.net).